LOST DEPARTMENT STORES *of* DENVER

LOST DEPARTMENT STORES
of
DENVER

Mark A. Barnhouse

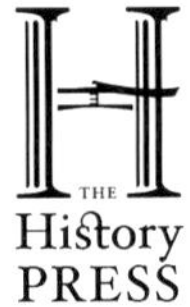

Published by The History Press
Charleston, SC
www.historypress.com

Front cover: Neusteters Cherry Creek (main image), History Colorado, Neusteter Collection, 10027909; A.T. Lewis & Son (*top left*), Denver Public Library, Western History Collection, X-24116; Fashion Bar architectural rendering (*top center*), Beck Archives, Special Collections, CJS and University Libraries, University of Denver; the Golden Eagle (*top right*), History Colorado, 10040053.

Back cover: May-D&F (*main image*), Bob Rhodes Collection; May-D&F (*color image*), Alan Golin Gass Collection.

First published 2018

Manufactured in the United States

ISBN 9781467138406

Library of Congress Control Number: 2018948043

To Janice Miller Wallington (1938–2017);
also, to Della, a dog with a nose for fashion.

CONTENTS

ACKNOWLEDGEMENTS

Writing a book is never a solitary effort. This my third book on Denver's department stores, and I'm grateful to everyone who has helped along the way. Although some of these names have not contributed directly to this volume, they have helped it nevertheless, as the two previous works inform this one.

For advice, tips, stories and encouragement; for facilitating connections with others; or for help in obtaining images, I am indebted to the following individuals: Kristen and Robert Autobee, Sandra Barnhouse, Mark Bochnak and Richard Bruce, Jean-Pierre Chardeaux, Kathleen Corbett, Sandra Dallas, Bill Eloe, Alan Golin Gass, Lois Harvey, F. Joseph Hayes, Richard Hentzell, Leslie Mohr Krupa, Linda Lebsack, Robert J. Levy, Red Nichols, Thomas J. Noel, Jim O'Hagan, Mary O'Neil, Heather Ormsby, Judy and Ron Proctor, Virginia Ronzio Owens, Susan Powers, Marilyn Quinn, Bob Rhodes, Tom Rowan, Tom and Laurie Simmons, Joe Sokolowski, Jodi Sokup, Judy Stalnaker, Shantelle Stephens, Matthew Sullivan, Israela Vera, Nan Walker and Roger Whitacre.

As usual, I have depended on Denver's archives for research and images. At Denver Public Library Western History Collection, I thank Coi Drummond-Gehrig and Katie Rudolph for excellent help, along with their colleagues at the fifth-floor desk and Mullen Manuscript Room. Thanks also to Melissa Lawton of the Stephen H. Hart Library, History Colorado. Jeanne Abrams and Thyria Wilson at the Ira M. and Peryle Hayutin Beck Memorial Archives of the Rocky Mountain Jewish Historical Society at the

University of Denver helped particularly with the Fashion Bar and Golden Eagle chapters, for which I am grateful.

I also thank those who have asked me to speak to audiences about Denver's department stores and other topics. These engagements have led to unexpected connections that made writing this book and the two previous interesting and fun, contributing to the process. These include Ryan Warner and Nathan Heffel (Colorado Public Radio); Steve Friesen and Reed Weimer (The Denver Posse of Westerners); Larry Bohning (Denver Rotary Club); Carol Hiller and Kyle Long (Doors Open Denver/Denver Architecture Foundation); Shawn Snow, Michael Vincent and Jack Wheeler (History Colorado); and Phyllis Larison (Bemis Public Library, Littleton).

Special thanks go to Artie Crisp at The History Press for his help, advice, enthusiasm and flexibility, as well as to Ryan Finn for his thoughtful editing.

Finally, thank you to Matt Wallington, for everything you do.

Author's note: Chapters are arranged in chronological order of each store's founding. Subtitles derive from advertising slogans used at some point during each store's history.

Introduction

ENTREPÔT OF THE WEST

The department store rose to prominence over a century ago in part because it satisfied some basic human needs beyond the desires of consumption.
—Richard Longstreth, The American Department Store Transformed, *1920–1960*[1]

THE DEPARTMENT STORE

In the twenty-first century, it is increasingly difficult for most Denver residents to remember the role that local department stores once played in their lives. Before online shopping, big-boxes and chain discounters, Denver's department stores were the first choices of the middle and upper classes. These emporia, sprawling across multiple floors on prime downtown corners, carried just about everything: complete lines of clothing, shoes and accessories for everyone in a household and myriad other items like cosmetics; jewelry; linens; china, glass and silverware; furniture; toys and games; fresh-cut flowers; gifts; stationery and books; sporting goods; candy and gourmet foods; televisions and radios; records and record players; luggage; small and major appliances; and, in the case of one Denver store, everything required by the professional working stockman, including saddles.

Denver's stores were about more than just the goods they carried, however. They also provided services. Businessmen could get their shoes shined in a few minutes or resoled in a few days. Marrying couples could set up gift registries. Women meeting friends for shopping could enjoy comfortable lounges, perhaps dashing off a letter with store-provided stationery. Arts patrons could pick up theater or symphony tickets. Vacationers could book tickets and rooms with a travel agent. Those with tight budgets could put items on layaway, paying a little at a time (they could also find great values in bargain basements). People could mail packages or letters instead of trekking to the post office. Gift-givers could have purchases wrapped elegantly. Families could have portraits taken in photo studios, and women could have their hair shampooed, cut and set. When everyone's needs had been met, they could meet for lunch or mid-afternoon nosh in genteel in-store tearooms before heading home. And if they had bought something too large to carry on the streetcar or just didn't want the burden, the store could deliver it.

No one Denver store offered everything, but what most had in common were service levels we would find unusual in the twenty-first century, even in luxury stores. In the late nineteenth and early twentieth centuries, customers sat in front of sales counters while clerks brought them items to examine—"self service" was unheard of. For the affluent, clerks brought goods to the lady waiting in her carriage so she would not have to mingle with the masses (several Denver stores claimed to have served Baby Doe Tabor, second wife of "Silver King" Horace Tabor, this way). All quality merchants followed the famous dictum of Chicago's Marshall Field: "give the lady what she wants," with the unspoken corollary, "she's always right, even when she's not." Purchases weren't just tossed into sacks, but were wrapped in paper and tied with string or placed in boxes with tissue paper. Clerks remembered customers' names and knew their tastes—if something came in they knew Mrs. Smith would like, they would send her a note. Great service engendered strong customer loyalty.

If department stores could be all things to all people (at least those with means), resembling a small city contained within one building, they reflected the unique circumstances of the time—the nineteenth century—in which they arose. New technologies allowed for mass production, with savings to manufacturers, retailers and consumers. Railroads made shipping efficient and cheap. New technologies—cast iron (later steel) for columns, new methods of manufacturing glass for large display windows and, most crucially, Otis's elevator—allowed for wide-open, well-lit spaces spanning multiple floors. Savvy "merchant princes" in eastern cities like Alexander Turney Stewart, John Wanamaker and Marshall Field came up with new innovations, including fixed, marked prices (eliminating haggling, allowing

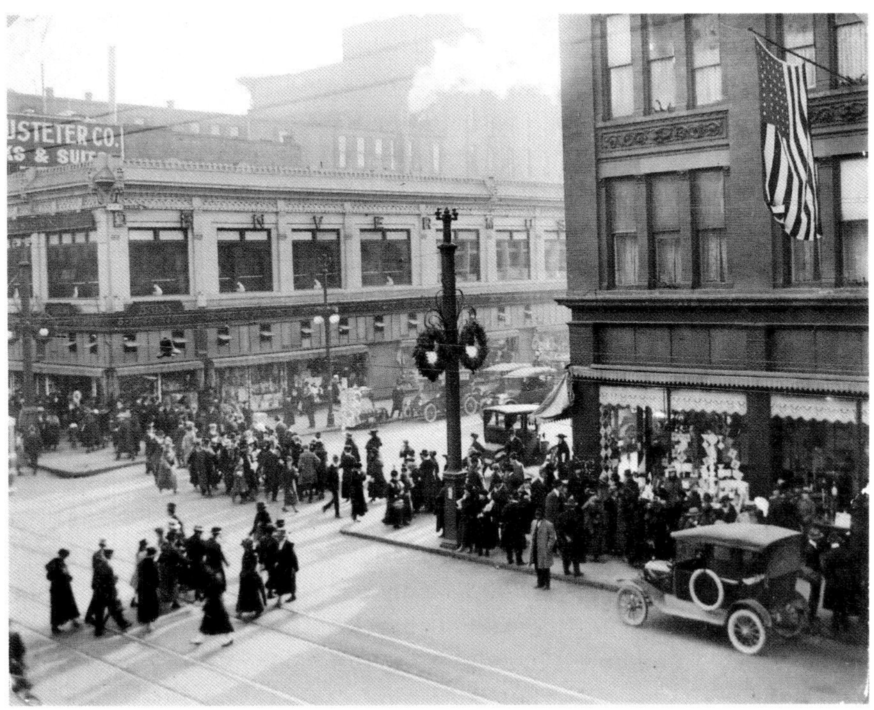

Holiday shoppers at Sixteenth and Stout Streets, circa 1920. A.T. Lewis & Son is at right, while the Neusteter Company and the rear of The Denver Dry Goods Company are visible in the distance. *Denver Public Library, Western History Collection, X-22697.*

people to browse knowing whether they could afford something) and management hierarchies that allowed departments to function essentially as individual businesses. Perhaps most importantly, men who founded early department stores discovered that clever marketing could entice middle- and upper-class women, formerly homebound, into coming downtown to a world long dominated by men—department stores were feminine refuges and perfectly respectable. Big-city innovations spread rapidly to hinterland burgs like Denver.

DENVER'S STORES

Founded by General William Larimer in 1858, Denver, thanks to its isolation from major cities, became the primary metropolis for a vast territory encompassing several sparsely populated states. Denver's department stores, with wholesale divisions serving retailers in smaller towns, grew into larger institutions than otherwise might have been justified by Denver's relatively small population. In this sense, Denver's stores and wholesalers collectively made the city an *entrepôt*, where goods shipped in bulk from distant manufactories were broken into smaller lots and shipped to the hinterland.

Denver's stores were not especially innovative, mostly cast in the mold set by pioneers like Stewart and Field, but they were beloved nonetheless. They reflected the city's character: somewhat utilitarian and not especially trendsetting but proud. Denver should not have achieved prominence, bypassed as it was by the first transcontinental railroad (which ran through Cheyenne instead). But its leaders persevered, creating a metropolis despite the transportation obstacle presented by the Rocky Mountains. So, too, did Denver's store founders persevere, establishing institutions that lasted, in several cases, for more than a century.

They did it the same way more famous department store kings did, by endearing themselves to the people. Denver's merchant princes were often great charmers, and they trained staffs to be polite without being effusive, to gently guide customers without appearing superior. They built impressive edifices on main streets—first Larimer and then Lawrence and up Sixteenth—that locals could show off to country cousins. They participated in parades and festivals and gave to charities. Every Denver store went all out for the holidays, with lavish decorations and other traditions that created warm memories. Through their advertising dollars, they forged symbiotic relationships with Denver's newspapers—never willing to upset stores, papers published flattering profiles and generally took stores' sides during labor disputes and other controversies. Denver people came to love their stores as much as New Yorkers loved Macy's, even without a Thanksgiving Day parade.

Denver's department stores, with vast floors filled with goods and staffs numbering in the hundreds, seemed permanent. Most assumed they would always be around, just as they always had been. Small stores might come and go, but big stores—with their tearooms, holiday windows, personal shoppers, fleets of delivery vehicles, end-of-month sales and daily advertisements—were part of every Denverite's mental map. If someone had been told in 1950 that by 2000, fifty years hence, none of Denver's department stores would still exist, she would not have believed it. After all, in 1900, fifty years earlier, Denver had its big stores, and most of them were still around, weren't they? Certainly, there was one spectacular failure

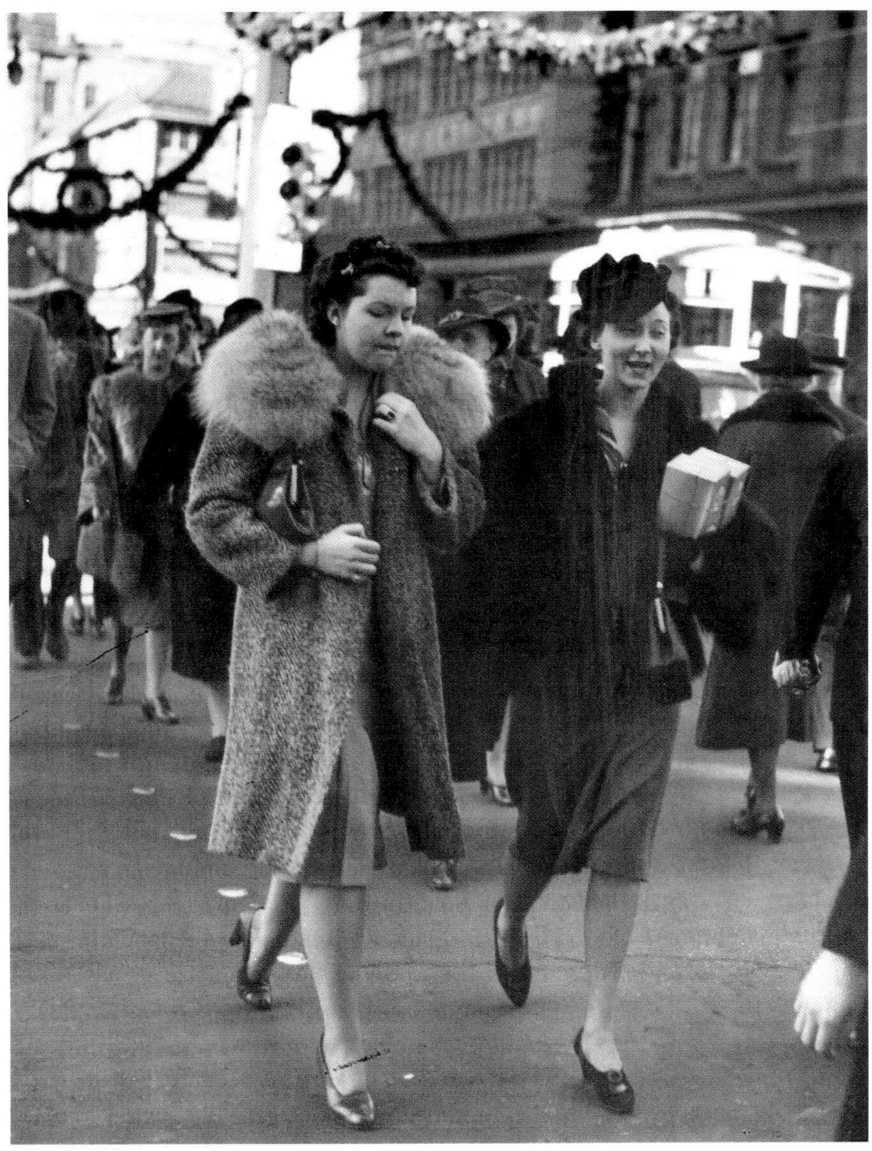

Two shoppers crossing Champa Street at Sixteenth during the 1939 holiday season. *Author's collection.*

in 1893 when McNamara Dry Goods got caught short during an economic panic, and another one forty years later, when A.T. Lewis & Son had to close during a cash crunch in the Great Depression. But The Denver, the May, Daniels and Fisher, Joslin's, Gano-Downs, Neusteter's, Fashion Bar—

their shutting up shop for good was unimaginable to the Denver shopper of 1950.

Yet they did close, one by one. Some stores responded to the changes in American life after World War II the way stores in other cities did, building suburban branches. Over time, there were fewer reasons to come downtown to patronize the parent stores, and these dinosaurs, with high overhead and upkeep costs, began weighing heavily on balance sheets. As other forms of shopping came into vogue (discount stores in the 1960s, off-price chains and outlet malls in the 1980s and online shopping in the 1990s), not only did downtown stores lose all economic viability, but many suburban branches did too. A wave of consolidations that gained steam in the 1980s led to the demise of local names Denverites knew and loved.

Was this inevitable? Yes. Denver's stores disappeared at the same time department stores elsewhere began merging or closing. Even Chicagoans lost their beloved Marshall Field's in 2006, with the big Loop emporium renamed Macy's on State Street (customers protested and boycotted, to no avail). But that Denver's stores died as part of a national trend does not take away the sting of their loss. Many thousands still remember going downtown in their finest attire (including gloves, hats and hosiery) to lunch at The Denver Dry Goods Tea Room. They remember Carl Sandell, the famous seven-foot, five-inch-tall Daniels and Fisher doorman. They remember bargains found at the always amply stocked May Company. They remember Bob Rhodes's animated windows at May-D&F and its skating rink, always worth a trip downtown in December. They remember May-D&F's "fortnights" of the 1960s and 1970s, two weeks of special events and exotic merchandise celebrating foreign cultures. They bought their children's back-to-school clothes at Joslins, and when those kids grew up and began shopping for themselves, they chose Fashion Bar for something stylish and fun. Those who could afford it patronized Neusteters, Denver's equivalent of Saks Fifth Avenue, with *haute couture* and stellar service. Well-heeled Denver businessmen bought suits and holiday gifts for their wives at Gano-Downs. And while few living now remember A.T. Lewis or the Golden Eagle, those stores were just as beloved in their time and mourned when lost.

This book exists because these institutions' stories deserve to be told. Many (not all) of them are mentioned in general Denver histories, but usually in just a sentence or two, even as accounts of banks, railroads and industries are given whole paragraphs and chapters. In their day, department stores were as vital a part of Denver's civic and business life as any of those more male-oriented institutions were, and it is probably because most

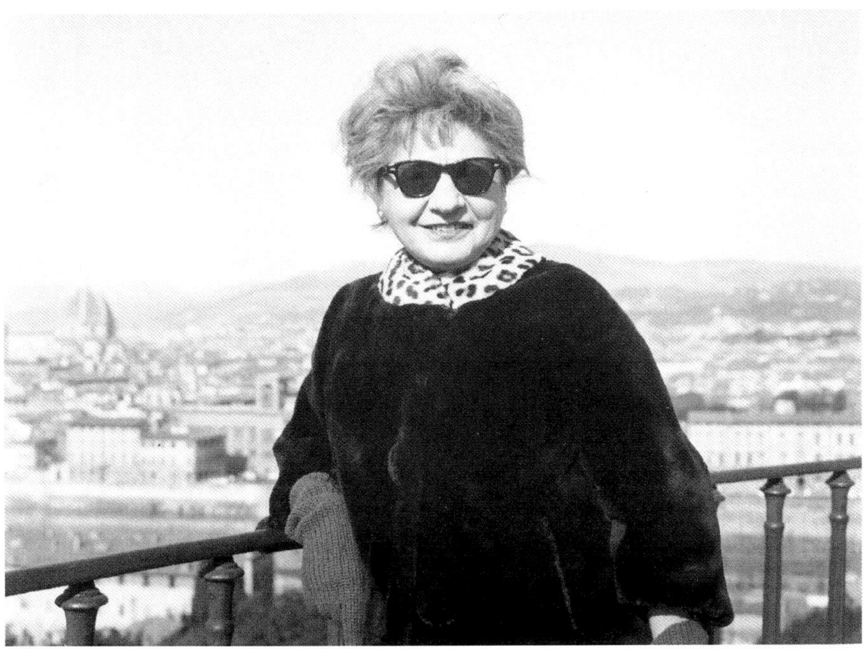

Fashion Bar co-founder Hannah Levy enjoys a view of Florence, Italy, during a buying trip, circa 1965. *Beck Archives, Special Collections, CJS and University Libraries, University of Denver.*

history writers have been men that the stores have not been better covered. Denver's merchant princes—men like William Bradley Daniels, William Cooke Daniels, William Garrett Fisher, Charles MacAllister Willcox, David May, Michael J. McNamara, Dennis Sheedy, Leopold Guldman, John Jay Joslin, the Neusteter brothers (Meyer, Edward and Max), Merritt W. Gano, William D. Downs, S. Nelson Hicks Sr. and Jr., Aaron Dennison Lewis and Jack Levy, along with remarkable women like Jack's sister, Hannah Levy—were, in their day, as celebrated *as businesspeople* as the "Seventeenth Street crowd," bankers, brokers and businessmen with names like Boettcher, Evans and Kountze. Here, then, is the story of Denver's lost department stores.

Chapter 1

DANIELS AND FISHER

Denver's Pioneer Store

If a stranger wishes to be thoroughly convinced of the great and rapid advance of Denver he can not do better than pay a visit to the "Stewart's of the West"—we mean Daniels & Fisher's dry goods establishment. This house was founded fourteen years ago, when Denver was in its infancy [and] *it has continued to grow and prosper. This firm is one of Colorado's landmarks.*
—Rocky Mountain News, *December 31, 1879*

TAKING A CHANCE ON DENVER

We still have the tower. The stately landmark at Sixteenth and Arapahoe Streets, modeled on the Campanile of St. Mark's in Venice, reigned for more than four decades as the tallest building in Colorado, but the Daniels and Fisher store to which it was once attached is gone. Denver-bound train passengers would look for the tower from their windows, its appearance on the horizon signifying that they would soon be home, but now it is hard to spot, crowded by taller and bulkier skyscrapers. Occupying a plot just 40 feet square, it rises, with flagpole uppermost, to 375 feet. Newcomers and visitors find its dimensions odd: why does such a thin tower stand by itself next to a park? If they walk around it, they notice that obviously there once was a building attached, its memory marked by darker brick that rises to five stories, describing the roofline of a structure long gone. Few Denver newbies realize that the tower was once the pride of the city, or that the story behind it goes back nearly to Denver's founding.

Leavenworth, Kansas merchant William Bradley Daniels was already successful as he approached his thirty-ninth birthday in 1864. His first wife had died young, but he had remarried in 1860 to Elizabeth P. Knox.[2] He was always looking to grow his businesses (including a store in Iowa City, Iowa), and sensing an opportunity in the rising young town of Denver (likely influenced by boosterish newspaper accounts of its potential), Daniels determined to take a chance. Funding the venture himself (without his Leavenworth and Iowa City partners), he sent west his wife's brother, William R. Kenyon, with a wagonload of goods and instructions to lease a suitable storefront. Kenyon arrived in October, after his wagon train had been delayed several weeks by fears of trouble with indigenous Cheyenne and Arapaho people (whose anger was stoked further a month after Kenyon's arrival by the infamous Sand Creek Massacre, perpetrated by a Denver militia). He rented space in the two-story Fillmore Block on F (today's Fifteenth) and Blake Streets, and on October 6, he opened the doors of W.B. Daniels and Company.[3]

Largely the creation of city boosters rather than the logical outcome of favorable geography (little water, no train service, abutting a formidable mountain range), Denver was just six years old, and the initial gold rush that had led to its founding at the confluence of the South Platte River and Cherry Creek had dissipated, just as the few flakes of gold in those streams had long been claimed by early miners. By 1864, three years into the Civil War, tiny Denver's future was anything but certain. Without a rail connection, journeying to Denver was arduous, across dry, windy prairies. Daniels's decision to open a store in Denver was decidedly risky.

Daniels soon sent out a protégé, John M. Eckhart, to run things so Kenyon could come home. Eckhart expanded the business rapidly and soon rented a second storefront. The new branch was two blocks away, on Larimer Street between F and G (today's Sixteenth) Streets, and as it was located nearer the residential district, it specialized in carpet and home goods, with the original store selling clothing and dry goods. In 1869, the Larimer store, now called Daniels & Eckhart, moved into more impressive quarters farther up the block closer to Sixteenth, and in 1870, Daniels sent out from Iowa City a promising young man, Civil War veteran William Garrett Fisher, to assist Eckhart. Fisher toiled long hours, sometimes sleeping in the store, justifying Daniels's faith in him. When in 1872 Eckhart reduced his role to silent investor, Daniels made Fisher his new Denver partner. Daniels and Fisher would stand for high-quality goods at fair prices for another eighty-six years.[4]

By now, Denver's fortunes were more assured. Railroads had arrived in 1871, the Denver City Railway had built a horsecar line and the population was beginning to grow after the stagnant 1860s.[5] New mineral discoveries in Colorado's mountains led to increased trade in Denver. The town, soon to be a city, was poised to boom, and its merchants, Daniels and Fisher prominent among them, were well positioned to take advantage of it.

Fisher's first significant move was consolidation: he sold the Fillmore Block operation to Eckhart and moved the Larimer Street store around the corner and up one block, buying the eastern corner of Sixteenth and Lawrence Streets and erecting in 1875 a two-story building, 50 feet wide by 125 feet deep. Four years later, this proved too small, and the partners (Daniels, as of 1878, residing in Denver) added another 25 feet along Lawrence and another two floors. Colorado's economy continued booming through the 1880s, growing so rapidly that Fisher built yet another addition in 1888, adding an atrium with "a massive skylight." In 1893, he added a fifth floor.[6]

By 1880, Daniels and Fisher had unequivocally become the most impressive store in Denver, employing 250 people as clerks and dressmakers and running a thriving wholesale operation. It even opened a branch in booming Leadville (Daniels, Fisher and Smith, their local partner being Joel W. Smith), where so many fortunes were being made.[7] Denverites familiar with the famous A.T. Stewart store in New York took to referring to the store as the "Stewart's of the West." It offered something for everyone, from utilitarian work clothes to fine suits and fancy gowns. Those with means found imported items from top European dressmakers and tailors. Fine Denver homes were filled with Daniels and Fisher's carpets, furniture and draperies, and to complete the scene, the store offered the full variety of ornate *objets d'art* considered essential for the proper home.[8]

On the first floor, busy counters filled eight aisles; upper floor and basement departments sold goods requiring more careful perusal. After the fifth-floor addition, the store was arranged as follows:

- first floor: men's furnishings, women's furnishings, umbrellas, stationery, photographic goods, notions, sundries, toilet articles, perfumes, laces, trimmings, handkerchiefs, dry goods, dress patterns, notions, table linens, bed linens, towels, books, jewelry, clocks, silverware, leather goods, shoes, potted plants and cut flowers.

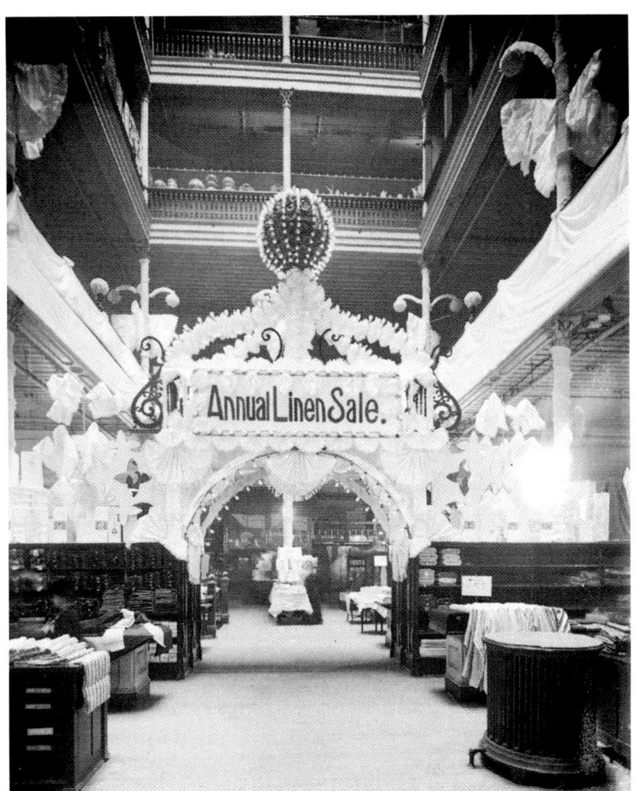

Right: Daniels and Fisher's atrium, circa 1902. *Denver Public Library, Western History Collection, X-22860.*

Below: Daniels and Fisher at Sixteenth and Lawrence Streets, circa 1881. *Denver Public Library, Western History Collection, X-24857.*

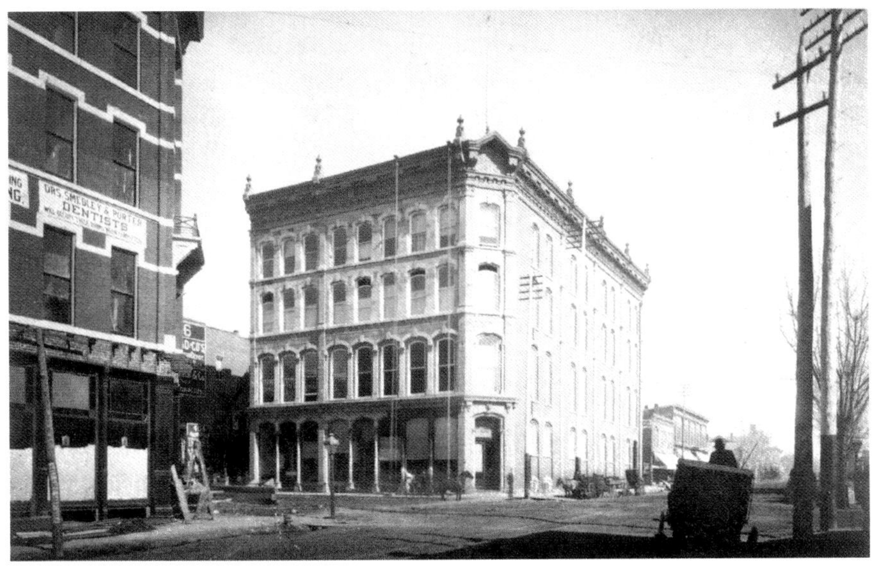

- second floor: women's cloaks, suits, furs, millinery and infants' clothing.
- third floor: bric-a-brac, Tiffany glass, marble statuary, Japanese art ware, candelabra, candles, pictures and framing, carpets and rugs, linoleums, lace curtains, draperies, men's clothing and custom tailoring and boys' clothing.
- fourth floor: crockery, china, cut glass, cutlery, lamps, furniture and mattresses.
- fifth floor: dressmaking and tailoring, along with clothing manufacturing.
- basement: baby carriages, sporting goods, toys, dolls, games, candy, fancy groceries, tea and coffee, traveling bags, trunks, china, glassware and lower-priced dry goods.[9]

The fourth floor also boasted a tearoom serving light meals, and the third housed a unique Daniels and Fisher institution: a classroom for juvenile staffers. Boys and girls moved stock and ferried cash from customers to a central cashier, working long hours and unable to attend school regularly. Qualified teachers instructed them, and class time was paid so children would have an incentive to attend lessons.[10]

Daniels died on Christmas Eve 1890. He was sixty-five and worn out. Elizabeth had died of tuberculosis in 1881, and he had married in 1882 the much younger Lilyon Donna Abbott, whom he had originally engaged to give speech therapy to his young son, Willie. The conservative Daniels and the artistic, temperamental Lilyon (who later adopted the stage name Donna Madixxa to highlight her Spanish aristocratic ancestry) were soon estranged, and the embarrassing public melodrama of their marriage and divorce took its toll on him.[11] When William Bradley Daniels died, Willie—William Cooke Daniels—was just twenty, already deeply engaged in his lifelong pursuit of knowledge, studying Buddhism in Yokohama, Japan. Fisher ran the store for several more years. However, when Fisher died in 1897, it was time for William, two-thirds owner, to take the reins.[12] For the next two decades, the dashing, sophisticated Daniels, who did not live in Denver for long periods, periodically blew into town and impressed residents with tales of his exciting life. In between adventures, he definitively put his stamp on the store.

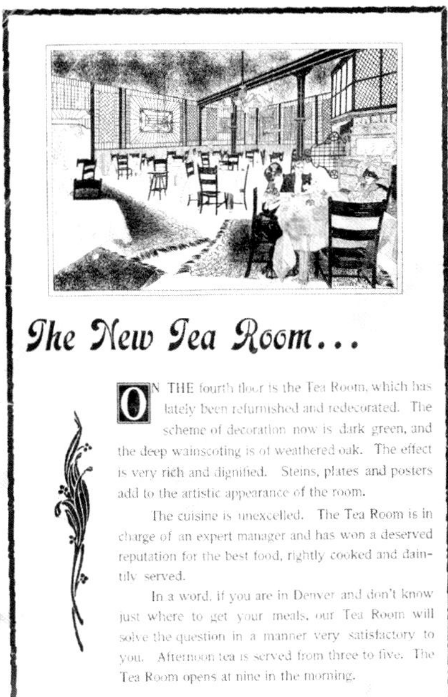

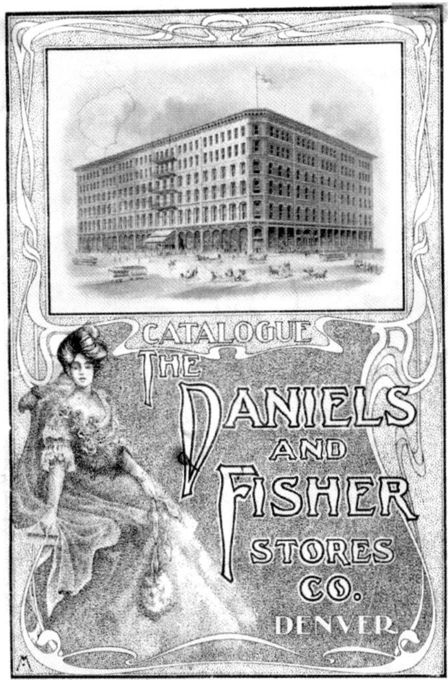

Left: Advertisement for the Daniels and Fisher Tea Room, circa 1902. *Right*: Catalogue cover showing the full extent of the Lawrence Street building, circa 1902. *Ron and Judy Proctor Collection.*

DENVER'S LANDMARK

Before Daniels had time to do much with the store, the United States declared war. The Spanish-American War of 1898 is associated with its most famous participant, Theodore Roosevelt, and the intensely patriotic Daniels was cut from the same cloth as the future president. When war broke out, he immediately volunteered for the army, securing a commission; for the rest of his life, newspapers referred to him as "Major Daniels." He saw action at the siege of Santiago, Cuba (and was commended for his bravery) but caught typhoid and had left the service by 1899.[13]

While he was away, Daniels required an able person to direct the store, and he appointed his good friend Charles MacAllister Willcox as general manager. After the war, Daniels and Willcox set out to upgrade the store—positioning it above rivals the May Company, The Denver Dry Goods Company and Joslin's—to win the carriage trade. They installed dramatic, bronze-framed show windows on Sixteenth Street. Inside, new departments included jewelry, bicycles and a floral shop; the tearoom was expanded and made more elegant. Upon the remodeling's completion in 1902, the store commissioned photographs to document its refined beauty: curved mahogany and beveled glass showcases, potted plants and oriental rugs accenting elegant merchandise displays.[14] Having previously purchased from Fisher's widow her one-third interest, Daniels also changed the store's structure, incorporating the Daniels and Fisher Stores Company to issue stock as a way of rewarding Willcox and others with shares.[15]

The changes complete, Daniels returned to his peripatetic life, voyaging to far corners (French Guiana, Martinique, New Guinea, Australia, London and Paris), with Willcox minding the store.[16] Having married and divorced previously, Daniels became enamored of an aristocratic young Englishwoman, Cicely Banner, whose ancestors included King Edward I. They married in 1907. In 1909, Daniels returned to Denver with Cicely, accompanied by her best friend, Florence Martin, an Australian. The Denver

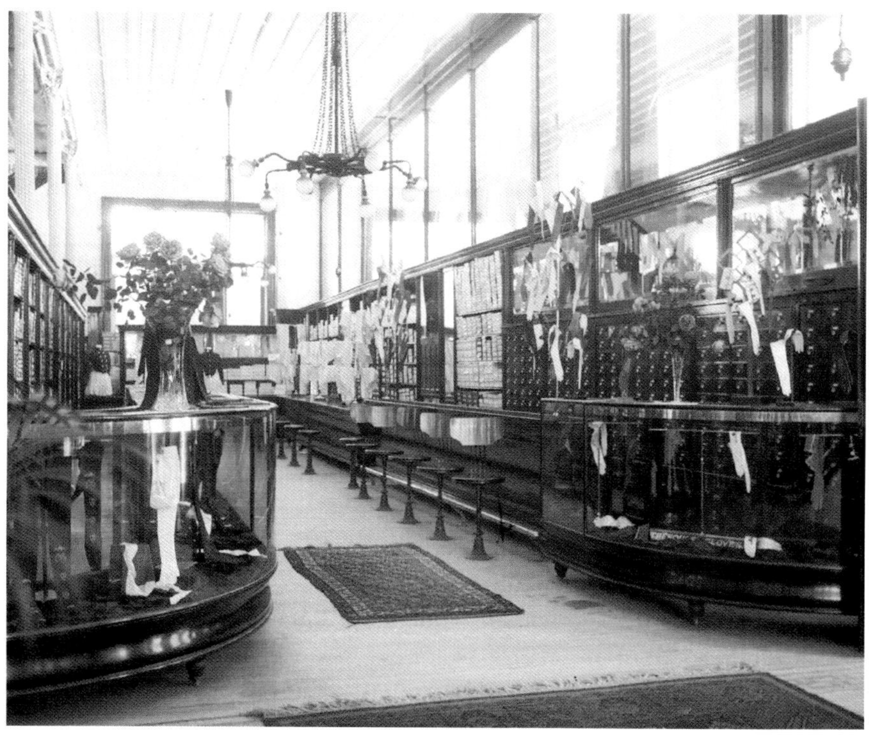

Ladies' stocking and glove departments, circa 1902. *Denver Public Library, Western History Collection, X-22825.*

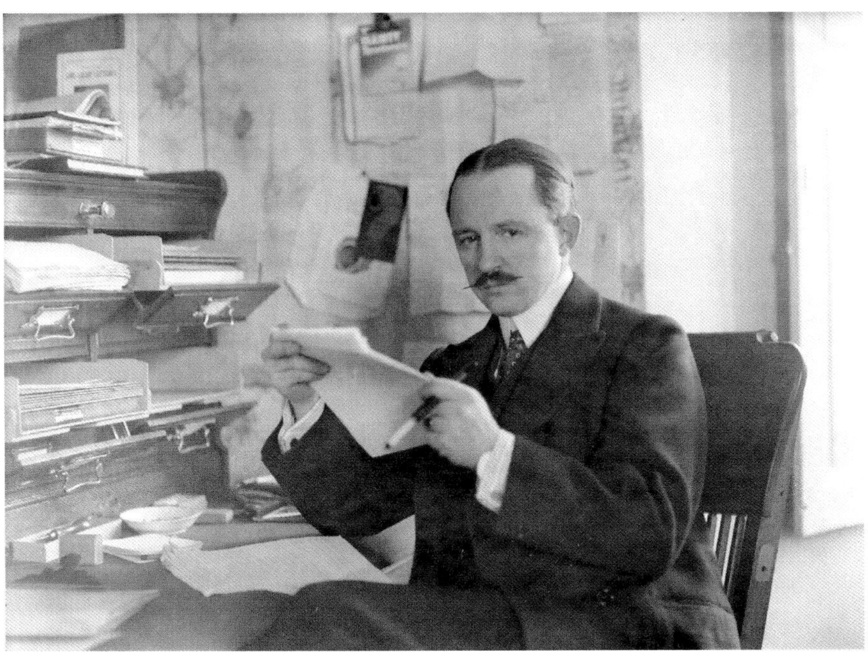

William Cooke Daniels, man of the world, circa 1907. *Ron and Judy Proctor Collection.*

press fawned over the new bride of the city's most glamorous merchant: "[She is] vivacious, extremely fair to look upon, and possesses a personality of unusual charm…she rides and drives and motors and is extremely fond of pets and wears beautiful gowns and is in love with America and the American people." Daniels and his wife soon returned to a thirteenth-century Loire Valley castle in France, the Chateau de la Motte-Sonzay near Tours, which Daniels had leased since 1906. Curiously, for a French census that year he declared his name as "Daniel Cooke." He may have wanted to remain anonymous, as Cicely Banner and Florence Martin were also listed as living with him as "governesses" (Cicely was not yet Mrs. Daniels, which might cause scandal at home). They enjoyed a *luxe* life, with Daniels indulging his love of fine automobiles, including a Daimler-Mercedes and several early Rolland-Pilain cars, built by a Tours manufacturer.[17]

Daniels had not lost interest in his store or Denver, however. In February 1910, all four Denver dailies published drawings of an "artistic improvement" planned by Daniels and Fisher. Needing more room and blocked from growing further on Lawrence Street, Daniels and Willcox jumped across the alley, with an addition stretching to the corner of Sixteenth and

Arapahoe Streets. This gave Daniels and Fisher 266 feet of Sixteenth Street frontage. More importantly, the addition included a tower that would come to symbolize Denver's status as "Queen City of the Plains"—the tallest building in a thousand miles and for a short period the sixth-tallest building in the United States.[18]

Daniels instructed architect Julius Sterner (of Sterner and Williamson) to design an edifice that would "get away from the inartistic 'warehouse' style of construction" of the original building and other Denver stores, providing Denver a monument to complement Mayor Robert W. Speer's "City Beautiful" improvements such as Civic Center and new tree-lined parkways. Venice's Campanile of St. Mark's had collapsed in 1902, and over the ensuing decade, there was worldwide interest in its rebuilding. Replica towers inspired by the original were popular, so Sterner designed for Daniels a tower that resembled, but did not exactly reproduce, the campanile. He specified a buff-colored brick instead of Denver's ubiquitous red, accented with terra-cotta Della Robbia medallions and other Neoclassical features, capped by a red-tiled sloping roof. Sterner rebuilt the Sixteenth Street façade of the original building to conform with the addition, and above the first floor, the new was joined with the old. The 330-foot tower (375 feet with flagpole) and addition were completed in 1911.[19]

The tower became a tourist attraction. An elevator ride to the observation deck (cost: one dime) provided an unequaled panorama of Denver and the mountains, viewable through telescopes. In addition to a twentieth-floor curio shop, the tower featured clocks on all sides and a bell ("the largest bell west of the Mississippi" per truth-guessing newspaper accounts) that tolled hourly. Above the five retail levels, each floor had a purpose, including the relocated schoolroom, gender-segregated employee lounges and executive offices.[20] But the tower's main role was to symbolize the store. For the next forty-seven years, Daniels and Fisher employed images of it in its advertising.

Also for that entire period, Daniels and Fisher employed Carl Sandell as its doorman. First recruited by *Denver Post* publisher Frederick G. Bonfils to star in his paper's Boys Band, the extremely tall (seven feet, five inches) Sandell became almost as famous a store symbol as the tower, although he generally opened the original main door on Lawrence Street rather than the tower doors. Another legendary employee was "the most beautiful model in Denver," Margaret Gessing. Initially a stock girl, Gessing's poise resulted in her modeling at fashion shows between 1912 and 1918 and appearing in newspaper spreads and even a silent film representing the store. Mary Alice Fitzgerald was yet another well-regarded employee, serving as book buyer

Right: Daniels and Fisher in its glory, as photographed from the top of the U.S. Post Office and Customs House at Sixteenth and Arapahoe Streets, circa 1912. *Thomas J. Noel Collection/Library of Congress.*

Below: View from the observation deck looking up Sixteenth Street toward the Colorado Capitol Building. *Denver Public Library, Western History Collection, MCC-1656; photograph by Louis Charles McClure.*

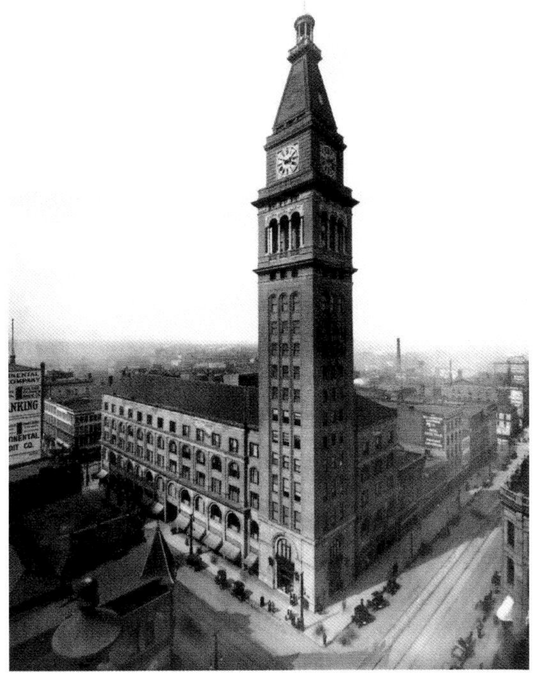

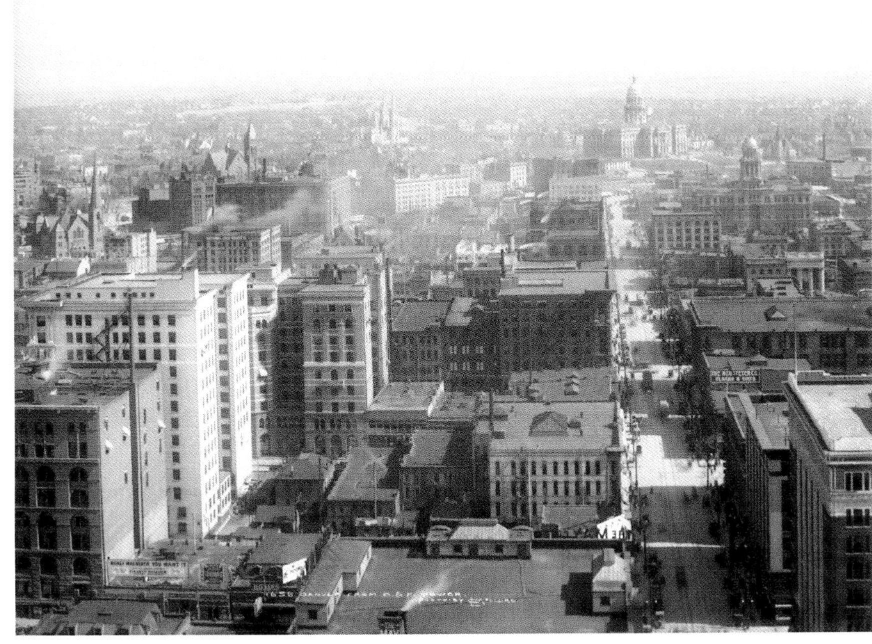

from 1927 until 1958 and, with her many book signing events, establishing Denver as an important stopping point for touring authors.[21]

William Cooke Daniels viewed his completed tower only once, in 1912. After World War I began in 1914, and particularly after the United States entered it in 1917, he wanted to serve his country again. Too old to serve in battle, the government accepted his offer of service regardless. In the spring of 1918, he traveled to Buenos Aires, Argentina, on some unspecified mission and died of a sudden fever; he was forty-seven. Cicely Daniels and Florence Martin still resided in Europe, running a facility in Switzerland for recuperating soldiers. The influenza pandemic of 1918–19 struck both women, and Cicely died six months after her husband (Martin survived).[22]

Daniels had no heir and had designated Charles MacAllister Willcox to receive his shares. Cicely willed her shares to Florence Martin and to Willcox's eleven-year-old daughter, Elaine. This kept the store in the hands of Denverites. Martin relocated to Colorado to keep an eye on her interest, although she never actively participated in store management. Honoring her friends Cicely and William, in 1937 she donated 1,040 acres, twenty-one miles south of Denver in Douglas County, to the Denver Mountain Parks system; Daniels Park, with expansive views of the South Platte River Valley, remains a popular destination today.[23]

Willcox kept the store's reputation strong by continuing to make improvements during the 1920s—he had to, as its chief rival, The Denver Dry Goods Company, was capturing an ever-increasing share of Denver's retail dollars, and new competitors vied for the carriage trade. In 1929, he decided to retire. After briefly entertaining an offer from newly formed Hahn Department Stores Inc. (later Allied Stores), Willcox and his now-adult daughter, Elaine, chose to sell to longtime employees Alfred Blake Trott and Walter Beans.[24] The new men continued burnishing the store's image, utilizing the slogan "Denver's Pioneer Store" in advertisements. They also reminded shoppers that the store was still locally controlled, in contrast to The Denver Dry Goods and Joslin's, both owned by out-of-town interests. Trott and Beans completed the final store addition, erecting in 1930 a parking garage abutting the Arapahoe building, with their architect designing a Neoclassical façade to match Sterner's from 1910 to 1911. The garage provided valet parking and gave women a reason to venture to a downtown section that was beginning to lose its luster. They could hand their cars off to an attendant and enter the store directly, without venturing outside.[25]

The Dowager of Sixteenth

Trott and Beans saw the store through the Depression and World War II, keeping expenses down while continuing to offer fine products and service (not an easy feat during wartime). Trott died in 1944, and Beans retired shortly after the war. Ownership was still in Denver hands, however, with various members of the city's old guard holding shares.[26] New president Edward C. Yourell announced a $2 million remodeling in 1946, to include the store's first escalator, connecting the first and second floors (for context, both the May Company and The Denver Dry Goods had had escalators for four decades).[27] In 1950, the store announced its first branch since the Leadville days, buying the Giddings Company of Colorado Springs. Daniels and Fisher's name replaced Giddings in that city's downtown and in its Broadmoor Hotel boutique.[28]

In July 1953, an announcement by colorful New York City developer William Zeckendorf, president of Webb & Knapp Inc., upended the store's future. Since 1945, he had been planning a project some distance up Sixteenth from Daniels and Fisher, on the block bounded by Sixteenth,

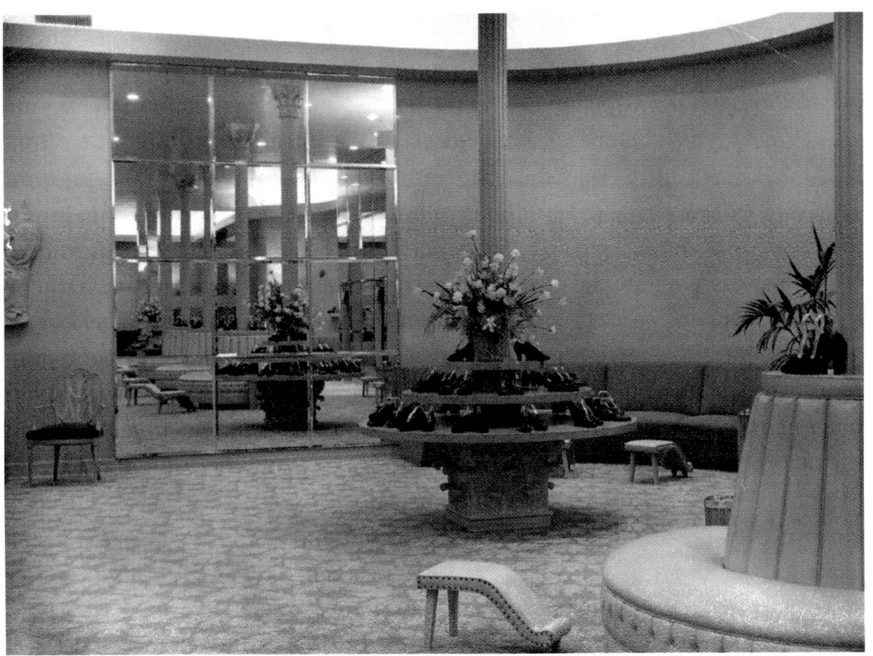

Ladies' shoe department as remodeled by J. Harford Ryan, circa 1950. *History Colorado, J. Harford Ryan Collection, 10055019.*

Fifteenth, Tremont Street and Court Place. It had once been home to the Denver County Courthouse (demolished in 1933), and Zeckendorf had bought it from the city to build Courthouse Square, a "second Radio City"—a sophisticated, urbane development with a department store, a hotel and other amenities. Rejected by Denver's old-guard retailers, he realized that he would only land an anchor tenant by buying one. Daniels and Fisher, with its diffuse ownership, seemed easiest to acquire, so he began accumulating shares. Once he won control and obtained a signed lease, he sold the store to a partnership of Des Moines, Iowa-based Younker Brothers department store and Jerome M. Ney of Fort Smith, Arkansas. The store with the tower would move to a modern landmark designed by Zeckendorf's in-house architect, a Chinese American named Ieoh Ming (I.M.) Pei.[29]

Daniels and Fisher's last years under Younker Brothers and Ney delivered a final burst of glory. Yourell had resigned earlier, and his successor, Albert P. Sonneman, resigned at the sale. To replace him, the owners chose a rising executive of Dallas's Neiman-Marcus, Joseph Ross. He had reported directly to Stanley Marcus, and he brought touches of the Texas emporium's elegance to Daniels and Fisher—William Cooke Daniels would have approved. After the war, sales had slid, largely because of the store's now-undesirable location near Larimer Street's "skid row." Forty years old, ambitious and talented, Ross soon "re-establish[ed] the store's greatness" through better customer service, more on-trend fashions, better merchandising and an elegant new logo. His borrowed ideas from Neiman-Marcus included an art gallery, a themed Italian "fortnight" (celebrating Italy's culture and hosting a personal appearance by Sophia Loren) and sophisticated giftwrapping. Ross's changes worked: sales rose dramatically (14 percent in his first year).[30] But Zeckendorf was not content with a signed lease. He needed success at Courthouse Square, and with other stores opening suburban branches, he decided that downtown had too many department stores.[31]

Zeckendorf felt that the best way to reduce downtown square footage was to engineer a merger between two or more stores. He approached The Denver Dry Goods, but it was not interested. The May Company was intrigued, mostly because it also recognized that downtown had too much square footage. Zeckendorf arranged for May to sell its Iowa stores to Younker Brothers and for Younker to sell Daniels and Fisher to May.[32] The new entity would be called May-D&F and would assume the Courthouse Square lease. After the merger announcement, Joe Ross departed, returning to his first employer, Macy's in New York; he died of a heart attack not many

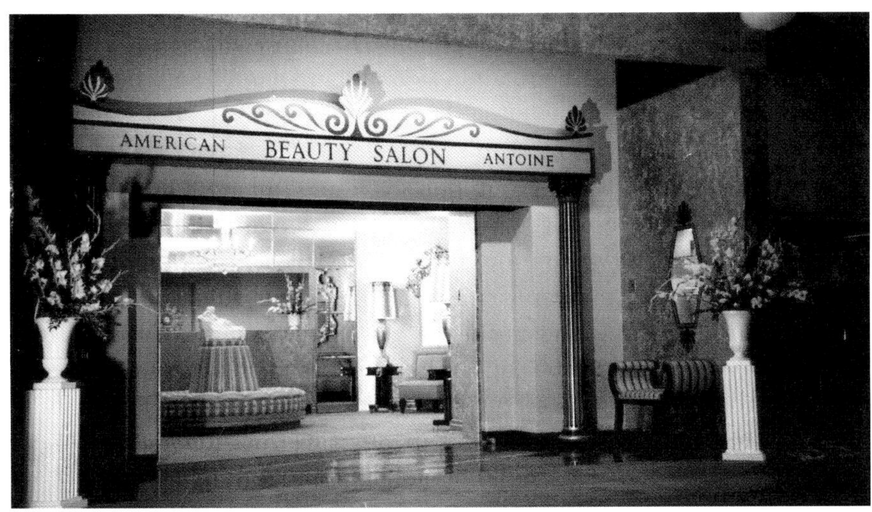

Entry to the American and Antoine beauty salons, designed by J. Harford Ryan, circa 1950. *History Colorado, J. Harford Ryan Collection, 10055020.*

years later. The merger was consummated in the fall of 1957, and for the last few months, May Company ran the store. Advertisements dropped the Daniels and Fisher name, replacing it with "D&F," to accustom shoppers to May-D&F. Daniels and Fisher closed its doors in late July, prior to May-D&F's August opening at Courthouse Square.[33]

Chapter 2
JOSLIN'S
The Friendly Store

I blink my eyes in amazement when I pause long enough to consider the remarkable transformation in the Joslin Dry Goods store of today over the little general merchandise store I founded....The changes of the years, however bewildering they may be, are all for the best.
—J. Jay Joslin, May 11, 1924[34]

THE GENIAL YANKEE

The grand old man of Denver retailing, John Jay Joslin managed to reach ninety-six years without ever retiring from the store he had founded in pioneer days. A Yankee of definite opinions, he never wavered from his belief in work. "Success in any line of endeavor means competency, strenuous work and integrity," he told the *Rocky Mountain News* on his ninety-fifth birthday. Also, he advised, "smoke moderately, if you must smoke at all; drink moderately, if you think you must. Above all, eat with discrimination."[35] Hoping to reach his centenary, he fell short, succumbing to influenza in early 1926. Obituaries expressed admiration for a man unaffected by fads, and the day after his death, seven Denver department stores published a joint advertisement paying tribute to a career that "has been, and will continue to be, an inspiration to us all."[36]

When J. Jay Joslin (his preferred styling) arrived in Denver in 1872 to visit his brother, Jervis, a successful jeweler, he had no idea beforehand that that the dusty young city would become his home. He was impressed by "the climate and the character of the people [he] met" and realized that "there was a great future here."[37] Joslin's enthusiasm for Denver was based not on boosterish tales but on what he saw with his own eyes. He had already built a successful business and recognized opportunity.

Born in Poultney, Vermont, on May 11, 1829, to Joseph and Caroline Ruggles Joslin, J. Jay was the second son of five, descended from Thomas Joslin, who had settled in Hingham, Massachusetts, in 1635. His grandfather Lindsey Joslin had participated in the Battle of Concord, which set off the American Revolution. As a teen, Joslin clerked in a local store, and after a year spent farming (at his father's behest), he decided that the mercantile life, not the agricultural, was for him. He married Mary E. Andrus in 1851 and, in 1852, opened a store in Poultney. He funded it with $500 he had saved, supplemented by $1,000 from his father, who saw that "he meant business," as well as another $1,000 in credit. By 1864, he had built "the largest and finest store" in Vermont, stocked with "the best general assortment of goods to be found north of Troy [New York]."[38]

So enthusiastic was Joslin about Denver that he sold his Poultney establishment and bought the New York Store, a two-story mercantile at Fifteenth and Larimer Streets owned by Jacob Deusch. J. Jay Joslin Dry Goods opened there on April 22, 1873, featuring a large assortment of "silks, epinglines, Lyons, poplins, striped poplins, cashmere d'ecasse, black silks, black alpacas, black grenadines, embroideries, parasols, shawls, gloves, cloaks, suits, white and linen goods, hosiery, laces, lace curtains, fans, ribbons, trimmings, notions, gents' furnishings, carpets," as well as myriad other goods. He soon developed a reputation for honest dealing. Unlike every other Denver merchant in these pages, he never took on a partner.[39]

Joslin quickly became a leading figure. By 1874, he was a director of the Denver Mercantile Protective Association and also spoke at the city council regarding the difficultly of conducting business when the street was cluttered with horses and drays awaiting passengers and freight. He petitioned to have this activity moved elsewhere, as the male drivers not only blocked the street but also made his female customers uncomfortable. Denver's unpaved streets could be unbearably dusty during dry summers; Joslin, with other merchants, agitated for sprinkling to keep down the dirt, which soiled ladies' dresses. Years later, Joslin filed police charges against automobile drivers going too fast for public safety. Yet despite his assertiveness in business and civil society, he was known best for his geniality. Per one account: "It seems to be a pleasure to him and to his assistants to gratify the eyes of those

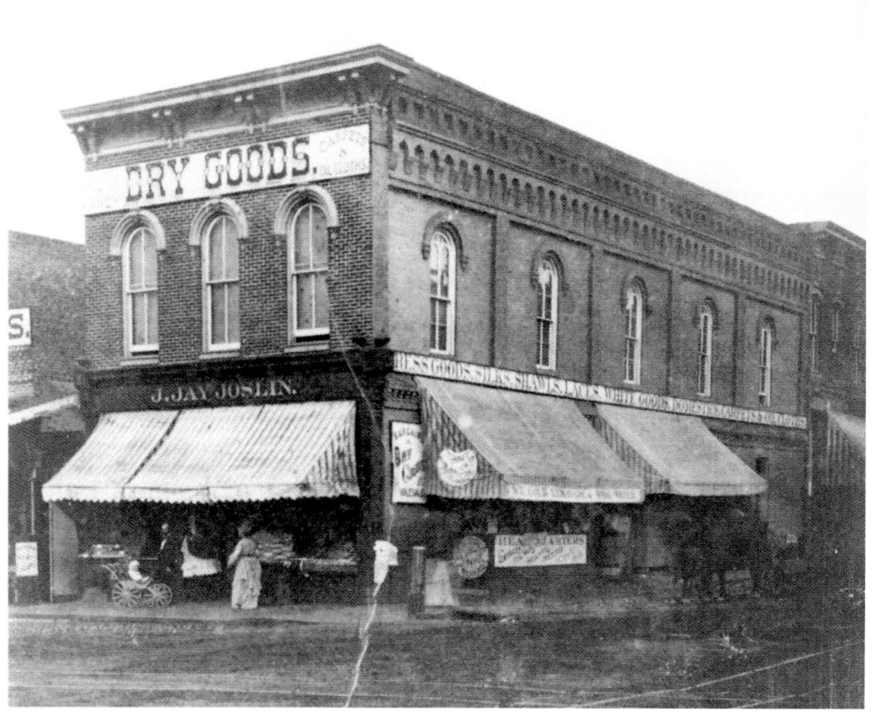

John Jay Joslin's first Denver store at the eastern corner of Fifteenth and Larimer Streets, 1875. *Denver Public Library, Western History Collection, F10860.*

who enter his store, though no purchase should be made. And herein likes the difference between an agreeable salesman and one whose actions drive custom from his store. No storekeeper ever lost money by a genial politeness, and our friend J.J.J. is well aware of this."[40]

Joslin's softer side also showed in extracurricular activities. He loved singing tenor in church choir (First Baptist), and in 1874, he co-founded the Handel and Haydn Society, a choral group. The society performed, often in the First Baptist Church, until 1883, when it merged with the Choral Union, of which Joslin was president. Before the merger, the two groups joined in 1879 to produce the Gilbert and Sullivan operetta *H.M.S. Pinafore*; Joslin sang in the chorus.[41]

Joslin's store thrived, and by 1879, his shop had become too small. Expansion was impossible, so he found temporary quarters at 376 Lawrence Street (in Denver's old address system), between Fifteenth and Sixteenth.

Later that year, he moved into a new three-story building four doors closer to Sixteenth, at 384 and 386 Lawrence. By September, this new store, fifty feet wide by one hundred feet deep (with the wholesale department in the basement), was ready, and in October, Joslin held a grand opening. While the Larimer Street shop was essentially a glorified general store (per Joslin's own remembrances several decades later), this new facility was a true department store, with "goods [that] are all classified into departments, each of which has a competent lady or gentleman in attendance." With Colorado's economy strong, Joslin catered not only to middle classes but also to the carriage trade, with "some elegant suits…ranging all the way up to $300—Paris make—and handsome enough to gratify the wealthiest lady in the land."[42]

Joslin conducted business here for less than a decade. Colorado's economy continued booming, and in 1887, he decided to move to a new four-story building at Sixteenth and Curtis Streets, opposite the 1881 Tabor Grand Opera House. Hardware merchant (and fellow Choral Union member) George Tritch had branched out into real estate, and the Tritch Block would

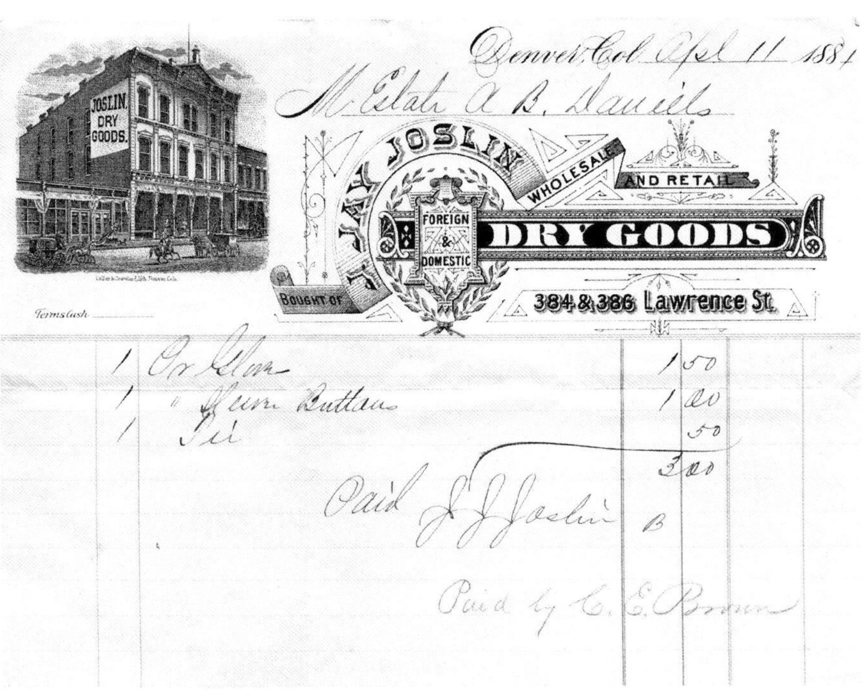

Denver, Col. Apl 11 1881
M Estate A. B. Daniels
JOSLIN DRY GOODS.
Terms Cash
Bought of
Jay Joslin
Wholesale and Retail
Foreign & Domestic
Dry Goods
384 & 386 Lawrence St.

1		1 50
1		1 00
1		50
		3 00

Receipt dated 1881 showing Joslin's second location on the southeastern side of Lawrence Street between Fifteenth and Sixteenth Streets (closer to the latter). *Author's collection.*

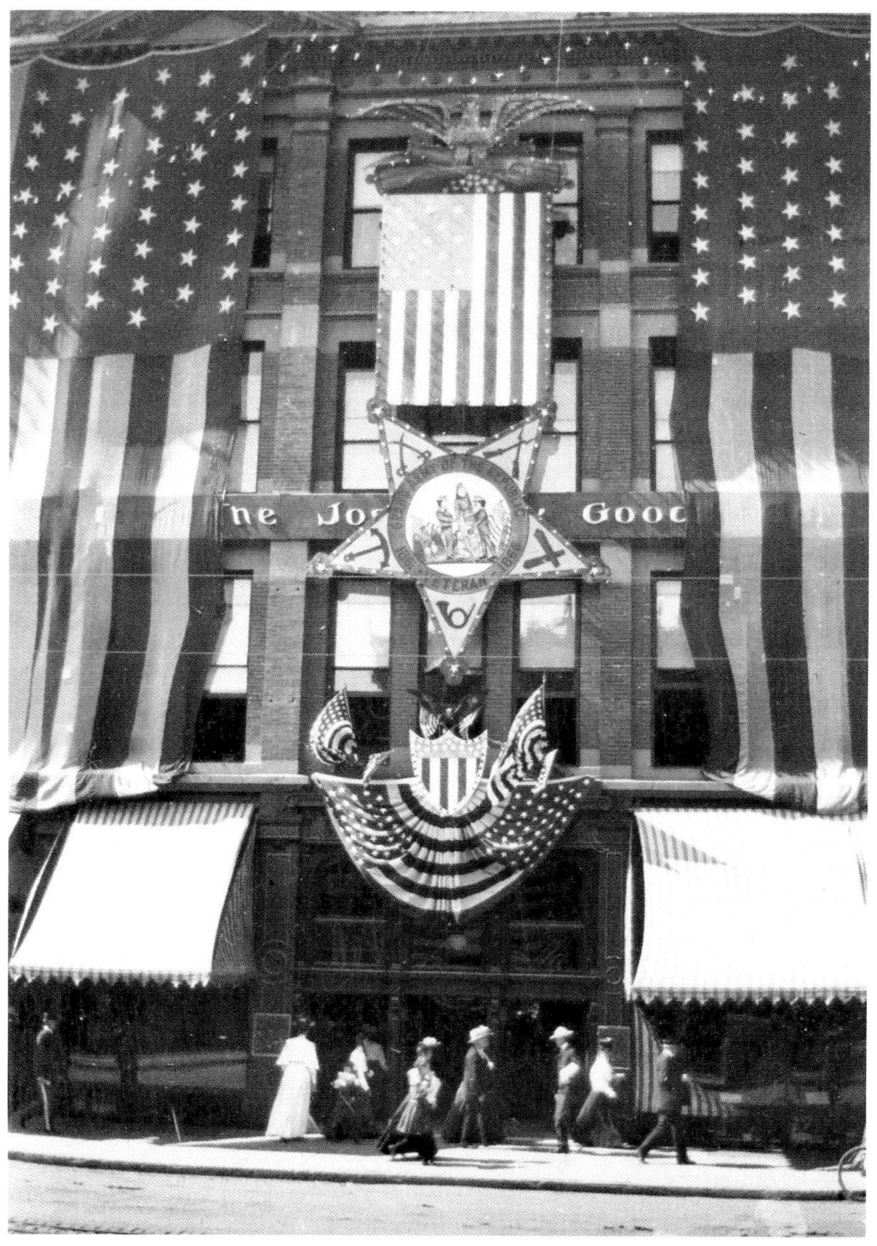

Joslin's Sixteenth Street entrance in the George Tritch Building, decorated for the Grand Army of the Republic Encampment, held in Denver in 1905. *Denver Public Library, Western History Collection, F6834.*

be Joslin's new home, along with another store called The Fair. The building was finished late in 1887, and Joslin opened "the most complete dry goods store in the west" on April 30, 1888. While The Fair occupied part of the first floor, Joslin took the larger portion, along with the basement and upper floors, encompassing forty-five thousand square feet. It took fourteen years, until 1902, for Joslin to obtain The Fair's space. Joslin's was organized similar to other department stores. Dry goods, handkerchiefs, notions, perfumes, gentlemen's goods and other high-traffic departments filled the first floor. On two, ladies perused linens, underwear and decorative items and enjoyed "spacious waiting and toilet rooms." Three beckoned with cloaks and suits, jackets and wraps, millinery and dressmaking parlors. Four housed carpets, curtains and draperies. In the basement, customers found domestics and bargain departments (the wholesale department had space downstairs). "Two commodious elevators" connected the floors. Joslin's soon adopted the slogan "the busiest store, on the busiest corner, of the busiest street, in the busiest city in the West."[43]

LAST OF THE MOHICANS

Joslin, with son Frank Andrus Joslin joining him as secretary and treasurer, continued to thrive after the turn of the twentieth century. Frank, also born in Poultney, was another well-liked, genial businessman, described by the *Denver Times* as "a fellow who assays clear to the limit as a royal prince of good fellows." In addition to his duties at the store, he also speculated in mining; both father and son had interests in mines and stamp mills in Idaho Springs and Central City.[44]

It was during this period that Joslin's briefly employed a young man who would later found a retail empire, one James Cash Penney. According to later store president Herbert M. Stoll, Penney, who had come west for his health and worked in the domestics department, was "a lively kid" and "a go-getter with a special gift for straightening out department tangles." After leaving Joslin's, Penney moved to Longmont, where he worked in a Golden Rule Store. He later bought that chain and, in 1902, renamed it the J.C. Penney Company. Another employee, Julius Garfinckel, "a little flip boy who had come to do rushabout chores," rose to a buyer position and then left Denver for Washington, D.C., where he founded the upscale department store Garfinckel's.[45]

Two of DENVER'S Important Institutions

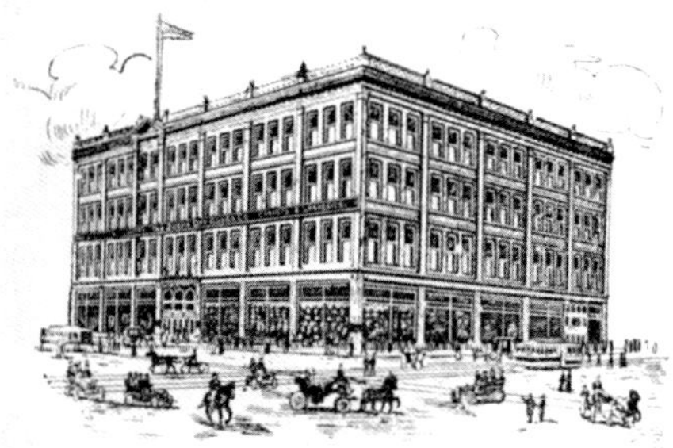

DENVER AUDITORIUM cost $550,000.00. Seating capacity 12,500; 266 feet long, 200 feet wide; built of brick, stone, concrete and steel. Lighted by 500 electric lamps.

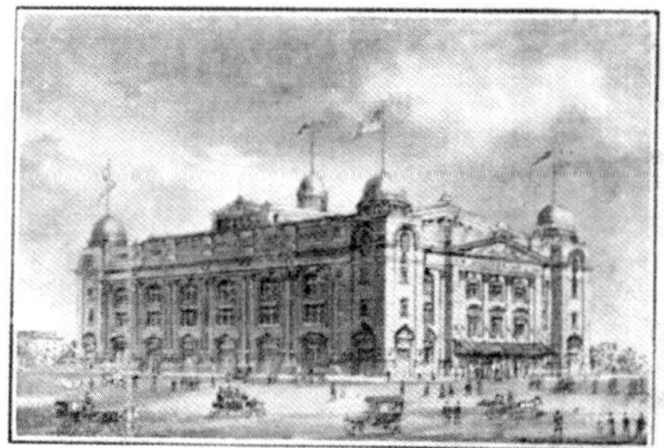

The busiest store, on the busiest corner, on the busiest street in the busiest city of the west—**THE JOSLIN DRY GOODS COMPANY.** Doing business in Denver for thirty-six years.

Monuments to Western Enterprise, Solidity and Growth

Joslin's postcard bearing its famous slogan "The busiest store, on the busiest corner, on the busiest street, in the busiest city of the west," 1909. *Author's collection.*

In 1910, Joslin sold his store to the H.B. Claflin Company. Horace Brigham Claflin had founded his firm in 1843, and for several decades, it functioned as a wholesaler (or jobber) of dry goods to stores. Claflin died in 1885, and in 1890, his son, John Claflin, reincorporated the business. With jobbing less lucrative (many merchants now bought direct from manufacturers), Claflin used the firm as a shell company, incorporating two other businesses, Associated Merchants' Company and United Dry Goods Company. He used these other entities ("wheels within wheels," per one postmortem) to buy department stores around the country, largely to prop up the wholesale division. Besides Joslin Dry Goods, Claflin-controlled stores included Lord & Taylor (New York); Scruggs, Vandervoort and Barney (St. Louis); the Jones Store (Kansas City); and dozens of others. Claflin overextended himself, and in June 1914, his empire came crashing down. After bankruptcy, two new companies emerged: Associated Dry Goods Company and Mercantile Stores Corporation (later Mercantile Stores Company). Associated won the "plum" stores like Lord & Taylor, while Mercantile absorbed the rest, including Joslin's. The largest shareholder of Mercantile was the Milliken family of South Carolina, whose primary business was textiles.[46]

Joslin's emerged from the Claflin disaster in fine shape; its profitability was never in doubt. John Jay Joslin, who had remained president of the store under Claflin, continued under Mercantile Stores—although controlled by a New York–based company, Joslin's was in every other respect a local store, run by local people. Denver newspapers began marking Joslin's birthday each May—this remarkable man in his eighties (later nineties) was financially comfortable and could afford retirement yet still worked every day. "I have worked hard," he said in 1916, "but who minds that when success follows? I have built up this business; it is a part of me just as I am a part of it. I want to stay with it as long as I may."[47] Yet his long life was not without sorrow. He lost Mary in 1911, continuing to live alone in their home at 2915 Champa Street (which the Joslins had occupied since its 1878 construction).[48] He lost Frank in 1922 after a months-long illness; he was only sixty-four.[49] Finally, it was the turn of "the dean of Denver business men," who referred to himself as "the last of the Mohicans," to leave the stage. After working a full day on December 12, 1925, he came down with influenza and died at home on January 7, 1926. Hundreds attended his funeral, held at First Baptist Church at Eighteenth and Stout Streets; Joslin was laid to rest at Fairmount Cemetery.[50]

Early Branches

Longtime employee Herbert Mortimer Stoll succeeded Joslin as president. He had arrived in Denver in 1887 from Omaha. Initially working for Daniels and Fisher, Stoll liked the atmosphere Joslin had fostered and began managing Joslin's curtain department in 1889. Like Joslin, Stoll was Baptist, believed in hard work and didn't retire. While Joslin was alive, Stoll rose to general manager (beginning in 1910), and after Joslin's death, he helmed the store until 1933, then becoming chairman, a position he retained until his 1948 death at eighty-four. During Stoll's tenure, in 1927 the store modified its façade, converting groups of three narrow windows on floors two, three and four to single, large panes by removing brick piers in between; Stoll also added a fifth floor.[51]

After some short-term presidencies, in 1938 Mercantile sent Clarence F. Beaglehole to Denver. It was under him that Joslin's began to assume the form most people remember, a chain of which the downtown store was merely one link. As had been the philosophy since early days, Beaglehole sold merchandise of good quality at reasonable prices, nothing too fancy or expensive. A youthful thirty-seven, he came to Joslin's after leading another Mercantile division in Pennsylvania.[52]

In 1944, Beaglehole opened the first branch, a shop on Eighth Street in Greeley (in 1973, a Greeley Mall store replaced it). In 1945, Joslin's opened in Englewood, and in early 1946, Beaglehole announced a third branch in "West Denver" (today's Lakewood) at 7308 West Colfax Avenue. In 1949, Joslin's opened in downtown Aurora at 9620 East Colfax Avenue, and in 1951, a fifth branch sprouted at Merchants' Park shopping center, 627 South Broadway. These branches were not large like later mall stores, and Beaglehole referred to them as "junior stores." West Colfax measured just 50 feet wide by 132 feet deep, with basement and mezzanine; Merchants' Park was the largest at 36,000 square feet on three levels. Regardless of size, these were the first branches built by any Denver department store—Beaglehole saw the future, and it meant proximity to middle-class customers and plenty of free parking. Nevertheless, downtown was still important, and Beaglehole knew that investments were needed to keep it strong. In 1950, he announced a complete remodeling of the second and third floors, designed to keep fashion-conscious women coming downtown.[53]

By 1952, Beaglehole was worn out after fifteen years and announced his retirement "on orders of his physician." Postwar prosperity, combined with his branch openings and downtown efforts, resulted in sales fifteen times greater than when he first came to Denver. To replace him, Mercantile sent out Paul C. McWilliams from the Jones Store in Kansas City. Originally from Cedar Rapids, Iowa, he was just as energetic as Beaglehole had been and found ways to further Joslin's growth.[54]

In 1953, he doubled the Aurora store's size by taking space next door. In 1954, he moved Englewood to a three-level building at 3315 South Broadway, at the Stop-and-Shop Center. Designed by local firm Fisher and Fisher, Englewood featured wrought-iron and gray oak fixtures, a beauty salon and an "outdoor roof-top beauty terrace" that afforded "a magnificent panoramic view of the Rockies." Affluent shoppers resided in nearby Cherry Hills Village, and McWilliams wanted their custom. Downtown, he acquired the building from George Tritch's heirs. He then bought the adjacent Rialto Theater on Curtis Street. Expanding onto that property was a dream to be realized later, however.[55]

McWilliams loved football and enjoyed watching Boulder's University of Colorado Buffaloes play. He realized that that growing city (up by ten thousand residents since the end of World War II) lacked a department store, so he opened one. Occupying the first three floors of a new nine-story office tower built by Boulder financier Allen J. Lefferdink at Fourteenth and Walnut Streets, the forty-two-thousand-square-foot Boulder branch

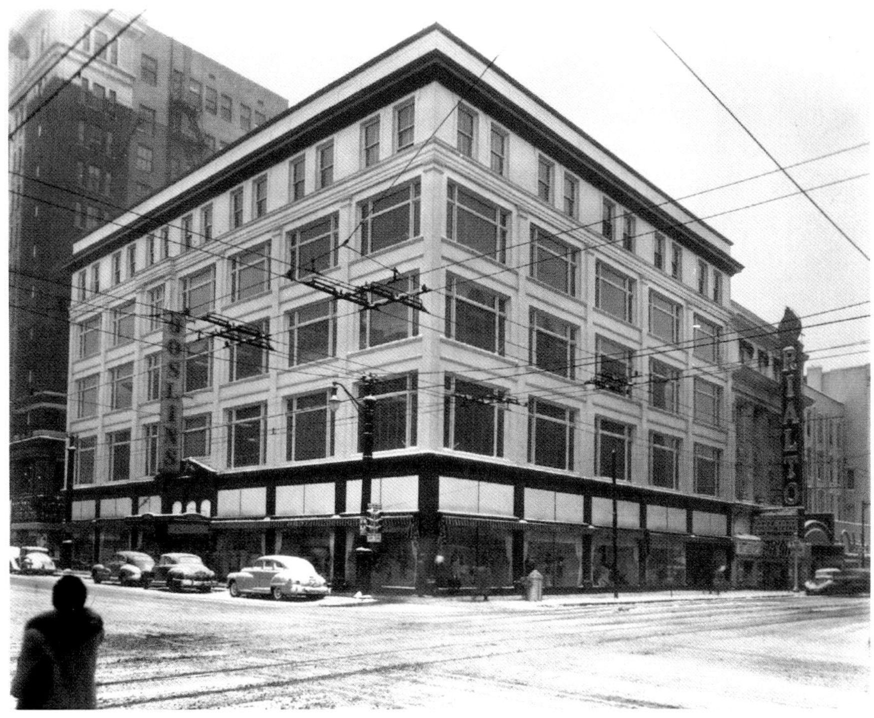

Joslin's, Sixteenth and Curtis Streets, February 1947, showing the larger windows installed on the second through fourth floors twenty years earlier; the original Fashion Bar store is visible at extreme right, past the Rialto Theater. *History Colorado, 10040067.*

opened in time for the holidays in 1956.[56] The last major expansion under McWilliams was the relocation, in 1957, of West Colfax to larger quarters nearby, in the new J.C.R.S. Shopping Center. A block-long, L-shaped center, J.C.R.S. included free parking, with the three-level Joslin's occupying prime space at the corner of the "L."[57]

McWilliams was then replaced by Norman Zilies, another executive transferred from a Mercantile division (Duluth, Minnesota's Glass Block). During McWilliams's tenure, Joslin's incurred legal expenses over some of his actions (likely endorsed by his Mercantile bosses). The first was a dispute with General Electric. In the 1950s, consumer products manufacturers favored a pricing regime known as "fair trade," which had been legislated by Congress in 1937 in the Miller-Tydings Act, supplemented by similar state laws. These were meant to protect small businessmen from unfair competition by larger retailers, specifically exempting manufacturers from antitrust action when they set minimum retail prices. Keeping prices at a specified level might have aided small businesses, but it hurt consumers. Department stores wanted to compete with discounters, which were flouting the Miller-Tydings Act by selling below the minimums. In 1954, Joslin's decided to price General Electric small appliances below stipulated levels, and GE sued. Simultaneously, consumer advocates favored abolishing fair trade laws, and the Colorado Supreme Court ruled the state's law unconstitutional. Ultimately, Joslin's could price products made by GE and other makers at any level it deemed competitive.[58]

The other conflict during McWilliams's time involved the International Brotherhood of Teamsters and National Labor Relations Board (NLRB). Previously, the Teamsters had organized Joslin's warehouse workers, truck drivers and appliance and television repairmen. The NLRB charged Joslin's with unlawful union-busting activities, including offers of money to refrain from union activities and threats of retaliation for engaging in them. Other Denver stores conflicted with the Teamsters and other unions during the early postwar era; McWilliams's anti-union stance was typical of most executives.[59]

In 1959, Mercantile bought Pueblo's Crews-Beggs Dry Goods Company. For the next eleven years, Crews-Beggs operated separately, but in 1970, Mercantile decided to merge it with the Denver division, initially retaining the Crews-Beggs name on the five-story, 100,000-square-foot store in downtown Pueblo. Eventually, Joslins signage went up, giving it an eighth branch and coverage along the Colorado Front Range for nearly 180 miles.[60]

COLORADO'S LARGEST STORE

Donald R. Chabot replaced Norman Zilies in 1963, and it was under Chabot that the store overtook its largest rivals, May-D&F and The Denver, in sales. His strategy was to "shoot the gap" between upscale department and specialty stores on the high end and chain discounters on the low. Chabot, like Zilies, had worked for Glass Block in Duluth (his birthplace) but was coming to Denver from a much smaller division in Terre Haute, Indiana; Denver was a big promotion.[61]

Six months into his tenure, Chabot announced a complete overhaul of downtown that would fulfill McWilliams's dreams of expansion onto the former Rialto property. Downtown would be modern: Chabot hired Denver architect Richard L. Crowther to completely reimagine what Joslin's could

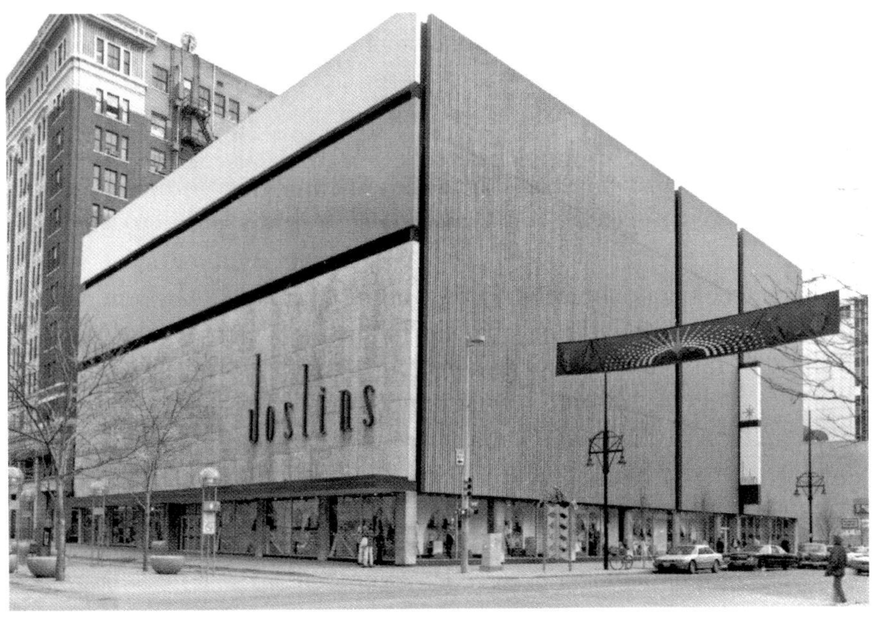

Joslins, now without an apostrophe, at Sixteenth and Curtis Streets, circa 1990, showing Richard Crowther's 1965 façade and logo design, along with the addition that took the place of the Rialto Theater. *Denver Public Library, Western History Collection, Z-10463; photograph by Roger Whitacre.*

look like, inside and out. Crowther began by eliminating the apostrophe: henceforth, it would be Joslins, not Joslin's. Along with the Rialto addition, the building was sheathed in blue anodized aluminum and white crushed onyx panels, with windows at street level only; a tall Joslins sign was visible from blocks away.

Lowered ceilings allowed for air conditioning ductwork, and escalators now connected all floors. To attract downtown businessmen, Chabot broadened the first-floor menswear offering with suits and sport coats. For the first time, Joslins would offer food service, the fifty-five-stool Coffee Kettle luncheonette on five. On the main floor, a new candy counter sold Colorado's own Jolly Rancher hard candies, and a new basement department sold major appliances. Chabot's decision to invest downtown, increasing its space by 50 percent, was inspired, he said, by many "improvements" near Joslins, which was now, after the closure of Daniels and Fisher, the northwestern-most department store on Sixteenth Street. The Tabor Theater across Curtis was gone, its site eventually sold to the Federal Reserve; Colorado National Bank demolished the vacant May

Company across Sixteenth; and one block away, F.W. Woolworth expanded its store to Fifteenth, becoming the "world's largest Woolworth's." The remodeling was complete by summer 1965.[62]

Chabot continued his predecessors' focus on suburban expansion. In 1964, he announced the first phase of "Operation Blanket Denver": Joslins would anchor developer Gerri Von Frellick's ambitious Villa Italia, an 800,000-square-foot mall in Lakewood, at West Alameda Avenue and South Wadsworth Boulevard. Chabot promised "bubbling fountains" in keeping with the center's Italian theme. New York architects Raymond Loewy and William Snaith designed the two-level, 87,000-square-foot store, which opened in March 1966. In addition to the usual departments, it boasted a ski shop and more upscale, fashionable merchandise (compared with other Joslins), but it was still "out to offer more shopping for your money than you will get in any store in the area," per Chabot.[63]

The next expansion was a 100,000-square-foot replacement for the Englewood store. Von Frellick's next project was initially called New Englewood and was later christened Cinderella City. The Denver, J.C. Penney and Neusteters would join Joslins as anchors of the 1.5-million-square-foot mall located at West Hampden Avenue and South Santa Fe Drive. Cinderella City was the largest Joslins when it opened in September 1968 and the first with a sit-down restaurant, the High Country Inn, featuring "a wall of live aspen trees with a photographic mountain backdrop." Other innovations included a Fanny Farmer candy shop, a two-thousand-title record and tape department, a ski shop, a "University Shop" (to "dress college students fashionably at moderate prices"), a "Career Shop" and a "Sophisticate and Bridal Salon," continuing Chabot's drive to make Joslins appealing to better-heeled consumers.[64]

His attention next turned eastward. Chabot had planned for some time to move Aurora to the new Buckingham Square, South Havana Street and East Mississippi Avenue, having purchased land there in 1964 in conjunction with developer Robert Hayutin. Buckingham was slow to start, however, even though Aurora was fast growing; a Kansas City developer eventually took it over. Colorado Day, August 1, 1971, would mark the new 130,000-square-foot, two-level store's opening day. With many young families populating Aurora, the Buckingham Joslins included a complete line of Boy Scout, Girl Scout and Campfire Girls uniforms, along with a "Grandma Shop," with "those hard-to-find gift items for infants and toddlers." As at Villa Italia and Cinderella City, a "Ski Haus" featured skis, boots, bindings and a repair service.[65]

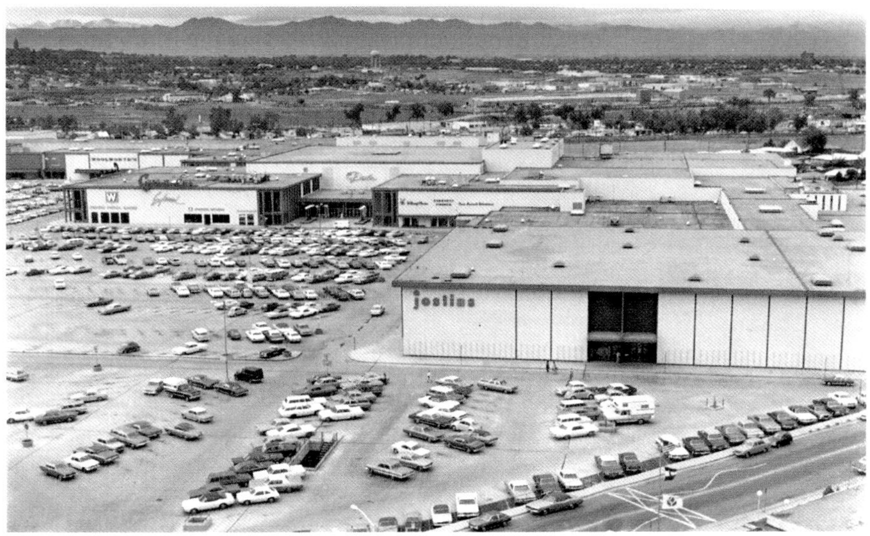

Joslins' Cinderella City store in Englewood, *right*, in 1971; signage for The Denver can be seen at the center. *Denver Public Library, Western History Collection, 332.*

Next came a store in a completely unexpected spot. Joslins did not open at Aurora Mall or Southglenn Mall, flashy new centers of the mid-1970s, but Chabot knew of an underserved market to the northwest. In February 1977, Joslins opened "in the boondocks" at West Eighty-Eighth Avenue and Sheridan Boulevard as the sole anchor of Westminster Mall. The isolated store looked like a "lighthouse standing on a lonesome knoll…with the smatterings of a half-finished mall trailing off to the west." There were few houses nearby, but Chabot correctly sensed that Westminster would grow. According to contemporaneous accounts, it was Chabot's idea to build there, and he had to convince the developer to build a mall to attach to the store rather than the other way around. Westminster's Joslins drew business from a wide area, from Arvada to Broomfield. In 1983, Chabot opened a large two-level store at Southwest Plaza, South Wadsworth Boulevard and West Bowles Avenue. After Southwest, he opened Cheyenne, Wyoming (1983); Colorado Springs (Chapel Hills Mall, 1985); and Longmont (Twin Peaks Mall, 1985), bringing the store count to eleven. Chabot continued to invest in older stores, adding floors (Buckingham Square with three floors now encompassed 210,000 square feet, the largest suburban branch of any chain in Colorado) and additional mall space.[66]

By 1986, Chabot's work had paid off: Joslins was now the top Colorado department store, with $205 million in annual sales to May-D&F's $172 million and The Denver's $145 million. Merchandise was more compelling, as Joslins now carried some brand-name offerings sold by competitors (usually at better prices). Undoubtedly, much of Joslins' success was also due to Chabot's understanding that "Joslins exemplifies middle America" and to his people: in 1986, store managers had worked for the company for twenty-seven years on average, and buyers and other important employees averaged fourteen years. Always encountering familiar faces in stores, customers tended to remain loyal. It was very much in the tradition of J. Jay Joslin.[67]

Chabot retired in 1990 after twenty-seven years. Replacing him was Roger Derr, who had begun his career downtown in 1959 and worked his way up. In 1985, Mercantile had transferred Derr from Joslins to its Billings, Montana division, where he turned around its fortunes. He presided over Joslins' 120th anniversary celebration in May 1993, but eleven months later, his short presidency was over. Effectively ending Joslins' status as a locally managed institution, Mercantile consolidated its operations with the Jones Store, eliminating one hundred Denver jobs and putting Derr in retirement. He was offered a position at Mercantile headquarters in Fairfield, Ohio (it had relocated from New York), but declined due to health problems. With no locally based management, Joslins was no different from Foley's, the May Department Stores division that had swallowed up May-D&F a year earlier, except that the Joslins name remained.[68]

THE LAST COLORADO STORE

Roger Derr's short tenure was not without its legacy, however. In 1993, he signed a lease at Southglenn Mall, South University Boulevard and East Arapahoe Road. This would be the nicest Joslins yet when it opened in October 1994. Filling 160,000 square feet on two levels, it featured upscale brands (DKNY, Estee Lauder, Clinique, Tommy Hilfiger and Nautica) not previously carried by Joslins. Southglenn was graced with three atriums, 18-foot waterfalls abutting escalators, marble floors and teak trim; the effect was spectacular. The children's department included a full-size airplane suspended from the ceiling. Sadly, Southglenn's opening meant that an older store would close: Cinderella City, which had been losing business, shut its doors in January 1995.[69]

That year would also see the downtown Joslins close, as Mercantile was looking to cut costs as the industry struggled to compete with myriad choices available to consumers, from discount stores to outlet malls. The pride of John Jay Joslin in 1888, the downtown location shuttered in early October, the very last Sixteenth Street department store to close. Mercantile had considered alternatives over the previous decade, including anchoring the never-built Centerstone enclosed mall (on today's Denver Pavilions site). Mercantile also considered buying an adjoining parking lot to expand the first floor (if not the whole building) and renovating the store to its nineteenth-century splendor. But after Joslins became merely the western outpost of the Jones Store, all momentum for reviving downtown ceased.[70]

The story was not quite over, however. Shortly before downtown's demise, Joslins announced that it would anchor the new Park Meadows mall, Interstate 25 and Colorado Highway 470. This came just a year after Southglenn's opening five miles away; retail analysts considered it a defensive move, as Park Meadows would likely eclipse the older mall. Opened in August 1997, the new store was almost as large as Buckingham Square at 200,000 square feet. To attract the wealthy, Mercantile created an environment even nicer than Southglenn, with a 5,700-square-foot day spa, two coffee bars and various musical backgrounds for departments, with sounds ranging "from Bach to Beck." Merchandise, taken up another notch, included Ralph Lauren and St. John.[71]

Less than a year later, none of this opulence mattered. On May 18, 1998, Dillard's Inc. and Mercantile Stores announced a merger, with the former acquiring the latter for $3.14 billion in cash. Dillard's already operated in Colorado, and most of the Joslins would be converted to the Little Rock, Arkansas retailer's nameplate. In malls with an existing Dillard's, Joslins would close. This was a lucrative payoff, approximately $1 billion, for Mercantile's still-largest shareholder, with an approximately 40 percent share, the Milliken family of South Carolina. Locally, it meant that the last department store associated with Denver's early days was gone.[72]

Chapter 3

THE MAY COMPANY

Watch Us Grow

"O! sir," she said, "I do not dream
Of days of long ago,
But I'm wondering how in Dickens' name
The May Company sells so low."
—early advertisement[73]

Levi's and Longies

Four years after John Jay Joslin founded Joslin Dry Goods, young David T. May came to Colorado to recover his health, not expecting to found a retail empire that would endure until 2006. Born in Kaiserslautern, Bavaria, May had immigrated to America in 1863 as a fifteen-year-old. He came without his financially struggling parents, who had decided he should go by himself. May was not entirely without resources, as an uncle had made his way to Cincinnati previously. He eventually landed in Hartford City, Indiana, where he worked in a dry goods store owned by Raphael Kirschbaum. Thanks to May's enthusiasm and entrepreneurial skills, Kirschbaum's business tripled, and he sold May an interest in the store, making him junior partner and changing the firm's name to Kirschbaum & May.[74]

One cold night in the winter of 1876–77, Hartford City caught fire. May spent hours hauling stock out of the store, getting drenched by firehoses, and he soon developed pneumonia. Fearing it would lead to tuberculosis, May's doctor ordered him to recover in a dryer climate. May sold his share of the shop and ventured to Colorado, lodging in Manitou Springs, a popular health-tourism destination. He soon met other guests, including Marshall Field, the Chicago merchant, who invited May to join his fishing party on the Arkansas River at Twin Lakes. The silver boomtown of Leadville was just a short distance north, and the party ventured there to take a look. May, sensing the opportunity of a lifetime, elected to stay.[75]

At first, he had no intention of getting back into dry goods. Instead, he joined another young man, Jake Holcomb (who, like May, had absolutely no knowledge of geology) to mine silver. They were certain that digging holes randomly would result in striking a vein. After weeks of fruitless prospecting, May realized that he had to return to what he knew and proposed to Holcomb that they enter into business together. May soon found someone who wanted to get out of dry goods and bought his inventory. The firm of May, Holcomb and Dean (a third partner for a short period) was born, housed in a wood and canvas structure. Their stock in trade comprised, as later company histories recounted, "Levi's and longies." The blue *serge de Nîmes* (denim) pants and overalls made by San Francisco manufacturer Levi Strauss & Company were prospectors' favorites, along with red woolen underwear ("longies"). Holcomb was not a natural businessman, so May bought him out and soon moved to a storefront at 318 Harrison Avenue that he named the Great Western Auction House and Clothing Store.

Boomtowns attract all sorts. Some, like May, seek riches; others look to make fortunes in other ways. One famous story of May's Leadville years demonstrated that he knew intuitively what people wanted. Hearing of a Chicago retailer (unnamed) overstocked in ball gowns and anxious to be rid of them, May cheaply bought several dozen of the fancy velvet and brocade dresses and had them shipped to Leadville. Other merchants had no notion that there was a demand for such goods, but May cleared them out quickly, selling them dearly ($200 to $400) to *nouveau riche* miners' wives and, quite possibly, to "brides of the multitude."

May had competitors. Among them were Joseph and Louis Shoenberg. Their brother, Moses, soon arrived to join them; May befriended Moses and soon made him a partner in what was now called May & Schoenberg. A fourth family member, sister Rosa, soon arrived, and May was smitten. They married in 1880, the same year that May (without his brother-in-law) began opening branches in other Colorado towns. A Pueblo store was followed by shops in Irwin (today a ghost town near Gunnison), Glenwood Springs and Aspen; most lasted only as long as area mines continued paying out.

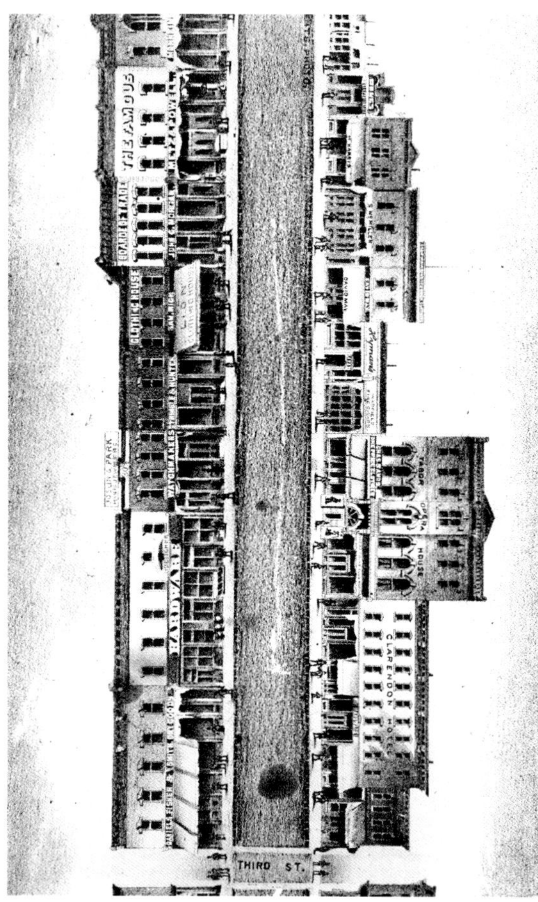

Harrison Avenue, Leadville, Colorado, circa 1880. David May's store was two doors to the left of the Tabor Opera House on the east (*right*) side of the street, while Daniels, Fisher and Smith operated on the west (*left*) side at the corner of Third Street. *Beck Archives, Special Collections, CJS and University Libraries, University of Denver.*

May was a serial entrepreneur, pursuing business in any likely spot. At least one branch, in Colorado Springs, remained open for several years, as it was mentioned as being destroyed by fire in 1900.[76]

David and Rosa May remained in Leadville for nearly a decade, becoming deeply involved with the community. They were prominent members of Temple Israel, and their first two sons, Morton J. and Thomas, were born in Leadville. He was friendly with hardware merchant Charles Boettcher and banker David Moffat (both familiar to readers of Colorado history). May ran for Lake County treasurer in 1881 and again in 1883, succeeding as a Republican in a largely Democratic district. Moses Shoenberg decided to seek opportunity elsewhere, so he and May dissolved their partnership in 1885. In 1888, it was May's turn to move on—Leadville was still producing silver, but living so high above sea level is taxing, winters are cold and the

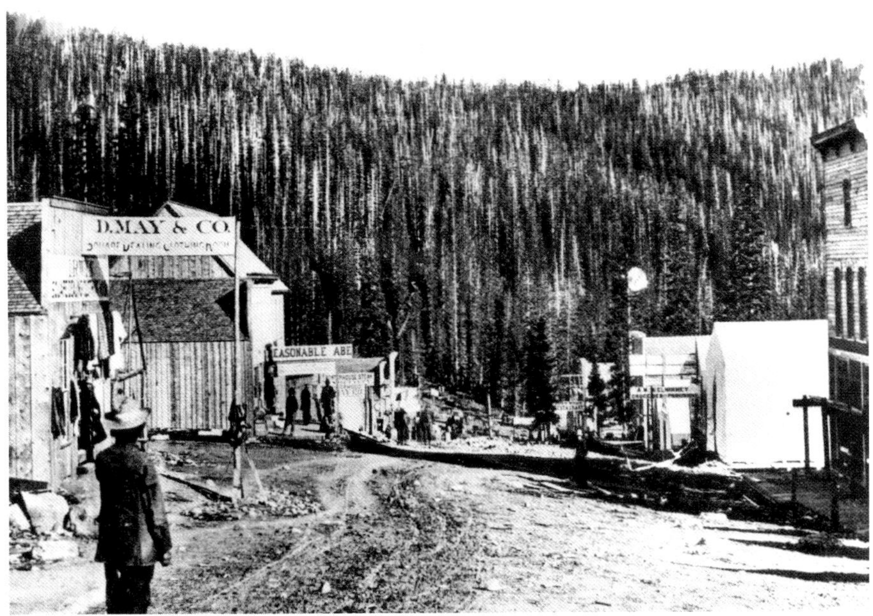

May's branch in the mining boomtown of Irwin, Colorado, near Gunnison, 1879–80. *Beck Archives, Special Collections, CJS and University Libraries, University of Denver.*

retail market is limited. He came to Denver on business, discovering that the J.S. Dreyfus Company at Fifteenth and Larimer Streets was closing. May decided to buy out Dreyfus and paid $31,000 for the stock. He slashed prices, hired a brass band to attract crowds and sold the merchandise within a week at a huge profit. Denver was the place to be.

TO DENVER AND BEYOND

May returned to Leadville, sold his inventory and brought his family to Denver. He located a space at 1614 Larimer Street, just a few doors up from Sixteenth, and opened the May Shoe & Clothing Company. Louis Schoenberg soon joined May, and together they conducted a store known as much for its lively attitude and competitive spirit as for its fantastic bargains. Early advertisements utilized purple prose:

> *We put a price upon these princely garments that'll paralyze and dumbfound all would-be and self-constituted competitors and prove a stumbling block to gray-brained imitators.*
>
> *Where on God's green earth outside of our house will you find men morally brave enough to place on sale, on the very threshold of the busy season, our sixteen hundred tailor-made, figured, seasonable and stylish $18, $16.50, $15, and $12.50 suits at TEN DOLLARS FOR THE CHOICE?*[77]

Perhaps Denver's merchants did not mind being branded "gray-brained imitators" by this upstart, but May succeeded hugely with this unsubtle approach and soon needed more room. He knocked through walls to neighboring storefronts and then leased space across the alley, facing Lawrence Street, connecting it to his Larimer Street store by a second-floor bridge. In 1895, May bought out his next-door neighbor on Lawrence, Skinner Brothers & Wright (a men's store), and then bought the Brunswick Hotel, which stood on Sixteenth abutting the Skinner building. He combined the two and had the assemblage remodeled to a single architectural style, with large plate glass windows on all floors for good illumination.

By the time May moved into the new building, opposite Daniels and Fisher and the Golden Eagle, Denver was not his only base of operations. Three years earlier, in 1892, May and his brothers-in-law discovered an opportunity in St. Louis, a department store for sale called The Famous. They bought it; in 1911, May bought another St. Louis retailer, William Barr Dry Goods Company, forming Famous-Barr, which grew into the largest-grossing single-location department store west of the Mississippi.[78] In 1896, May and the Shoenbergs replaced their partnership with a corporate structure.

May Company landed lucrative contracts during the Spanish-American War of 1898, providing thousands of blue flannel shirts and blue pants for soldiers. It kept growing in other ways, buying that year the Hall & Dutton store in Cleveland. In 1899, May Company opened a buying office in New York at 722 Broadway. It was home to buyers when they visited the city and housed textile workers who manufactured goods for the three-store chain. The *Denver Times*, like other Denver papers fond of hyperbole and boosterism, crowed that the New York facility and May stores elsewhere "contributed not a little to the fame of Denver." Like today's tech titans, by growing so quickly and not shying away from publicity, May became well known, with President William McKinley offering him a diplomatic

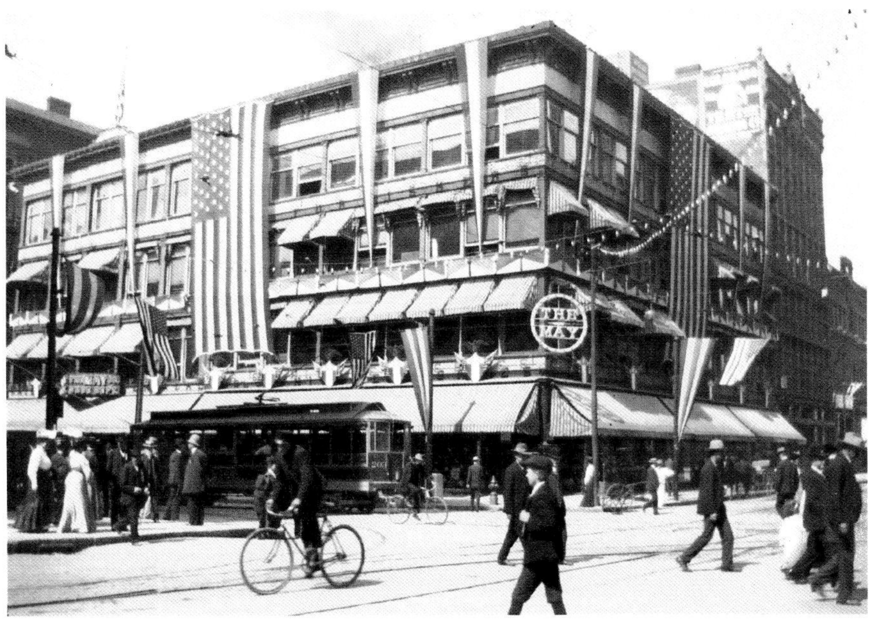

The May Company on the northern corner of Sixteenth and Lawrence Streets, circa 1905. *Denver Public Library, Western History Collection, X-24124.*

post in Frankfurt-am-Main, Germany. May respectfully declined—he had an empire to build.

Despite his now far-flung operations, May continued living in Denver. When he first moved from Leadville, he lived at 2546 Champa Street, but as he grew wealthier, he bought a mansion at 2135 East Colfax Avenue. In 1900, he bought the Horace Bennett mansion at 1304 Logan Street. As he had in Leadville, May established ties with Denver's Jewish community, becoming close to Rabbi William Sterne Friedman of Temple Emanuel. The rabbi, a towering figure, was concerned for tuberculosis sufferers who came to Denver to recover their health in the dry climate. He was the moving force behind the establishment of the National Jewish Hospital for Consumptives at East Colfax Avenue and Colorado Boulevard (today's National Jewish Health). May, and later son Morton and nephew Alfred Triefus, contributed greatly to National Jewish, helping fund building programs. Even today, the campus includes a May Building, and plaques with May's name and that of May-D&F can be found in various corners.

In 1901, May Company became a chain of four by buying the M. O'Neil Company of Akron, Ohio. Two years later, May moved to St. Louis, May Company's operations base. In Missouri, successful men in those days were often referred to as "colonel," regardless of military service, and St. Louis newspapers began calling him "Colonel May." During World War I, anti-German sentiment caused brother-in-law Louis, who also lived in St. Louis, to change his name to Beaumont (the French translation of Shoenberg, "beautiful mountain"), and he was known as "Commodore Beaumont" for the rest of his life.

Big White Palace

Even though May had moved to St. Louis, he kept close tabs on Denver. He sensed a shift in the momentum of Sixteenth Street. In the early 1890s, it had seemed perfectly sensible to invest in the corner of Sixteenth and Lawrence, with two leading merchants thriving there. But by the mid-1900s, a relative newcomer, The Denver Dry Goods Company at Sixteenth and California Streets, was pulling trade southeastward, away from the traditional heart of the city on Larimer and Lawrence. May decided to move uptown, and in 1905, he bought the northern corner of Sixteenth and Champa Streets, the midpoint between Daniels and Fisher and The Denver Dry Goods. Construction began in early 1906, and by December, it was open for business. The new May Company spread across 90,000 square feet on five levels (four stories plus basement, with a mezzanine above the main floor), with 125 feet of frontage on Sixteenth Street and 150 along Champa.[79]

Architect Edwin H. Moorman favored the Beaux-Arts style, and he created an elegant showplace, with a brilliantly white-glazed terra-cotta façade trimmed in dark-green marble—the *Denver Post* called it "a big white palace." This was the City Beautiful era, inspired by the 1893 World's Columbian Exposition in Chicago, when white Neoclassical architecture conveyed progressive modernity, casting aside fussy, heavy Victorian architecture. The interior was no less elegant, and shoppers enjoyed the very first escalator in any Denver store, although it connected only the first floor to the second. White marble drinking fountains ran with "ice cold mineral water" from May's artesian well. Two bronze "electroliers," male and female bronze figures titled *Faneuse* and *Faucheur* by sculptor Auguste Moreau, illuminated the main stairway from their positions atop Corinthian-carved newel posts.[80] The bronzes may have come from France, but advertisements emphasized that the store had been "builded [*sic*] by Denver capital after ideas furnished by Denver brain and erected of Denver-made material." A "swaying mass

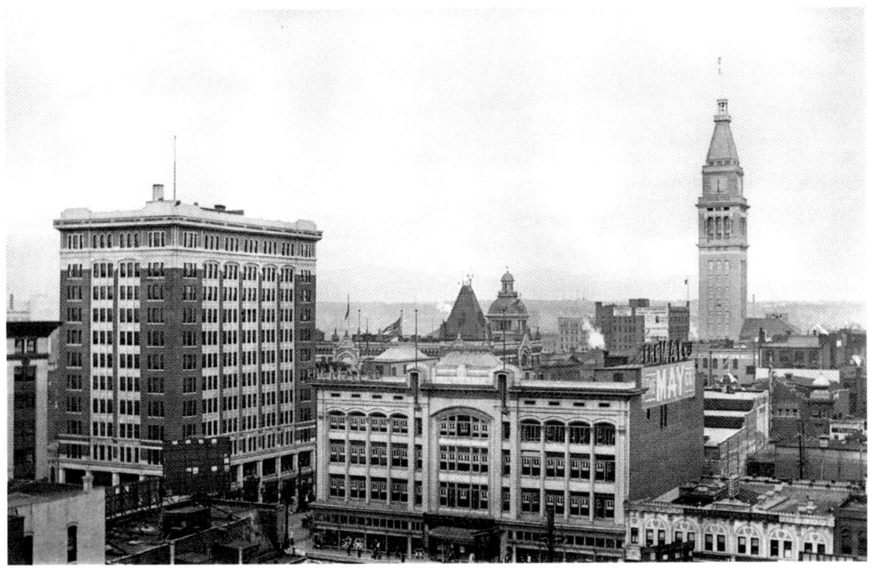

The May Company's Champa Street store, *center*, circa 1912, with the Daniels and Fisher Tower visible in the distance. *Denver Public Library, Western History Collection, X-24125.*

of humanity," estimated at more than twenty thousand people, turned out for the grand opening, which the *Post* described as an affair "of vastly more importance than a mere affair of state."[81]

May Shoe & Clothing Company became May Department Stores Company in 1910, publicly traded on the New York Stock Exchange. David May retired from active management in 1917, with son Morton J., who had begun his career at the Larimer Street store, taking over as president. The elder May never lost his focus on the business, however, and when a 1923 opportunity came along to buy A. Hamburger & Sons of Los Angeles, he jumped. With this acquisition, May Department Stores Company was now a chain of five, with fourteen thousand employees and annual trade "in excess of $100,000,000."[82]

Based in St. Louis, May felt it important to have a family member overseeing the Denver operation. That man was his nephew, Alfred E. Triefus. Like his uncle, he had suffered from lung problems, and May brought him to Denver for his health. Starting as a clerk in the Lawrence Street store one year before the move to Champa, he rose through the ranks, becoming general manager in 1922. It was a perfect time for an ambitious man to make his mark. Triefus witnessed The Denver Dry Goods adding two more floors in 1924, a year that also saw Neusteter's expand into a five-story building. Triefus knew that he needed more space if May was to compete, so in 1925 he added a six-story wing along Champa Street.

Opening in time for the holidays, the wing was designed by Denver architects William A. and Arthur E. Fisher, and it gave May 250 feet of frontage along Champa. Modern merchandising philosophy dictated extensive show windows to entice shoppers, so the entire length became "Fashion Lane," 10,000 square feet of plate glass through which shoppers admired smartly dressed mannequins. The original store was modernized inside to match the addition (with American walnut used lavishly for fixtures and trim), and the store added new departments and expanded others. Compared to other stores, May's roots as a men's store were still apparent, with clothing for men and boys occupying most of the first and second floors, with ladies' wear on three and part of four (which also included a children's playroom overseen by a nurse, allowing mothers to shop without hindrance). May's publicity again emphasized the use of Colorado materials and labor and proclaimed that while the St. Louis and Los Angeles operations might be larger, the Denver store was still the "parent" of the chain.[83]

David May did not attend the opening, his advanced age inhibiting travel, but he continued working in his office above Famous-Barr. In July 1927, he died, aged seventy-nine. With his lungs compromised as a young man, it was pneumonia that proved his undoing, contracted after a severe cold while at his summer home in Charlevoix, Michigan. He would likely have approved of Morton's next move, the acquisition of the financially distressed Bernheimer-Leader store of Baltimore two months after his death.[84] As good of an opportunity as this was, Morton May and his board decided it would be the last purchase for a long time, as they wanted to consolidate their position in their various markets. This conservative management style proved their salvation during the Depression, when so many other stores went into bankruptcy or liquidation. They followed David May's original philosophy: a broad range, deep inventory and quick markdowns when merchandise wasn't selling. May Company not only survived the 1930s, it thrived—it was one of the few large retail companies to continuously pay quarterly dividends throughout the Depression.[85]

As conditions improved near the end of the 1930s, May Company began exploring expansion again and opened its first non-downtown store in 1939, a large (270,000 square feet) branch in Los Angeles on "the Miracle Mile" of Wilshire Boulevard, complete with ample parking.[86] In 1940, it was Denver's turn for expansion, a seven-story, $1.5 million wing facing Curtis Street, across the alley from the 1925 addition, connected by a wide

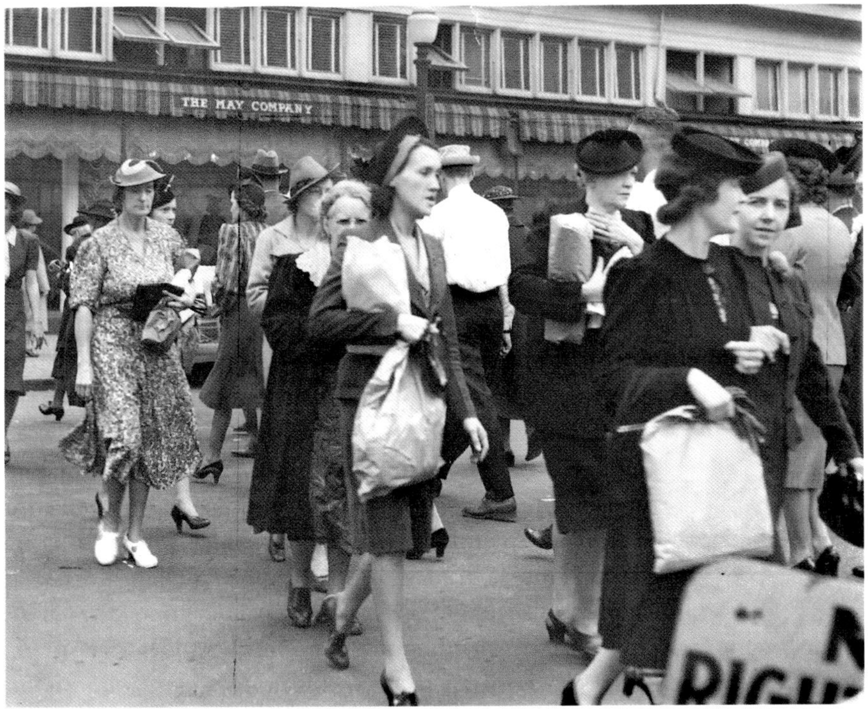

Shoppers crossing Champa Street in front of the May Company, 1940. *Author's collection.*

bridge on floors two through six. Designed by Denver architects Fisher, Fisher & Hubbell, the addition exemplified May Company's new love of modern architecture, favored over ornate styles of the past. It featured a clean-lined façade of limestone and glass blocks and brought total square footage to 261,000. Staff now numbered nearly one thousand, and once again May Company highlighted the fact that the addition utilized Colorado materials and Colorado workmen. The Curtis annex occupied the site of a former theater, and May also bought the theater next door to demolish for customer parking.[87]

STRIKE!

After World War II, May Company began planning for more suburban branches and improvements to downtown stores, but like many other large employers at the time, it had to face dissatisfied employees. May's Denver clerks had first voted for unionization in 1942, and after the war, they were struggling under postwar inflation. Organized as Local 454 of the Retail Clerks Union of the American Federation of Labor (AFL), May's employees voted to strike on August 20, 1946, the first-ever strike against a Denver department store. The union had asked for a twenty-six-dollar minimum weekly wage, along with a 25 percent raise for all, a freeze on sales quotas and a closed shop (all non-management employees would be required to join the union). Negotiations stalled; Triefus made a counteroffer but could not condone a closed shop.[88]

The union began picketing and told the press that it was hurting the store's business. May pooh-poohed this, claiming that traffic and revenue were normal and that most employees had chosen to remain on the job. Newspaper classified advertising sections told a different story, with May seeking replacements for striking employees. Representative Samuel Meyers of the AFL organized a mass meeting at the Denver Auditorium, with speeches by Denver mayor Benjamin Stapleton and local playwright Mary Coyle Chase (*Harvey*).

Workers enjoyed momentum during the early days, but management gained the upper hand as the strike wore on. According to the company, some strikers resorted to petty acts of violence (smashed windows, stink bombs), which the union denied had ever happened. Triefus did not want the strike to compromise the crucial holiday shopping season and asked the Colorado Industrial Commission to arbitrate. The commission ruled on December 11 that the local's demand for a closed shop was untenable, but union representatives countered that the commission lacked jurisdiction, as May was a national company involved in interstate commerce—not a strictly Colorado concern—and that the National Labor Relations Board was the proper authority. Local 454's leaders likely counted on better results from the federal board.

Upping the ante, on December 12 the AFL threatened to call a general strike of all twenty thousand of its Colorado members. The union attacked May's employment of strikebreakers, decrying its efforts to "break down the economic conditions necessary for human beings to exist under the present economic structure." The *Rocky Mountain News*, once a liberal paper but no longer, took May's side, labeling the strike "a threat to our community" and "an attempt to put a gun at the community's head." The typical Denver shopper probably did not feel too threatened by strikers but at the same time did not relish crossing a picket line.

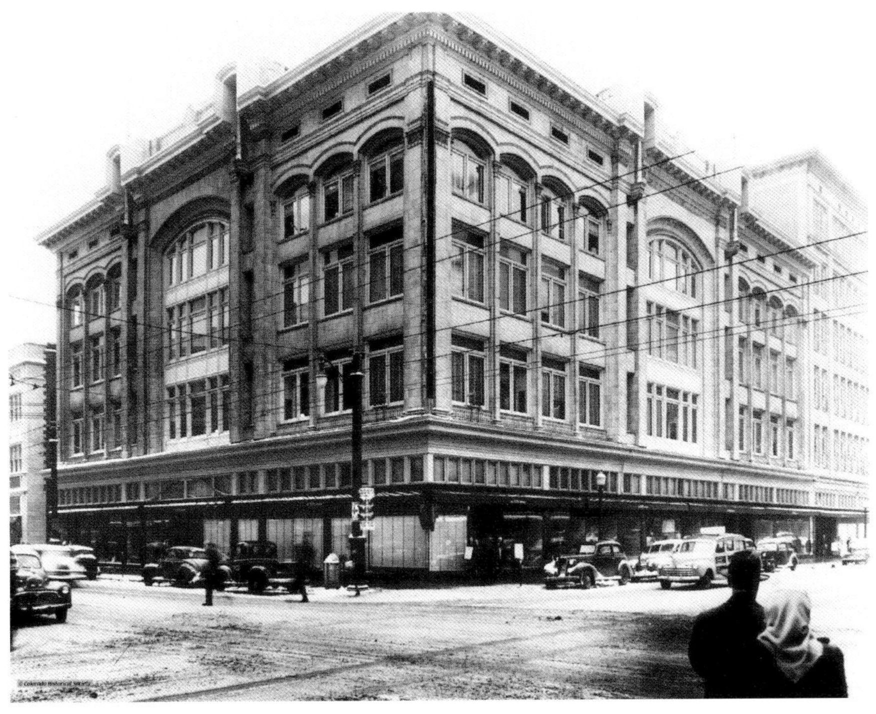

The May Company's Champa Street store on a cold day in February 1947. The 1925 addition is visible at far right, and four striking workers, one of them holding a placard, huddle near the Sixteenth Street corner. *History Colorado, 10027781.*

Triefus did not get his holiday wish, as the strike continued into 1947. Union representatives talked to Mayor Stapleton, who did not want to take sides and so did nothing. Finally, at the end of March 1947, thirty-two weeks after the strike had begun, the parties reached agreement. May won on the closed shop—there would be no requirement for employees to join the local. Pay would improve to levels even better than the union had originally asked for, holiday hours worked would be paid double time and sales quotas were abolished. The AFL's Meyers proclaimed that strikers should be regarded "not as conquerors or victors, but as something much better, as the unconquered." He also opined that the strike would have been settled much sooner had "certain anti-labor forces in the background had stayed out of the early negotiations"—he was referring to May Company's Denver attorney, whom Triefus had made lead negotiator. It was only after he replaced the lawyer with the manager of the Cleveland May Company that the store and the union were able to break the deadlock.

FINGERING THE MERCHANDISE

With happier, better-paid workers, Denver's May Company began to plan for the postwar era. Morton J. May still headed the growing chain, with its twelve downtown stores and twelve suburban branches, occupying 3.7 million square feet. May had purchased Pittsburgh's Kaufmann's just after the war, helping the company realize $358 million in sales in 1947. Despite its size, however, May Company remained a collection of local stores, managed by local people with local tastes in mind. Individual buyers in each department made decisions with little direction from above. If merchandise didn't sell, the buyer could slash prices without seeking permission, even if the store took a loss. A 1948 *Fortune* profile of May noted that "the store buyer has the last word, and no goods are ever planted in his department without his nod." It continued: "May regards the independence of its stores and the autonomy of its store managements with almost savage fetishism." Samuel Rosenberg, an executive in the Cleveland division, told *Fortune*, "We don't figure the merchandise. We finger it." This was a "chain run by buyers," merchants who knew their business, not by accountants. Animating all stores was David May's original philosophy of stocking as much merchandise as racks could hold, with wide assortment and deep inventory—something for everyone. Stores were not spacious and open—"calculated clutter," Morton J. and his team believed, made customers comfortable and more apt to buy.[89]

Two years after the strike, Alfred Triefus, like his Sixteenth Street compatriots, announced modernization plans, finally augmenting the single 1906 escalator with seven new ones connecting the four principal floors. May Company was not finished, however. In 1954, it had decided that the modern look of the 1940 addition should be applied to the 1906 building, a face-lift that would cover the ornate white palace with simple panels of light-gray mosaic stone, giving the building the appearance of a giant box. The design, by Raymond Harry Ervin and Robert Berne, featured huge block letters forming the word *MAY* vertically on the corner—no mere sign, but an architectural element. Inside, May found even more room for merchandise, extending the mezzanine over more of the first floor. A previously announced air conditioning project would complete the update. All of this was necessary if the downtown May was to compete with suburban shopping.[90]

Elsewhere, May Company was a primary force behind that very suburbanization, and in 1953, it announced its first Denver satellite store, on South Colorado Boulevard and East Yale Avenue, in the new University Hills Shopping Center. Initially planned as 110,000 square feet on three levels (two above ground plus basement), the building was engineered for an eventual third floor, which it received some years later. The branch opened in September 1955, as the thirty-first in the May chain. It paid tribute to its Colorado roots in naming its second-floor restaurant the Leadville Room, featuring views of the Rocky Mountains. Ervin and Berne, who had designed the downtown remodeling, were architects of the new store, built of Roman rose-tan brick and trimmed with Colorado travertine marble and stainless steel at its main (western, mall-facing) entrance.[91] A second Denver-area branch was announced in 1955 on West Colfax Avenue between Miller and Owens Streets, but it would not open until 1960.[92]

Even with the new branch, downtown continued drawing shoppers. *Cervi's Journal* found 2,150 customers entering May's main Sixteenth Street entrance on Friday, November 11, 1949, and this pattern continued mostly undiminished through most of the following decade. It all ended on July 31, 1958, however, when May Company on Sixteenth and Champa Streets closed its doors to prepare for the impending opening of the shining new May-D&F at Sixteenth and Tremont.[93]

Chapter 4

THE GOLDEN EAGLE

Denver's Bargain Centre

He is what may be described as a Good Citizen. *While Time takes toll of physical strength, Mr. Guldman's interest in social, business and civic affairs is* [as] *keen as the blade of a steel sword.*
—Denver Post, *December 7, 1933*

LAND OF OPPORTUNITY

Old-timers who remember shopping at the Golden Eagle are rarer with each passing year. In its time, however, the emporium founded in 1879 was immensely popular. A democratic store, it attracted everyone from the poorest to the richest, the latter loving a bargain almost as much as the former. The Golden Eagle emphasized price over everything, although it did not sell shoddy goods—quality always counted. It operated on strictly cash basis, neither accepting nor extending credit. Due to this policy, it not only amassed large cash reserves that it could tap in bad times, but it could also swoop in wherever bargains were to be had, obtaining goods so cheaply from manufacturers closing out odd lots or distressed retailers selling off their inventory that its retail prices were Denver's lowest.

The genius behind the Golden Eagle was Leopold Henry Guldman. Born in Harburg, near Nordlinger, Bavaria, in 1852, his early life was not unlike that of his later competitor and friend David May, although at eighteen years of age upon his arrival in America in 1870, he was not as young as May had been when he immigrated. Son of a butcher and *schochet* (ritual kosher slaughterer), Guldman had no desire to follow in his father's footsteps—he listed "merchant" on the passenger list for the ship that brought him across the Atlantic, and he had plans to become one. He was not the first of his family to immigrate, his sister, Fanny, having arrived in 1861. She, in turn, was following older relatives who had settled in the Midwest earlier. After arrival in New York, Leopold immediately joined her in Watertown, Wisconsin, between Milwaukee and Madison. She was married to dry goods merchant Morris A. Hirsh, who invited his brother-in-law to work for him. Guldman spent seven years in Watertown, learning the trade and art of running a successful business and developing fluency in English.[94]

He eventually saved enough to venture out on his own. With no family, he decided to try his luck in a young city known as a place where men could find fortunes: Leadville, Colorado. He arrived in 1878, a year after David May, and like May, he may have tried prospecting for the silver-bearing lead carbonate ore that lay buried under surrounding mountains. He may have also briefly engaged in retail trade. Unlike May, he did not stay—he sensed greener pastures in Denver and came down from the hills in early 1879. He had met another German Jewish immigrant with retail ambitions, Simon Winneman. At 3:00 p.m. on Monday, March 24, 1879, the two opened the doors of the Golden Eagle Dry Goods House, in a rented space at 391 Lawrence Street, at its western corner with Sixteenth. The *Rocky Mountain News* described its opening the next morning, a scene "of splendor, rivaling the richest bazaars of the orient," with "bright eyed ladies…eager to inspect the new goods," which included "costly shawls, elegant laces, handsome silks and other beautiful goods in endless profusion—all arranged with remarkable taste and skill."[95]

The store's name, Golden Eagle, reflected Guldman's love for his adopted country. He later told the story of hiring a carpenter to carve an eagle out of wood, which he then had gilded, mounting it on the front of the store. Denver shoppers grew to love the Golden Eagle because they soon learned they could buy goods "at eastern prices" (meaning lower). Thanks to these bargains, by the end of 1880 sales had more than doubled over 1879, leading the *News* to christen the store's proprietors the "Leaders of popular prices." By this time, however, Winneman was out of the picture, no longer partner. Instead, Guldman had brought on Bernhardt Heller as partner, although this, too, would last only a short time, with Guldman the sole owner by 1883. Although it is not possible to know from extant records the reasons for the dissolutions of the two partnerships, it is likely

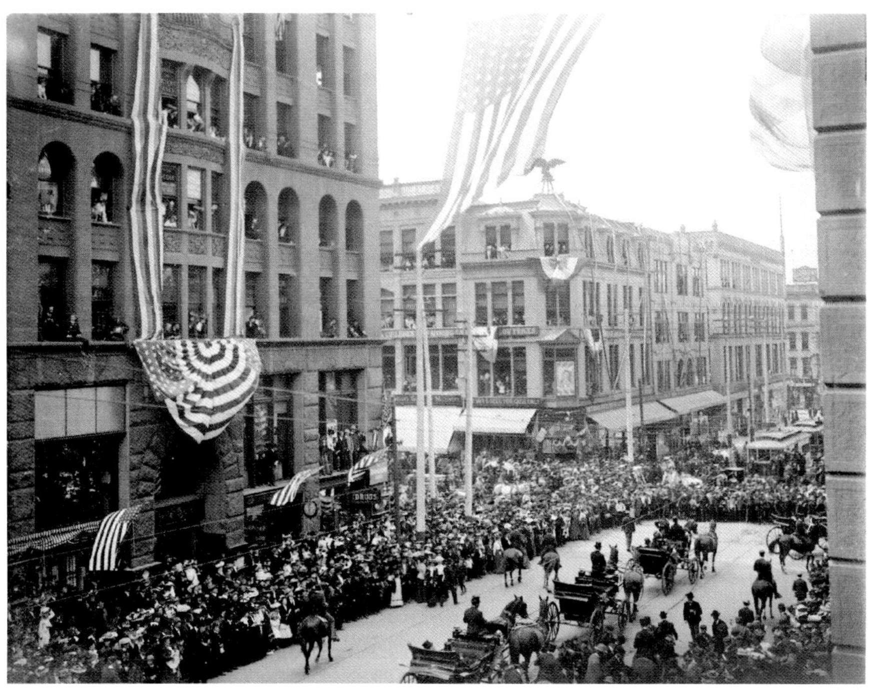

The Golden Eagle is visible at center, prior to remodeling, during a parade probably for Spanish-American War soldiers in 1898. Every store window is filled with parade watchers. *Denver Public Library, Western History Collection, X-23790.*

that Guldman simply preferred being sole decision-maker. After Heller, he never took on another partner.[96]

Guldman expanded in 1882, adding a "large and well-lighted room" for suits and cloaks. More expansion came in 1898–99 when Guldman, now owner of his building, took over an adjacent structure owned by William and Moritz Barth, knocking through walls to create a larger store. He also commissioned a new, larger golden eagle (with a nine-foot wingspan) to be mounted on the corner of the building above the cornice, decorated with two hundred lightbulbs. By the store's twentieth anniversary in March 1899, the enlargement was complete, and "immense crowds" attended its opening, the store bedecked with arches of violets and roses for the occasion. Expansion continued in 1901, when Guldman took over another adjacent building, that of the *Denver Times* newspaper. With this addition, Guldman modernized the assemblage significantly, adding three elevators (two for passengers, one for freight), large plate glass show windows on both the Lawrence and Sixteenth Street sides and pneumatic tubes for sending customers' cash to the cashier's office; he also added a fifth floor. Windows on floors two through five pivoted for maximum air circulation.

The Golden Eagle may have been a bargain hunters' paradise, but its fittings were as elegant as any store, including maple floors and oak fixtures fitted with French plate glass. The expansion included a 5,000-square-foot shoe department, which the store claimed was the largest in Denver. Further expansion came in 1905, when Guldman rebuilt the Sixteenth Street side, with bay windows on upper floors and the illuminated eagle uppermost. Altogether the Golden Eagle now spread over 100,000 square feet. Guldman's designer was Denver's leading commercial architect, Frank E. Edbrooke, who had by this time also been employed by May Company, Daniels and Fisher and The Denver Dry Goods. The final expansion came in 1916, when Guldman bought the three-story Kistler Stationery Company building next door and incorporated it into the store, adding two more floors to it and reworking the ground floor on the Lawrence Street side of the combined buildings to incorporate elegant arcade-style windows.[97]

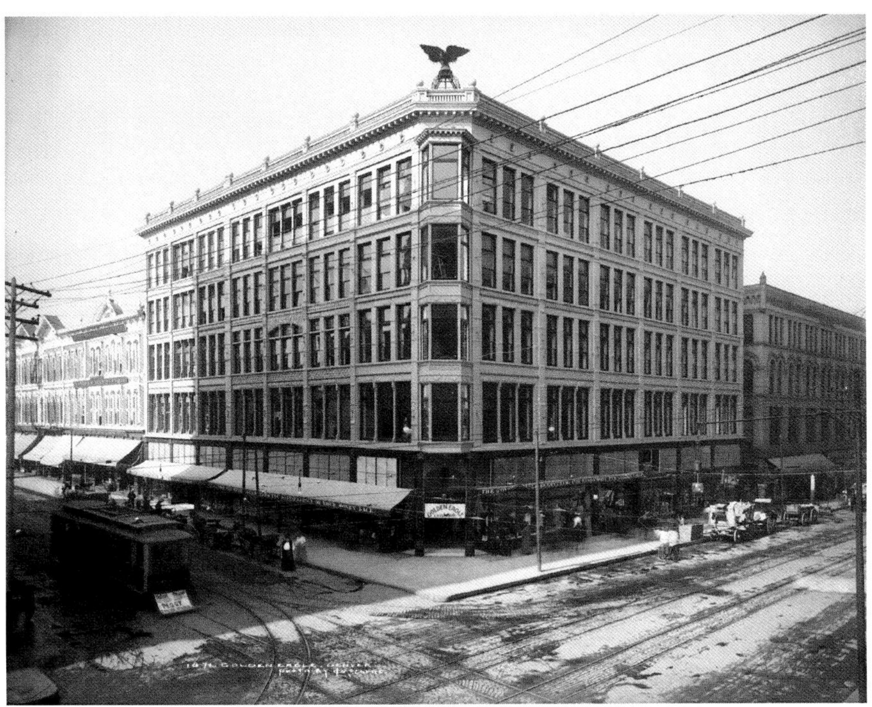

The Golden Eagle on the western corner of Sixteenth and Lawrence Streets, circa 1905. *Denver Public Library, Western History Collection, X-24066; photograph by Louis Charles McClure.*

GRATITUDE

In his several expansions, Guldman specified that contractors employ unionized workers exclusively. He was unusual in this; it was the era when relations between capital and labor were arguably at their very worst in American history, and most businessmen were staunchly anti-union. But above everything, his sharp practices aside, Guldman was a humanitarian at heart and believed in fairness and opportunity.

He had demonstrated this in 1880, when he had been in business for just a year. On October 31, an incident on Wazee Street near Sixteenth, involving white off-duty railroad workers harassing Chinese men playing pool in a tavern, resulted in a gun being fired by one of the Chinese, precipitating an anti-Chinese riot. Fueled by false rumors that "a Chinaman had shot and killed a white man," angry white mobs formed and began harassing Chinese living in Denver's small Chinatown (Sixteenth to Eighteenth, Blake to Wazee Streets). Whites pursued Chinese residents, even lynching one on Seventeenth Street opposite the Markham Hotel, just one block from the Golden Eagle. One Chinese man, seeking safety, ran into the Golden Eagle. Guldman, sensing his fright and hearing the mob approaching, told him to hide inside a crate, which Guldman then closed. The mob arrived, and when asked if he had seen a "Chinaman," Guldman shrugged and responded, "Is he in here?" He hid the man inside the store for three days, providing refuge during the riot's aftermath. In gratitude, the Chinese man sent boxes of dried fruits to Guldman "every Chinese New Year and Jewish New Year."[98]

Where Guldman really made his mark in Denver was in philanthropy, possibly the most giving of all of Denver's merchants; his obituaries referred to him as a philanthropist first and a businessman second. When Rabbi Friedman of Temple Emanuel established the National Jewish Hospital for Consumptives in 1899, Guldman was there with money and blankets for the beds; he would serve on the hospital's board of directors for more than thirty years, and after his death National Jewish would name a solarium in his honor. In 1923, when Beth Israel Hospital and Old Folks Home at West Sixteenth Avenue and Lowell Boulevard lacked sufficient funds to open its doors, Guldman provided $50,000, enough to fully equip it; in gratitude, its board named the structure the Leopold H. Guldman Building. In 1932, Guldman paid for a large home at 1601 Irving Street to house the Louise Guldman Community Center (named for his daughter), serving Jewish children and adults with classes, recreation and other activities. It had been founded ten years earlier, but his gift allowed significant expansion of its programs (it later moved to southeast Denver and operates today as the Staenberg-Loup Jewish Community Center). Additionally, Guldman gave generously to the Jewish Consumptives' Relief Society (JCRS), the Community Chest (today's United Way), Children's Hospital and both synagogues of which he was a member, Temple Emanuel and Beth Medrosh Hagodol (BMH). After his death, his will provided gifts to Catholic charities in addition to the usual Jewish ones, including the Queen of Heaven Orphanage in North Denver and the House of Good Shepherd.[99]

DYNAMO TO THE END

The Golden Eagle was not Guldman's only source of income. Early on, whenever he spotted a real estate opportunity that suited him, he bought. One of his properties was a four-lot tract at the eastern corner of Sixteenth and Champa Streets. When he purchased the first two lots in 1899, he announced that he would move his store there within a few years' time but later changed his mind; in 1902, he was quoted as "holding the same view" as William Cooke Daniels and David May, who believed it important to remain on Lawrence Street so as to be accessible from the northwest side of town as much as from the southeast. Guldman held on to the Champa property and later added two more lots, collecting rents from tenants of the older buildings that stood there. In 1935, in his eighties, he announced plans for an "ultramodern" three-story structure that would be known as the Guldman Building. Its primary tenant would be J.C. Penney, which lacked a Sixteenth Street presence.[100]

In 1902, Guldman, along with a number of other Denver businessmen (David May among them) formed the Continental Trust Company to operate a bank in the former People's Bank Building directly across Lawrence Street from the Golden Eagle; Guldman was on the Continental's board until the late 1910s, when it merged with Interstate Trust Company. The People's Bank was one of many that had failed in a hot, frightening summer years earlier, when the Panic of 1893 caused more than half of Denver's banks to fail. Guldman showed his generous side then, too, tapping into his cash to buy clearinghouse certificates issued by remaining Denver banks to shore up their reserves. It is likely that his doing so greatly helped stabilize Denver's economy, although it would suffer through Depression for several years. As another analysis points out, however, "the Golden Eagle had a major stake in the economic stability of the community," and his actions were not perhaps entirely altruistic.[101]

Through the decades, Guldman's popularity remained high in his adopted city. He continued offering the best bargains in town, buying out stores that were going out of business. In 1905, for instance, he bought the stock of The Leader department store in nearby Arvada for thirty-five cents on the dollar, transferred it to Sixteenth and Lawrence and, after marking it up slightly, held a huge clearance sale. Denverites were greatly concerned, then, when in August 1914 he was said to have been "lost" in Germany, which had commenced hostilities that month, beginning the Great War. To foil German communications, the British had cut the Germans' undersea cable to the United States on August 5, making it impossible for Americans to hear from anyone in Germany. After Milton and Bertha Guldman relayed their fears for Leopold's safety, the *Rocky Mountain News* cabled the State Department to find him. Nine days later, with the "personal aid of Secretary of State William Jennings Bryan," Guldman was located, perfectly well, at the Hotel Europe at Heidelberg. He had been visiting relatives in Bavaria; his relieved son and wife cabled thanks to Bryan, Colorado senators John Shafroth and Charles Thomas and Representative Charles Taylor for their help. So beloved was Guldman that by 1930, Denver newspapers began celebrating, as they had with John Jay Joslin, the birthdays of Denver's "Grand Old Man."[102]

Denverites were also concerned in 1931 when three "yeggs" (burglars in the newspaper parlance of the day) attempted a dramatic armed robbery. They made their move on a Sunday, when the store was closed. Being shut did not mean that it was empty, however. Having previously cased the store, they watched for Leopold's nephew, Max Guldman, who as office manager regularly came in on Sundays to catch up on work. They held a gun to him while the Sunday watchmen let them in, and once inside, they rounded up other employees and went to work on the safes with nitroglycerin. Large downtown stores at that time employed watchmen who made rounds, regularly "pulling watchman's boxes" at various locations to indicate that all was well. One of the robbers accompanied a store employee, silk salesman John Rudden, for more than an hour pulling these boxes until Rudden, feeling brave, coolly pulled a lever in special box that silently activated a burglar alarm. Police swiftly arrived, and a gun battle ensued, injuring one robber and an employee. Meanwhile a large crowd, estimated at two thousand, gathered outside, attracted by sounds of exploding safes and gunshots. The criminals—who were also wanted in St. Louis, Cincinnati and elsewhere—were quickly apprehended, and all served time.[103]

As charmed as Denver was by Guldman's public persona, it was to his family that he devoted his attention. Guldman had married not long after his arrival in Denver, to Sarah Schoyer of Milwaukee; possibly he had first encountered her when he worked in Watertown, Wisconsin. Leopold and Sarah had two children, son Milton (born in 1882) and daughter Helen (born in 1884). Sarah died in 1889, and in 1891, Guldman married her sister, Bertha G. Schoyer. Guldman and Bertha had three children: Corinne (born in 1893), Florence (born in 1896) and Louise (born in 1898). After he had enjoyed financial success with the Golden Eagle, Guldman employed William Lang and Marshall Pugh, Denver's finest residential architects, to design a Queen Anne–style home at 1549 Washington Street, replete with Richardsonian Romanesque arches and a second-floor balcony topped by a conical roof (the house survives today, somewhat modified). In 1912, he commissioned architects Aaron Gove and Thomas Walsh to design a massive, three-story, forty-room Neoclassical mansion at the southeast corner of East Tenth Avenue and Humboldt Street; this elaborate domicile symbolized how far Guldman had come from his humble beginnings. But it was perhaps too much—he sold it to *Denver Post* publisher Frederick G. Bonfils in 1918 and moved to a slightly less elaborate home, the former Herbert Collbran mansion at 1277 Williams Street.[104]

On June 2, 1936, eighty-three-year old Leopold Henry Guldman died at Denver's Mercy Hospital after a series of heart attacks the day before. Most of his children and his wife, Bertha, were with him at the end; his death was front-page news in Denver's papers. He left an estate of $1.85 million, the equivalent of $32 million today; this was after he had already given various downtown properties to his children in the year before his death; these were valued at $1 million. But there would be no replacement for him at the Golden Eagle—he had never designated a successor.[105]

Almost six months later, just in time for holiday shopping, store officers announced that Golden Eagle would hold a huge going-out-of-business sale. These men were all part of Guldman's family—his son, Milton, and three sons-in-law, Jacob L. Wolff, Lester Friedman and Melvin H. Schlesinger. Denverites with deep connections to their community, they had no desire to leave, but they also did not want to continue operating the store. The Golden Eagle had been a one-man show, and none wanted to fill Leopold's shoes. Except…there was one who did. Just three months later, in early 1937, Lester Friedman, husband of the former Louise Guldman, announced his

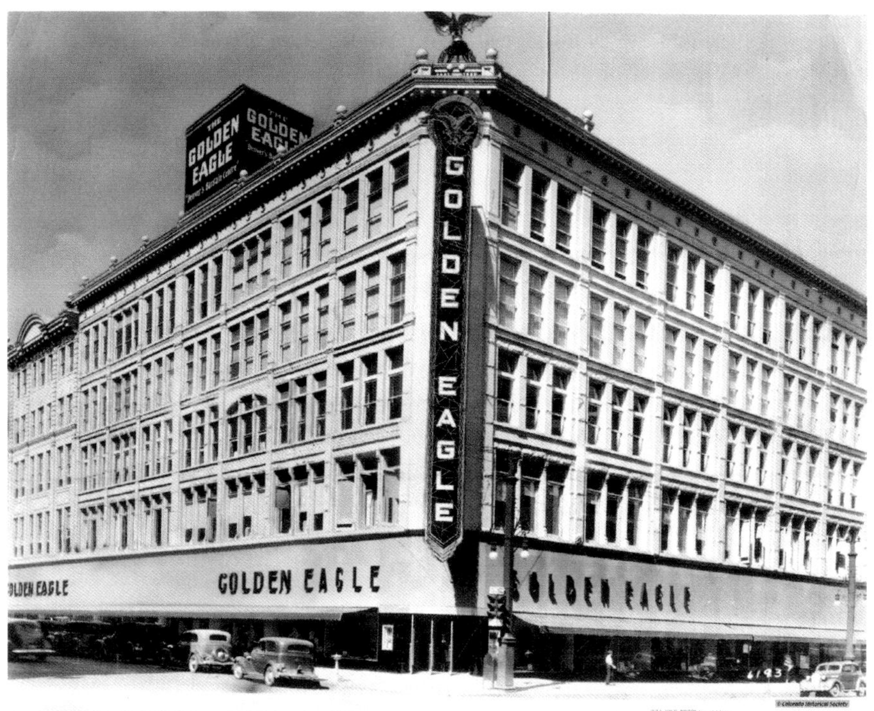

The Golden Eagle after its 1937 remodeling. *History Colorado, 10040053.*

intention to reopen the store. It could have simply been a case of wanting the Guldman estate cleanly closed out—the new entity, financially unrelated to the old, would be officially known as the New Golden Eagle Dry Goods Company—but the heirs never said so. Friedman brought in new executives to help him run the store and spent over $100,000 remodeling the building. He modernized the interior and street-facing show windows (bordered by shiny, black glass Vitrolite tiles) and added a free parking lot mid-block on Lawrence, demolishing a building to do so. He gave the store an impressive neon Golden Eagle sign running vertically on the corner but also kept Leopold's original carved eagle on top.

Despite the store's new slogan, "Everything New but the Name," it would still be a cash store, and low prices would still be the draw. By midsummer, all was ready, Mayor Benjamin F. Stapleton cut the ribbon, and crowds poured in. By all accounts, it was a smashing success; in 1938, Friedman announced plans to create additional departments and hire more staff. Three more years went by. In late 1941, on the eve of World War II, Friedman closed

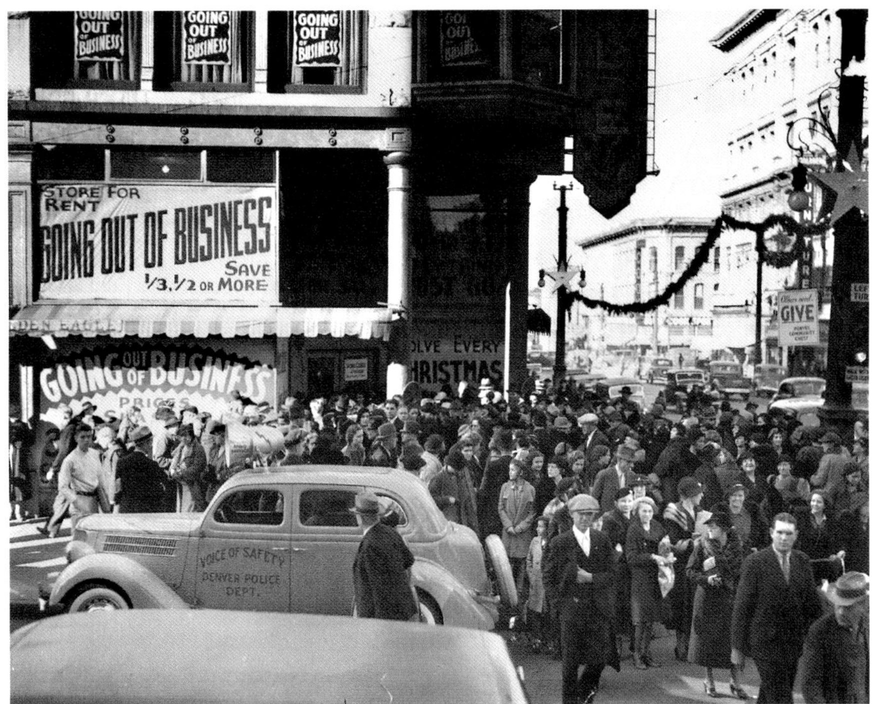

Golden Eagle's liquidation sale attracted large crowds in December 1941. *Beck Archives, Special Collections, CJS and University Libraries, University of Denver.*

the Golden Eagle for good, holding another closeout sale just in time for the holidays. He had been tapped to serve the government in some capacity in Washington but would later return, remaining a Denver figure until his death in 1970. Even though the Golden Eagle is now long gone, Leopold Guldman's benevolence toward his community remains a living thing. To this day, Denverites and strangers alike can still feel it whenever they visit National Jewish Health or take a class at the Jewish community center, quite the legacy for a humble butcher's son.[106]

Chapter 5

GANO-DOWNS AND COMPANY

The Store with the Shadow Box Windows

Here we cater to the man of substance, he who is both quality-conscious and fashion-conscious. Ours is a gentleman's shop, not necessarily oriented to sharp fashion, but rather to good taste.
—Robert Berry, 1972[107]

ONLY THE FINEST IN MENSWEAR

Gano-Downs' earliest days are shrouded in legend. The official story, per the store's publicity department in later years, is that in 1882, Merritt William Gano opened a small menswear shop off the lobby of the Windsor Hotel. At that time the Windsor, at Larimer and Eighteenth Streets, reigned as Denver's finest hostelry, and there was probably no better place to capture the trade of discerning gentlemen. It had opened two years earlier, under the management of William "Billy" Bush and his patron, silver tycoon Horace Tabor, who, flush with cash, had leased it from its English builder to provide Denver a hotel as impressive as his recently built Tabor Block and Tabor Grand Opera House. The Windsor featured nineteen-foot ceilings on the first floor, a stained-glass rotunda and diamond dust mirrors. The ballroom "floated," thanks to steel coils underneath the dance floor, and Denver's businessmen patronized the Windsor's bar, famous for three thousand silver dollars embedded in its floor and tended by future *Denver Post* publisher Harry Heye Tammen.[108]

The real story is that Merritt W. Gano began as a clerk at George H. Bramen & Company; it was only in 1887 that Bramen made him partner in Bramen & Gano. Eventually, the Windsor space proved too small, Bramen & Gano removing in 1887 to the Alkire Block at Sixteenth and Arapahoe Streets (later demolished for the Daniels and Fisher Tower), where it remained until 1889 or 1890. At about this time, Bramen decided to sell out to Gano, who became sole proprietor of Gano and Company, Clothiers, later Gano Clothing Company; Bramen later opened a competing shop at 927 Sixteenth. In 1893, Gano, now with silent partner Stephen G. Shaw, moved across Arapahoe to the Jacobson Block. By 1896, he had decided to move farther uptown, to the Steele Block at the eastern corner of Sixteenth and Stout Streets. This was a three-story building, built in 1882 by pioneer Dr. Henry K Steele (for whom Steele Street is named and whose son was Colorado chief justice Robert W. Steele). He had built his eponymous commercial block on the site of his 1872 home, on land purchased from

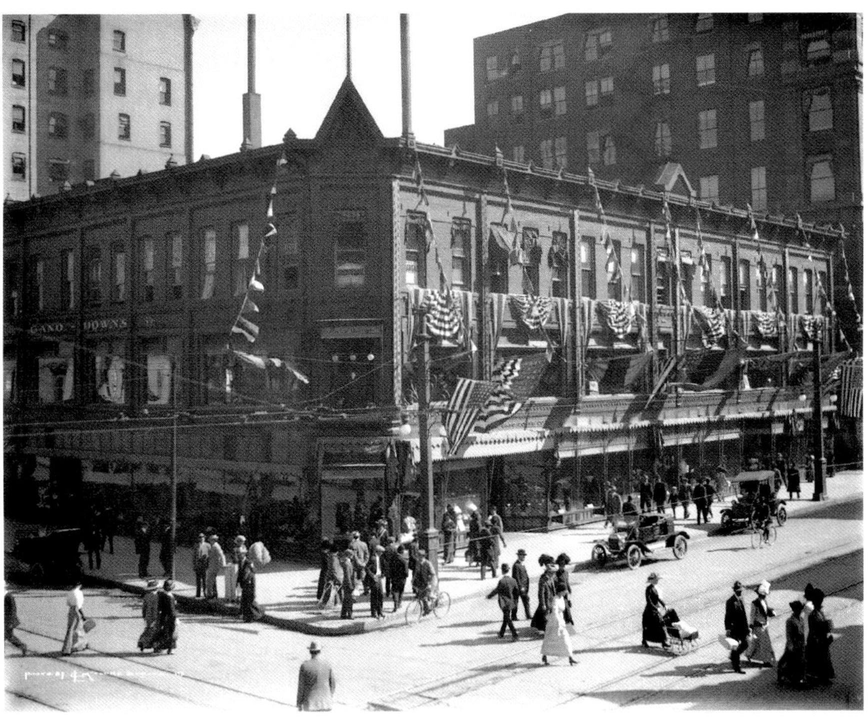

Gano-Downs occupied the first two floors of the three-story Steele Building on the eastern corner of Sixteenth and Stout Streets, circa 1910. *Denver Public Library, Western History Collection, MCC-3771; photograph by Louis Charles McClure.*

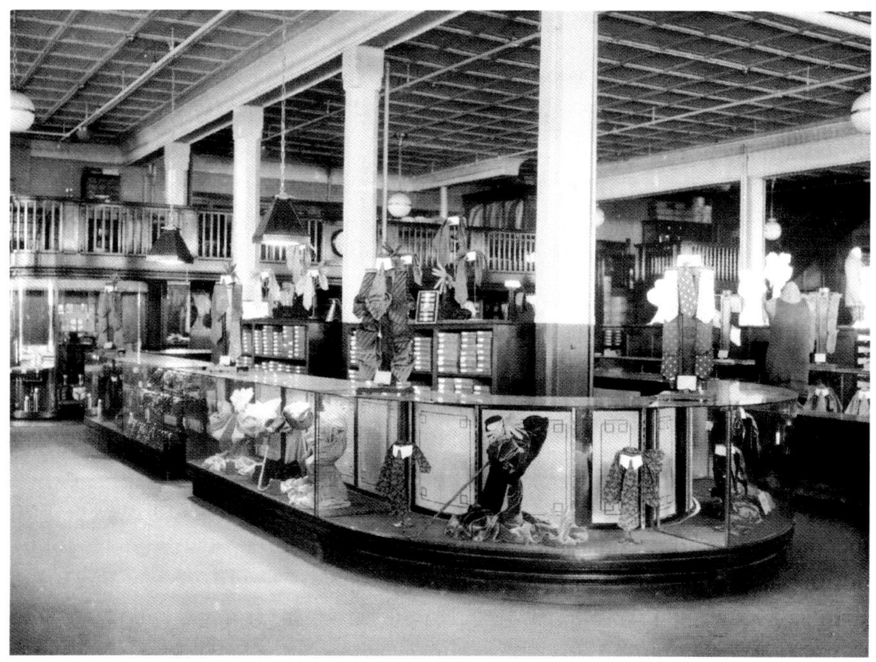

Gano-Downs' first-floor tie department, circa 1905. *Denver Public Library, Western History Collection, X-23952; photograph by Louis Charles McClure.*

former territorial governor John Evans. Gano & Company moved into a portion of the first floor, with upper floors leased to other entities. Here the store would remain for most of its history.[109]

This was a brilliant move. In settling here, Gano was following the trend uptown, pioneered by Michael J. McNamara, who had moved to California Street in 1889. Stout, once mostly residential, was rapidly gaining importance as a commercial street; at the other end of the block, at Seventeenth, the city's finest commercial edifice, the Equitable Building, arose in 1892, and Gano likely chose his new home based on proximity to it and other new upper Seventeenth Street edifices that housed banks, brokerages and law firms. Gano's forte was not, like David May's or Leopold Guldman's, the bargain suit—his customers came from the ranks of Denver's elite businessmen, who required finer attire. Also, locating so near the Equitable, he was near his own family. Brother George A. Gano, who had arrived in Denver before Merritt (1874 or earlier), was then partner, with the aforementioned Stephen G. Shaw, in an investment company headquartered on the Equitable's second floor; these two had also formed Queen City Coal Company, of which Merritt was treasurer. That was not the only extracurricular business in which Merritt was engaged—he also held the Denver franchise for Columbia Bicycles and in the 1890s ran a thriving trade selling and repairing them from the Stout Street side of the Steele Block. Gano & Company was a family concern—George A.'s son, George W., worked for his uncle in the clothing store.[110]

The Depression that followed the Panic of 1893 winnowed out weaker retailers; Gano, perhaps because of his other businesses, survived. By 1898, he could boast of significant growth over 1897, thanks to a concentration on "medium priced goods" during the lowest point of the crisis. As conditions improved, he returned to his original emphasis on only the finest menswear, and his advertising in the early 1900s emphasized Gano's commitment to "correct styles," meaning conservative and well made. In 1904, Gano brought on a new partner, William D. Downs, who was coming over from Daniels and Fisher, where he had begun as a clerk and risen to its board of directors. Upon acquiring a share of Gano's company, he resigned from that board, and Gano-Downs Clothing Company was born.[111]

TRANSITIONS

Gano-Downs grew rapidly in the new century, eventually occupying the entire Steele Block. In 1917, the store, which had previously displayed wares in conventional show windows along Sixteenth Street, decided to create a unique street-level identity by installing new windows, curving inward from the top. These "shadow box" windows had never been seen before in Denver, and their massing in a long line across the Sixteenth Street façade gave Gano-Downs a unique visual identity. They were expensive, no doubt—bending glass is difficult—but the feeling of elegance they imparted made them worth the money spent. Additionally, they eliminated sun glare, making it easier for passersby to view the goods within, visible from three sides thanks to hidden mirrors.[112]

Just a year after the window installation, those goods included fine ladies' clothing alongside menswear. Reasons for this change are not entirely clear, but most likely Gano and Downs looked out their office windows across Sixteenth toward Neusteter's and A.T. Lewis and saw their best customers' wives giving those stores their trade. By offering something for women, they could capture some of that business and forge closer ties with whole families. Women had often shopped Gano-Downs to buy for husbands and sons; now

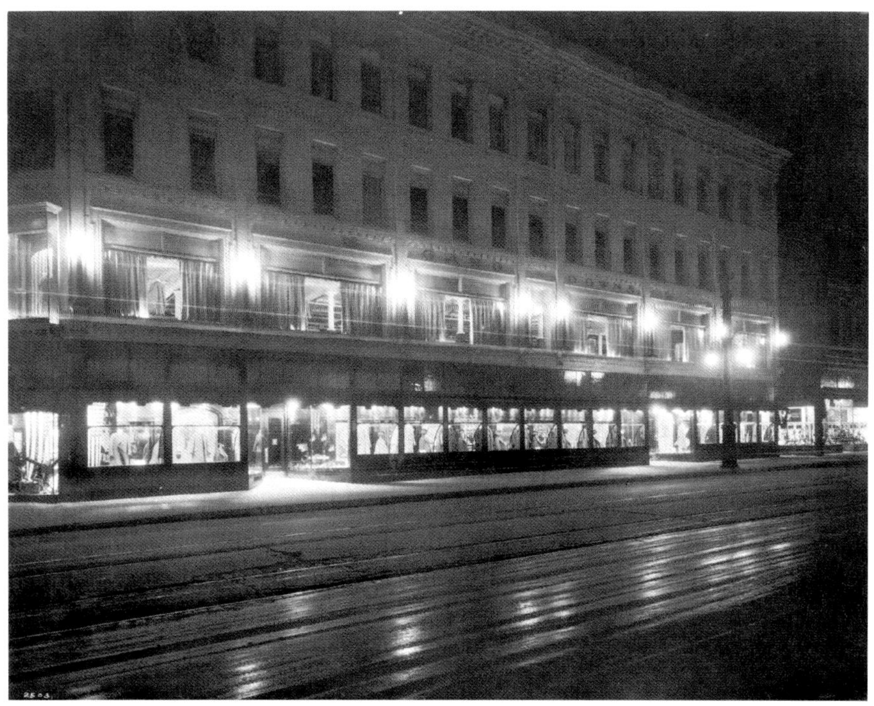

Nighttime view of Gano-Downs, now with four floors, after installation of its famous curved "shadow box" street level display windows, circa 1920. *Denver Public Library, Western History Collection, Z-6881; photograph by Louis Charles McClure.*

they would have reason to visit more frequently. The move into women's clothing was canny, but it necessitated more room, prompting the addition of a fourth floor in 1919.[113]

Gano-Downs thrived in the 1920s. In 1926, Merritt W. Gano and William D. Downs jointly retired, turning the store over to their sons, Merritt W. Gano Jr. and William H. Downs, with the elders remaining on the board of directors, along with George A. and George W. Gano. All three of the younger men had worked at the store for some time, their fathers grooming them to take over. It was surprising, then, when eleven years later, in 1937, Gano-Downs underwent its first significant ownership change: two Daniels and Fisher executives and board members, S. Nelson Hicks and W.L. Hillyard, bought a controlling interest (at first, Denver papers mistakenly assumed this meant that Daniels and Fisher was buying Gano-Downs, but the men soon announced their resignations from the big store). Reasons for the sale are unclear, although it is not likely that Gano-Downs was in financial trouble—the worst years of the Depression had passed. It is more likely due to the ambition of the acquirers, who, like William D. Downs before them, wanted to run their own store; buying the smaller Gano-Downs was less of a hurdle than buying Daniels and Fisher would have been. Merritt W. Gano Jr. retained minority ownership and became chairman. Joining Hicks were two of his sons, S. Nelson Hicks Jr., who had been chief buyer of men's furnishings at Daniels and Fisher and would become vice-president and general manager of Gano-Downs, and Alfred C. Hicks as treasurer.[114]

BUILDING ON THE LEGACY

World War II came and went, and like other Denver stores, Gano-Downs felt the urge to modernize, embarking in 1949 on a three-year modernization program. S. Nelson Hicks Jr. became president in 1951, and in 1952, he was proud to show off the changes, completed just in time for the holidays. A new fifth floor was entirely given over to fur storage for customers, and air conditioning now cooled the building. On the sales floors, lower acoustical ceilings now hid the original tin ones, and new fixtures, lighting, flooring and paint colors updated the store in the latest style. Various departments relocated. In the new layout, the first floor featured men's and women's accessories. Riding two new side-by-side elevators (two earlier lifts were located in different parts of the building), shoppers encountered men's and boy's apparel on two; women's shoes, furs and lingerie on three; and women's ready-to-wear on four. The biggest change was outside. It was new, gleaming and modern, with white, porcelain glazed-enamel steel tiles as shiny as a new refrigerator. Instead of ordinary windows, narrow panes were "joined in vertical lines accentuating the height of the building…built in twin sections with the center projecting out like automobile windshield," an apt metaphor for auto-centric times. Wisely, however, Hicks did not allow architects to touch the store's display windows, which remained as they had been since 1917. In fact, even with its new look, Gano-Downs accentuated its role, reminding shoppers in its advertising that it was "the store with the shadow box windows."[115]

In addition to modernizing, the other postwar trend among the store's peers was branching out to serve customers closer to where they lived. The first two satellites, however, catered more to well-heeled travelers and echoed the store's 1882 genesis at the Windsor. The first was a small shop in the lobby of Writer's Manor, a new, luxury suburban hotel (*not* a motel) at Interstate 25 and South Colorado Boulevard; it sold a small selection of men's and women's apparel and gifts. The second involved a 1957 purchase of the MacNeil and Moore's menswear shop at the Broadmoor Hotel in Colorado Springs; renamed Gano-Downs, it would continue to offer fine menswear exclusively.

The third branch, however, would be a full-line store, in Cherry Creek. Here it was following The Denver Dry Goods and Neusteters, both of which had already opened in the district by the time Gano-Downs opened there just before Thanksgiving 1960. Occupying the southwest corner of East Second Avenue and Fillmore Street, the Cherry Creek Gano-Downs would not be visible to drivers on busy First Avenue (another building, housing fashion boutique Cates First Avenue, stood in between Gano-Downs and First), but Hicks was certain that customers would find it. Occupying thirty-four thousand square feet on two levels and a small penthouse, it reflected the architecture of its downtown parent, with vertical slit windows on the upper level, spaced across white steel exterior panels. Upstairs was devoted to women's and girls' clothing, gifts, accessories, cosmetics, millinery, women's shoes and some men's departments. The street level featured men's and boys' suits, slacks, shoes and overcoats; the boys' department was six times larger than its downtown counterpart, as mothers were more apt to bring sons here thanks to the seventy-two-car parking lot on the roof. An open stairway, accented by a tiled waterfall, connected the floors. Street-level show windows were conventional, rather than replications of downtown's shadow boxes.[116]

Less than a week after Cherry Creek's opening, S. Nelson Hicks died at home, aged sixty, after a three-month illness; he had made a will eighteen days earlier, so he must have sensed that his end was near. Ownership passed to his wife, Dorothy Hicks, and sons S. Nelson Hicks III and David Foster Hicks. For Dorothy, the logical next president was Gano-Downs' vice-president, fifty-four-year-old Alfred R. Schumann, who had been with the store during the entire Hicks era, serving as controller, secretary, treasurer and merchandising manager. Schumann saw the company through the Christmas season, but on the evening of January 1, 1961, stress apparently took a toll. Absenting himself from a New Year's party he and his wife were hosting at their Lakewood home, he took a revolver from a bedroom drawer and shot himself in the head, dying the next day at St. Anthony's Hospital; he left no note. In mid-January, Dorothy named W. Cyrus Wilson as store president; in little more than six weeks, Gano-Downs had had three presidents. Wilson, a Denver native and World War II veteran, was younger than Schumann, having started in 1953 as a buyer, managed the Broadmoor shop and opened Cherry Creek as manager and vice-president.[117]

Wilson led Gano-Downs in much the same way Hicks Jr. had done, investing to keep the store current, as clothing styles and shopping patterns evolved rapidly during the 1960s. In 1963, he announced a major remodeling downtown, following numerous other stores making significant investments, hoping to stem the tide of suburbanization that was reducing profitability with each passing year. The remodeling, staged over three years, emphasized differences between the sexes: second-floor men's departments were given "thick red carpeting" and dark walnut paneling to evoke masculinity, while women's areas on three, in what the store called "mood merchandising," featured "bright, feminine colors and contemporary designs," with better lighting and lots of mirrors. Responding to the trendy "mod" style, Wilson established several boutiques on one, with cute names like "Sport Shed" (sportswear), "Knit Nook" (imported knitwear) and "Rain Drop" (raincoats).

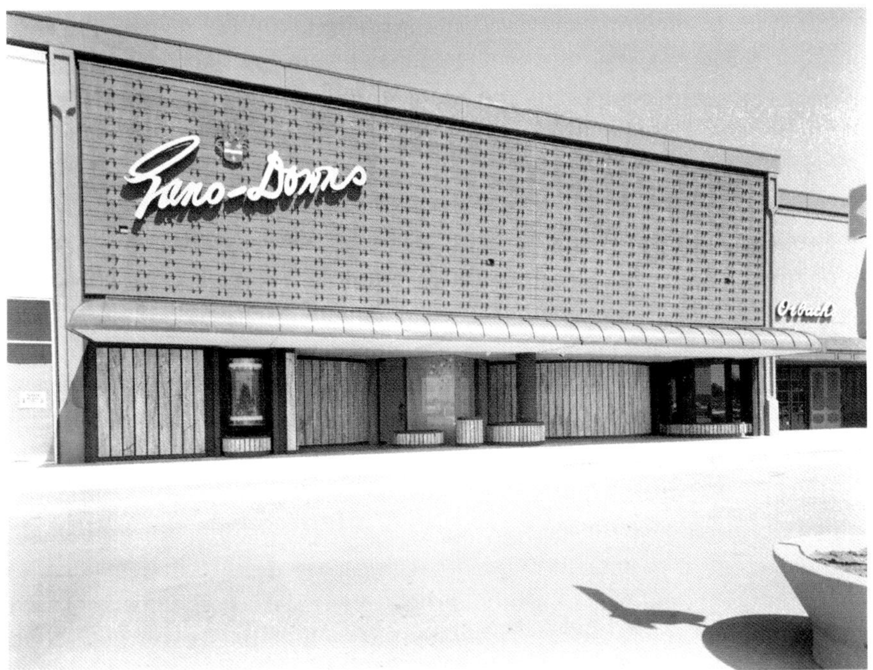

Gano-Downs' Cinderella City branch, 1968, with a vertically curved show window that nodded to the downtown store's horizontally curved ones. *Denver Public Library, Western History Collection, 346; photograph by Otto Roach.*

In first-floor men's furnishings and sportswear departments, shoppers encountered flooring that "looks like brick, feels like brick when you walk on it—but is actually the newest in vinyl tile" and perfectly on-trend.[118]

Like peers at other stores, Wilson felt the "call of the mall," the urge to continue expanding because competitors were doing so. In 1967, he leased fourteen thousand square feet at Cinderella City, in the "Rose Mall" section. Gano-Downs opened during the mall's second-phase grand opening in July 1968. The design, by Wilson's architect brother, Joseph Wilson, featured circular elements in its ceiling and floors; shoppers could enter through the mall or directly from the parking lot. Curiously, despite its suburban setting, it did not include children's departments, only men's and women's offerings. A year later, Gano-Downs announced in August 1969 another new branch, anchoring a new center across 28th Street from Boulder's Crossroads Shopping Center, a full-scale department store, unlike the Englewood shop. It was to open in 1970.[119]

Dismantling the Legacy

It would never open. Less than six months later, on February 18, 1970, W. Cyrus Wilson died from a heart attack, just shy of his forty-ninth birthday. Dorothy Hicks again promoted from within, elevating vice-president Harold W. Leonhardt, who had been an employee since 1955. He would serve as president less than two years. Two days before Christmas 1971, store employees and Denver shoppers learned that Gano-Downs was to be sold, for an undisclosed all-cash price, to Joseph Magnin, a San Francisco–based chain owned by a Honolulu entity known as Amfac Inc. With Hawaiian roots dating to 1849 (as one of the "Big Five" members of the kingdom's sugar oligarchy), Amfac in the 1960s and 1970s behaved like other conglomerates, buying up forty-two companies in mostly unrelated industries (conglomerate theory held that a downturn in one area could be compensated for by an upturn in some other division).

One Amfac segment was not dissimilar to Joseph Magnin and Gano-Downs—it also owned Hawaii's Liberty House department stores. But the odd mix also included sugarcane plantations, pharmaceuticals, real estate, electrical parts, the Fred Harvey hotel and restaurant chain and Denver's Wilhelm Foods, purveyor of processed beef to schools. Joseph Magnin's roots dated to 1913, when its eponymous founder, irked at being passed over by his mother in favor of his brothers to run the fashionable I. Magnin store in San Francisco, set up his own shop. When his son, Cyril, took over after World War II, he steered Joseph Magnin toward high fashion, opening numerous branches before selling out to Amfac in 1969. When it bought Gano-Downs, Joseph Magnin had thirty-two stores, primarily in California.[120]

When the sale closed in February 1972, Joseph Magnin president Robert Berry, a Neiman-Marcus veteran, wasted no time implementing changes. His plan retained Leonhardt as regional manager for Colorado, but the Gano-Downs name would come off the three locations, replaced by Joseph Magnin, and stores would cater to a younger, trendier shopper than Gano-Downs had done. The Gano-Downs name, synonymous with quality, would live on, in separate quarters. Berry leased a two-story property at 1630 Stout Street, abutting the Equitable Building. The sixteen-thousand-square-foot space, featuring menswear only, was a comedown from the fifty-thousand-square-foot structure Gano-Downs was vacating, but Berry announced plans to open additional Gano-Downs locations, in Denver and elsewhere in the West, generally located near existing and planned Joseph Magnin stores.

While these additional Gano-Downs branches never materialized (save for a small Second Avenue shop adjacent to the Cherry Creek Magnin store), the new downtown shop would carry over more than just its name and legacy for quality: it would sport two of the shadow box windows. Berry replaced the famous windows along Sixteenth Street with ordinary, but taller, plate-glass ones, allowing for full-height mannequins. This made perfect sense from a merchandising standpoint, but it did not endear Joseph Magnin to Denver shoppers. The new Gano-Downs Store for Men opened for business in October, five months after the Joseph Magnin name went up on the former Gano-Downs façades. It was technically competing with the "J-M for Men" department inside its former quarters, a first-floor boutique featuring trendy imported clothing, but it is likely that the overlap between the two operations' customer bases was small. With these changes, the two Denver stores could offer the city's shoppers two exclusive lines never previously available here: Joseph Magnin boasted a boutique for the prestigious Italian leatherwear maker Gucci, while the new Gano-Downs prominently featured a tweedy, "reminiscent of the 1930s" Polo Shop featuring the suits, slacks, shirts, knitwear, overcoats and luggage of young New York designer Ralph Lauren.[121]

With Berry's ambitious expansion plans not paying off, something had to give. In October 1975, former Macy's executives took over leadership, with plans to remake Joseph Magnin to appeal not only to its core younger shopper but also to older women who still desired stylish fashions. To this new team, Gano-Downs, a pet project of Berry's, was a poor fit. In late 1976, Amfac announced that it would return Gano-Downs to local ownership, selling it to Max Grassfield, effective in January 1977. Grassfield had operated a small menswear shop near the University of Denver since 1960, adding a second storefront for women, Distaff of Grassfield's, in 1966. He planned no changes to Gano-Downs' offering other than introducing to it some lines carried by his original store; the shops would henceforth be called Grassfield's Gano Downs (*sans* hyphen).

The downtown store, much larger than either the Cherry Creek or University Park boutiques, proved difficult to operate, especially when downtown was rapidly losing upscale shoppers to Cherry Creek; Grassfield closed its doors on August 1, 1982. He continued to operate Cherry Creek for several more years, finally closing it in the 1990s. This was a quiet end to what had once been one of Denver's finest stores, beloved not only for fine clothing and service but also, perhaps most of all, for its shadow box windows. Even the last two of them, at 1630 Stout Street, are gone, removed in a subsequent remodeling.[122]

Chapter 6

THE DENVER DRY GOODS COMPANY

Where Denver Shops with Confidence

Why, to come in here you had to be dressed, *honey.*
—Tea Room server Dorothy Howard Kenny, 1986[123]

AN IRISH DANDY

If there is one store that embodied Denver's old personality—solid, stolid, not too adventurous—better than any, The Denver Dry Goods Company was surely it, and this is the emporium that longtime Denverites miss most. Downtown's fifth-floor Tea Room comes up first in any conversation about "The Denver," memories of dressing up (including white gloves) to dine and its famous chicken à la king, inevitably what people remember best. But it was more than a tearoom—before the advent of suburban shopping, it was the largest store in Colorado and the busiest, the one place where nearly everyone (middle class, mostly white) shopped. It offered everything: the usual departments for women's, men's and children's clothing and items ranging from monogramed stationery to western saddles, from bargain-priced underwear to pricey furs, from books to bodices to boots to blenders. When it closed in 1987, Denverites were both saddened and outraged; in some ways, its loss that year presaged many other losses to come, as "old Denver" transformed itself into today's "new Denver." The Denver, as it was officially known after 1965, embodied the true "heart" of Denver.

Officially, the store was born in 1894, but this tale begins much earlier, with the Irish potato famine of the 1840s—two major figures in this store's history became Americans because of it. The first was Michael J. McNamara, who at age six immigrated with his family in 1849. At age twelve, he entered into his life's work in dry goods, taking a job with a Philadelphia linen importer. Upon reaching eighteen, he followed his ambitions west to St. Louis, where he clerked in a dry goods house for a few years before deciding to open his own store. With competition in St. Louis fierce, he looked for a newer, less well-established spot, trekking across Missouri to open a shop in Liberty, near Kansas City. In 1870, McNamara chose Denver as his next home.[124]

Instead of immediately establishing a business, McNamara first worked at an existing store, Brooks, Giddings and Company. Here he clerked for several years, becoming friends with Edgar H. Drew. In 1877, the two decided to strike out on their own, leasing a space at Fifteenth and Larimer Streets from two brothers, George Washington and William M. Clayton, who had operated a general store there on the site of Denver founder General William H. Larimer's 1858 log cabin. The new concern, Drew & McNamara, was not a general store but a true dry goods house, democratically catering to all classes and "filled with goods of every grade from the finest to the cheapest."[125]

In 1880, Drew sold out to his partner; the store was now M.J. McNamara & Company. On his own, the popular, genial Irishman (described as "a wit, a dandy in a broadcloth Prince Albert wing collar with opulent Price de Joinville tie, lilac colored waistcoat, gray striped trousers creased to a razor's edge, needlepoint and patent leather shoes" in one admiring profile) embarked on an expansion, leasing the next-door space and knocking openings through walls to double the store's size. It paid off; by the first day of 1881, McNamara claimed he had doubled his business in a year. Yet this was not enough. By 1883, his store bursting at the seams, McNamara and his landlords announced a plan that would transform the mercantile into a true emporium. The original two-story brick building gave way to a grand new edifice of four stories plus basement, faced in granite, rhyolite and red sandstone, to a design by architect John W. Roberts. M.J. McNamara would occupy the whole building, its wares visible through huge plate glass windows, framed in cast iron, on both the Larimer and Fifteenth Street sides. Two elevators linked all levels; upper floors housed the wholesale division and dressmaking.[126]

Yet this was not enough. In the 1880s, Denver changed rapidly, fueled by a rising population and a silver boom in the Rockies. The city's retail

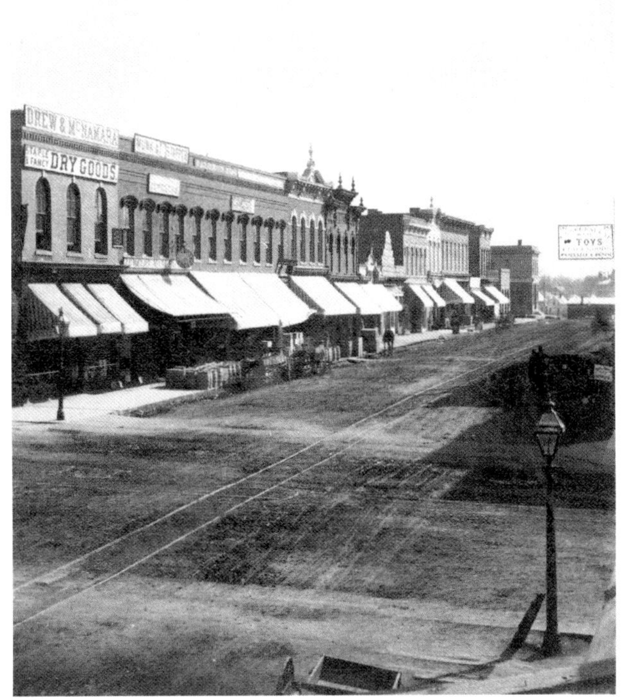

Drew & McNamara's store on Fifteenth and Larimer Streets (*left*), in a building erected in the 1860s by William M. and George Washington Clayton on the site of General William Larimer's log cabin, circa 1877. *Bill Eloe Collection; stereoview photograph by William Gunnison Chamberlain.*

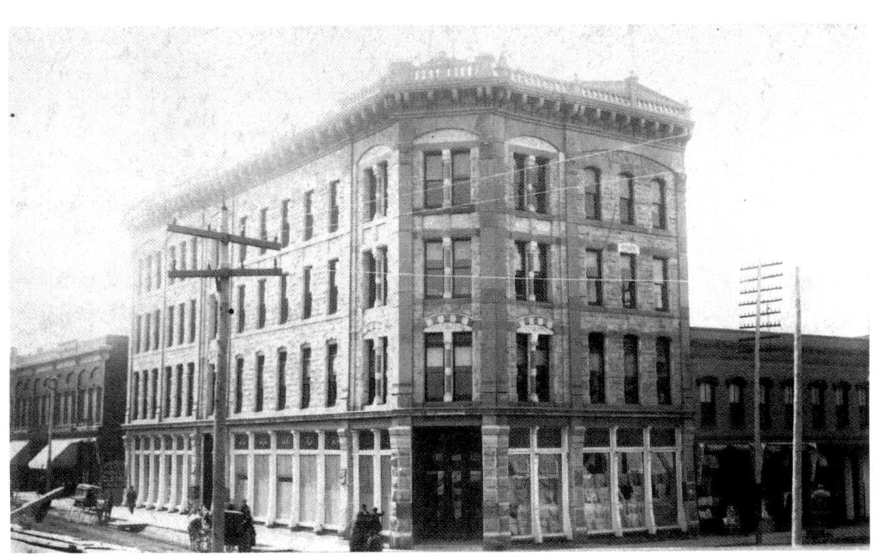

The Clayton Block, today known as the Granite Building, replaced the original two-story brick building on the southern corner of Fifteenth and Larimer Streets. All four floors were leased by M.J. McNamara and Company, circa 1883. *History Colorado, 10052743.*

geography, once centered on lower Fifteenth Street, next on Larimer, now on Lawrence and creeping up Sixteenth, was evolving too. When Swiss immigrant John J. Reithmann, resident in Denver since 1858, approached McNamara with an idea for getting ahead of the competition that would inevitably move uptown, the Irishman was all ears. Reithmann, originally a druggist but by then a real estate baron, owned various properties, including one diagonally across the street from his own house, at Sixteenth and California Streets. Here, he proposed to McNamara, he would build him "the finest department store building west of St. Louis."[127]

And so it came to be: in 1889, just six years after the opening of his emporium at Fifteenth and Larimer Streets, McNamara Dry Goods Company (so named after its 1886 incorporation) moved to California Street, occupying a three-story pressed brick and limestone building designed by the city's leading commercial architect, Frank E. Edbrooke. While not quite as tall as the Larimer Street structure, the new facility was significantly larger, as it extended down California Street for more than twice the distance that the previous one had extended on Larimer. Store histories written in the twentieth century claimed that McNamara had moved "out in the country," but this was stretching truth: while some residences still stood nearby, in 1889 Sixteenth and California Streets was rapidly becoming a preeminent location, thanks to the rapid growth of street railways and migration of its wealthier classes to the southeast. Remaining on Larimer Street would have been folly.[128]

The new store immediately attracted trade, and McNamara continued growing his business and charming customers. However, he had taken a big risk—not by moving, but by opening such a large building, requiring vastly more inventory than the Larimer store. When the financial Panic of 1893 hit, McNamara owed money to various Denver banks and vendors. In hot, dusty July, he was caught short, running newspaper ads that begged customers to come downtown and buy ("Must Raise Cash!" they shouted). All city merchants felt the pinch, as did banks—more than half of Denver's closed that month. Other department stores survived, either because they had been longer established, did not borrow or were still relatively small. McNamara's Irish luck ran out along with his money, and in September, he shut his doors. The Arapahoe County sheriff auctioned the store and its contents, with two Denver businessmen associated with Colorado National Bank winning the bid: its president, Charles B. Kountze, and its vice-president, Dennis Sheedy (the other Irish potato famine immigrant important in The Denver's history). Colorado National was one of McNamara's largest creditors.[129]

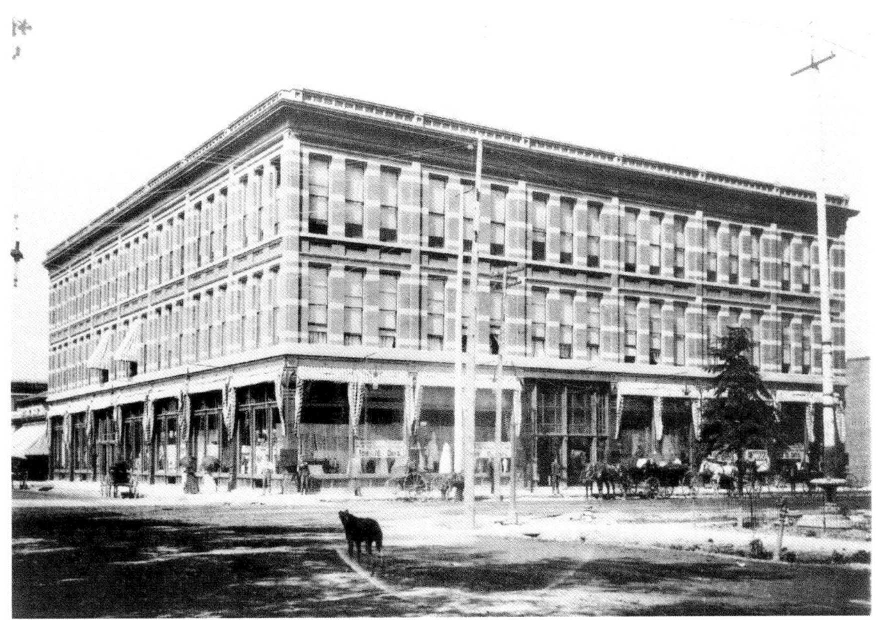

McNamara Dry Goods, the "finest department store building west of St. Louis," built in 1889 on the western corner of Sixteenth and California Streets to a design by Frank E. Edbrooke. *Thomas J. Noel Collection.*

The new owners, busy with other business interests (besides the bank, Sheedy owned and operated the vast Globe Smelter north of Denver), decided initially to keep McNamara at the helm—he knew how to sell, and they had no other candidate. They reopened on Monday, September 11, with McNamara greeting customers, many of whom had been greatly worried for him, reassured now that his future was bright. The new firm's advertisements were signed "M.J. McNamara, Manager for Sheedy & Kountze," with his name prominent. Over the winter, however, Sheedy and Kountze found themselves increasingly displeased by his management. Spring ads featured "Sheedy & Kountze" in large type, with McNamara's considerably downsized. Finally, on May 22, 1894, he was gone—and so was the name "Sheedy & Kountze." With Kountze still a financial partner, Sheedy had formed a new corporation, with himself as president: The Denver Dry Goods Company was born. The new manager was William Roland Owen, the sole McNamara executive that Sheedy found sensible. (Owen had previously operated his own store in Leadville, before selling it to Daniels, Fisher and Smith, and was well grounded in the fiscal side of retailing.)[130]

An Irish Mogul

Sheedy, in the three decades he led The Denver Dry Goods Company, was one of Denver's most prominent businessmen. He divided his days between desks at the bank and the store, also overseeing the smelter's operations until he sold it in 1899. His efforts paid off handsomely—his huge, Queen Anne–style mansion on Capitol Hill was a jewel on "Millionaire's Row," and his fortune allowed him to give generously to Mount St. Vincent's Orphanage, St. Leo's Church (the Irish parish), St. Joseph's Hospital and the Cathedral of the Immaculate Conception.[131]

His early story was not unlike that of David May and Leopold Guldman—he was an immigrant, and like them, he worked hard and employed his wits. His path to wealth led him on a very different route, however. It was "the call of the west" (as he named it in his *Autobiography*) that led him in 1863 to leave Lyons, Iowa, where his family had settled, and come to Denver. He soon found employment with Alvin B. Daniels, who partnered with J. Sidney Brown in a general store. In Daniels (unrelated to William Bradley Daniels), the teenage Sheedy found a father figure and mentor as well as a friend. Sheedy left

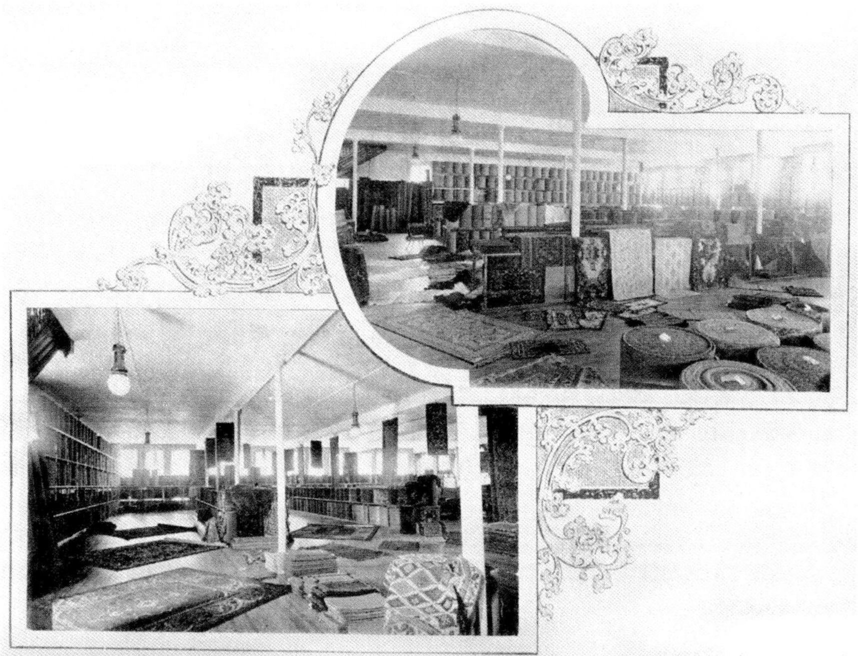

Two views of The Denver Dry Goods third-floor carpet department from a 1902 catalogue. *Jim O'Hagan Collection.*

Denver in 1864, embarking on a busy career, ranging all over the West, from Montana to Utah, to Montana again and Utah again, stopping in Chicago to take business courses. He traded merchandise at first, buying goods cheaply, hauling them over great distances to hinterland settlements and selling dearly. In 1868, Sheedy discovered another calling when he bought three hundred head of cattle. He was soon buying, driving and selling cattle all over the West, from Texas to Wyoming, from Arizona to Kansas.[132]

In 1880, Sheedy decided to get out of the cattle trade—it was time to settle down, but he had another reason. He had often returned to Denver to visit Daniels and his wife, the latter of whom had extracted a promise that if she died he would "look after" her husband. She passed in 1879, but it was Daniels's death in 1880 that brought Sheedy permanently to town, to raise their son until he grew to adulthood. He made friends with Kountze, who sold him a share in the bank and made him its vice-president; Sheedy also married and had two daughters. He bought a failing smelter and turned it around, and in 1893, he bought McNamara's store.

In many ways, Sheedy was McNamara's opposite—rather than for geniality, he was known as the bank's strictest debt collector. Instead of

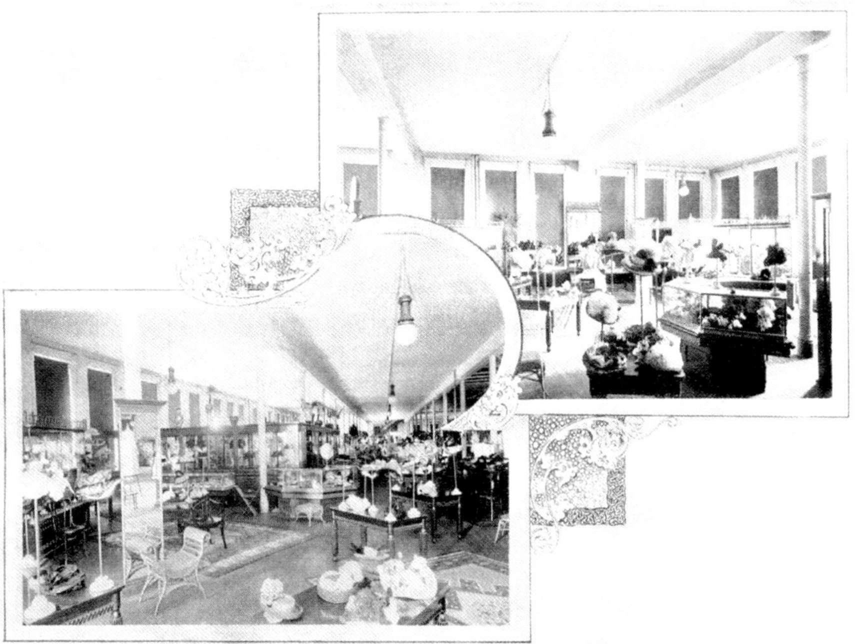

Two views of The Denver Dry Goods second-floor millinery department from a 1902 catalogue. *Jim O'Hagan Collection.*

losing during the Panic, he gained the source of a new fortune. Instead of conducting business from the sales floor, he operated behind the scenes. Per historian Phyllis J. Doner, he "was not the urbane cosmopolitan retailer such as a John Wanamaker of Philadelphia," but rather was "comfortable with and well suited to cope with the rough and tumble atmosphere of an early frontier community…maintain[ing] firm control over The Denver Dry Goods Company for over twenty-nine years and [running it] as he would have bossed a wagon train, driven a herd of cattle or issued orders to workers at the Globe Smelter—with an iron grip."[133]

Sheedy and Owen, once the Depression began lifting, rapidly grew The Denver Dry Goods into Denver's most important, and largest, store. By 1898, McNamara's building proved too small. Sheedy bought two lots next to it, hiring Edbrooke to extend his original design by fifty feet and top the whole with a fourth floor; he also bought the original building and land from Reithmann. The expanded store rivaled Daniels and Fisher for impressiveness. Its street level, "a puzzling labyrinth of aisles that checquer the great floor like the streets of a city," included shoe and furnishings departments for both sexes, stationery and books, notions, confectionery, jewelry, linens, laces and gloves, silks and dress goods and access to a mezzanine with comfortable seating and writing desks where women could relax between purchases. Millinery, children's, furs, cloaks, suits and the art department filled the second floor, while the third featured carpets, draperies and furniture. The top floor housed dressmaking and tailoring operations, while the basement included china, glass, silver, toys, coffee and tea; two passenger elevators linked all five levels.[134]

In 1906–7, Owen expanded again, growing the store all the way to Fifteenth Street, after Sheedy, with great patience and increasingly greater funds, acquired adjoining lots. The new Fifteenth Street wing, designed by Edbrooke again but very different from his 1889 and 1898 work, rose six stories, with much larger windows than the older building. Upon opening in the summer of 1907, it gave the store more square footage than Daniels and Fisher, crowning it the city's largest department store. It also featured something that previously only Daniels and Fisher offered: a tearoom, on the new wing's fourth floor. The store now also boasted an escalator, one way up to the second floor from the first. Unlike rivals, only The Denver Dry Goods could claim entrances on *two* major downtown streets—although Fifteenth was never as prestigious an address as Sixteenth, several streetcar lines ran along it, and in the 1900s and 1910s, it boomed, with new office buildings and hotels. The four-hundred-foot first floor main aisle, running from the

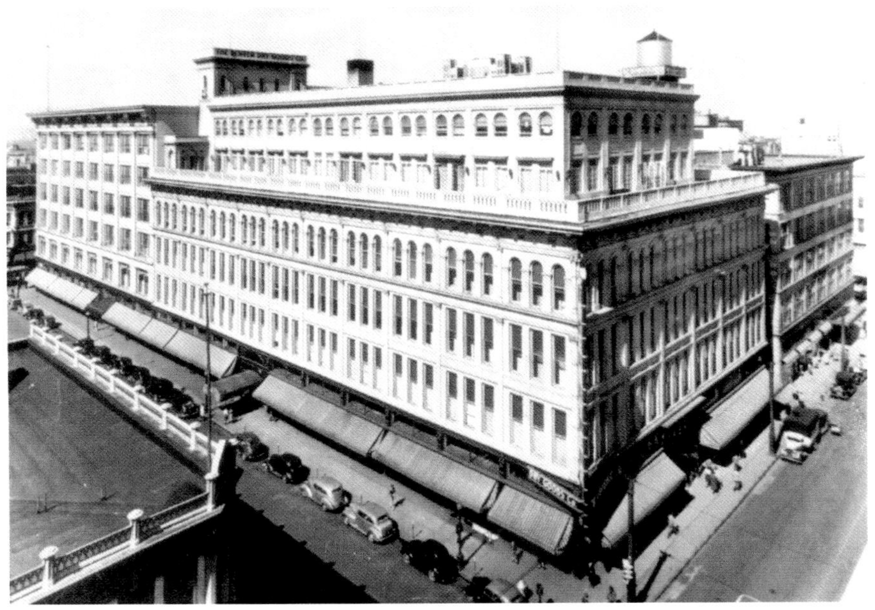

A 1940s view of The Denver Dry Goods Company from the roof of the Mack Block diagonally across the intersection of Sixteenth and California Streets. The building has been painted white; Neusteter's is visible at far right. *Thomas J. Noel Collection.*

Sixteenth Street door to the one on Fifteenth, was, the store boasted (with no small amount of hyperbole), "the longest department store aisle in the United States."[135]

It was during these years that The Denver built its reputation for service. Owen ran a tight ship, requiring staff to be at their posts promptly each morning and demanding of department heads strict accounting of profit and loss. In 1902, he instituted a dress code for female employees (but not men) that stipulated plain, sober dress so as not to compete with customers' finery—the women complied, even if some bristled at the double standard. Despite the strict environment, most staff served loyally, many for several decades. Owen also pioneered motorized delivery—while the store had previously maintained a stable of fine horses with carriages, in 1901 he bought steam-powered trucks from the White Automotive Company and in 1910 he replaced those with twenty-six Model T–based trucks from local Ford agency O'Meara Company. Owen likely also initiated The Denver's famous Lost-and-Found Book, a large, red leather-bound journal located near the Sixteenth Street entrance in which shoppers could leave messages for one another regarding their whereabouts.[136]

NEW TRADITIONS

Dennis Sheedy died on October 16, 1923, aged seventy-seven. His second wife, Mary (his first having passed in 1895), sold the company in early 1924 to a St. Louis store, Scruggs, Vandervoort and Barney, whose president, Melvin L. Wilkinson, had been friendly with her husband. This coincided with the beginning of a great wave of consolidations and mergers in the American department store industry; selling to an out-of-town entity was not unusual. Wilkerson and his son-in-law, Frank M. Mayfield (appointed general manager), immediately capitalized on their new purchase and the 1920s department store boom, adding two more floors to the Sixteenth Street building. At the beginning of the holiday season in late November, just eight months after they had bought the store, the new owners introduced Denver to one of its enduring institutions: the fifth floor Tea Room, replacing the earlier one on four.[137]

Seating nearly eight hundred, it was not only the largest non-hotel foodservice operation in Denver but also, instantly, the place to see and be seen. It occupied the entire fifth floor of the Sixteenth Street building, its vaulted ceiling supported by a forest of octagonal columns. French doors opened onto a balcony, the Promenade, where diners could stroll after eating. At the Sixteenth Street end, a glass-and-mahogany partitioned "Grill Room," with two large, round tables and several smaller ones, catered to Denver's old-guard businessmen, a mostly all-male environment contrasting with the larger Tea Room. Two new express elevators next to the California Street entrance ensured that male diners could access the Grill Room quickly.[138]

The Tea Room became a much-beloved element in Denverites' lives. In the 1920s, it conducted annual "Doll's Tea Parties" for little girls and their dolls. Later, it hosted "Breakfast with Santa" on December Saturday mornings, with entertainments for children and chances to tell Santa what they wanted. The Tea Room also hosted countless events for adults, including fashion shows and business luncheons. Dining at the store was an occasion—children wore their best clothes, and their mothers donned white gloves. Inevitably, nearly everyone enjoyed its signature dish, chicken à la king; other fare included salads, sandwiches, pot roast, prime rib and various soups. Dessert might be house-made ice cream, pies, pudding, peach cobbler or bread pudding, all created by store chefs. While the food was familiar and comforting, it was also high quality and made from scratch. While its original purpose may have been to provide sustenance for shoppers, over the

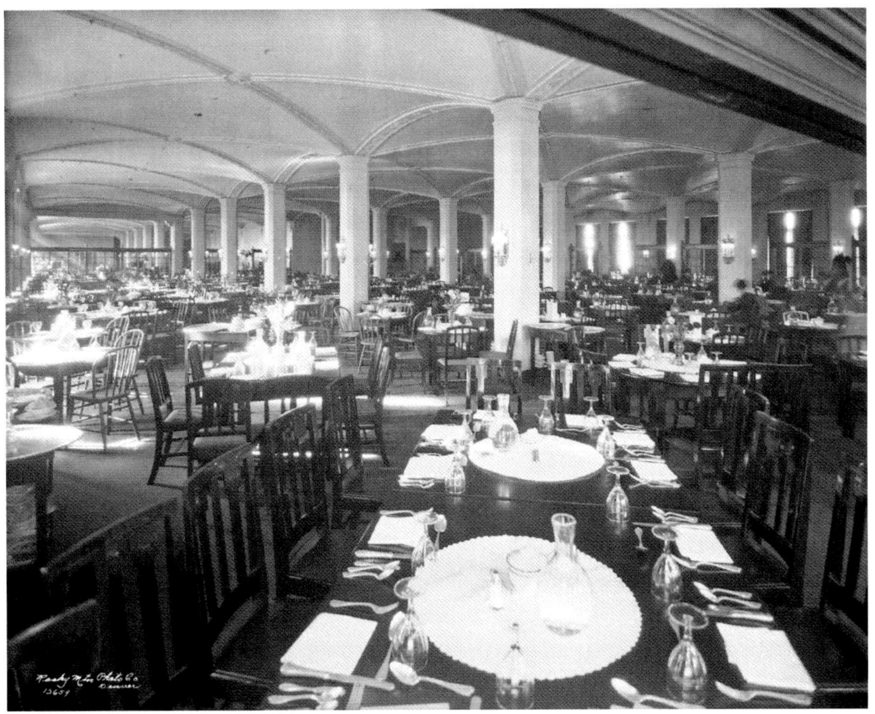

The Denver Dry Goods Tea Room at about the time of its 1924 grand opening. *Denver Public Library, Western History Collection, X-24058.*

decades the Tea Room took on a life of its own, cementing The Denver's place in the hearts of Coloradoans.[139]

The Tea Room was not the store's only point of differentiation. Opened during the Sheedy era, the Western Shop (later the Stockmen's Store) operated as a business within a business, initially on the fourth floor of the Fifteenth Street building and later on six. Offering a substantial array of clothing suitable for working cattlemen (or women), this unique department also sold saddles and gear made by the store's own Powder River Saddlery; from 1945 to 1950, it also owned Denver's storied Herman H. Heiser Saddlery, a pioneer concern dating from 1859. Not confining itself to Denver, the department operated a large mail-order business, with semiannual catalogues billing the store as "Western Outfitters to the Nation" and advertisements in national publications such as *Western Horseman*. For many years, the Stockmen's Store operated a booth at the annual National Western Stock Show.[140]

Concurrent with the Tea Room's relocation to the fifth floor, the store expanded and relocated various departments. First-floor counters sold

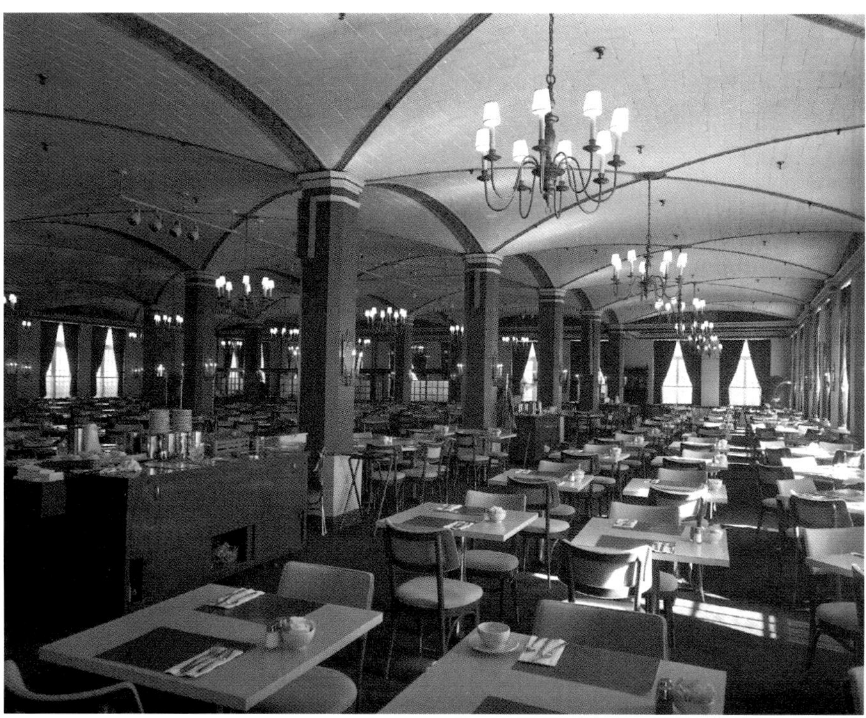

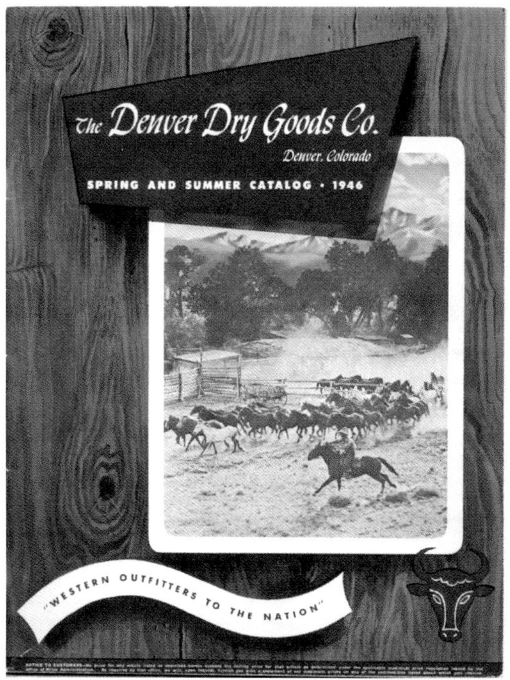

Above: The fifth-floor Tea Room showing closely placed tables for two and four, circa 1965–70; the Grill Room enclosure is visible at the far end. *Denver Public Library, Western History Collection, photograph by Morey J. Engle.*

Left: Mail-order catalogue for the Stockmen's Store, the store's department for all things western. *Linda Lebsack Collection.*

cosmetics, toiletries, handbags, gloves, handkerchiefs, scarves, umbrellas, hosiery, jewelry, casual millinery, knit underwear, budget hosiery, dry goods, notions, laces, buttons, ribbons and dressmaking patterns. Also on one were men's suits, ties, shirts, socks, underwear, shoes and casual clothing, along with books, stationery, vacuum cleaners, cameras, drugs, baked goods, candy and services (watch and clock repair, theater tickets and so on). The mezzanine now featured a portrait photography studio. On two, women shopped for dresses in various price ranges, sportswear, shoes, millinery, foundations, lingerie, coats, suits, furs, bridal and "stout wear." The third floor housed furniture and children's clothing. On four were draperies, rugs, floor coverings, linens and domestics, hardware, paint, radios (later adding televisions), record players, records and small and major electric appliances. The Fifteenth Street side's fifth floor offered gifts, art needlework, china, glass, silver, lamps, luggage and a beauty salon. The sixth floor of both buildings housed executive offices and operational departments, along with the Stockmen's Store. The basement Budget Store contained many of the same departments found upstairs, along with a post office substation, philatelic and numismatic counters and shoe repair. More than any Denver store, The Denver Dry Goods, almost a city within a city, had something for everyone.[141]

POSTWAR BOOM

Through the Depression and World War II, The Denver continued capturing the largest share of the city's department store trade. After Frank Mayfield retired in 1944, yet another Irish American, Charles A. Shinn, a store employee since 1906, replaced him as president; he served four years and then ascended to chairman of the board. In 1948, the board named his right-hand man, Kansas native Frank J. Johns, as president. Together, these two would oversee a multi-decade expansion, expending significant capital for upgrades and modernization and opening the first of several branches to capture the growing suburban trade. Deprivations customers endured through the 1930s and the war meant that sitting still was not an option—Shinn and Johns knew that if they did not grow, others would.[142]

Before the store could be modernized, its physical plant required major upgrades. In 1947, Shinn replaced the single wooden 1907 escalator with a new set of eight steel ones connecting floors one through four in both directions. In 1955, Johns had the entire building air-conditioned. Significant remodeling began with a re-imagination of the second floor in 1952. The old utilitarian atmosphere was now decidedly passé; new trends called for a total-design environment, with coordinated color schemes and dramatic lighting. Windows disappeared behind walls, allowing for vertical merchandising; mirrored pillars now encased Victorian cast-iron columns, and new drop ceilings hid older tin ones. Merchandise also received an upgrade with a new "Columbine Room" where well-heeled women could purchase better dresses in an elegant setting. Johns systematically modernized other floors year by year, concluding with the basement in 1962. In the 1960s, the store stayed relevant by introducing new departments for baby boomers—"Miss Denver" for young women and "the Bailiwick" with mod clothing for young men.[143]

In the 1970s, management saw a need to revive interest in downtown, which was competing not only with other retailers but also with its own suburban branches. One tool department stores then utilized was the "fortnight," a two-week period between the busy back-to-school and holiday shopping seasons. Fortnights carried specific themes, often around a foreign country (usually with help from that country's export trade office) but sometimes closer to home. Events—including performances, craft demonstrations and other happenings—took place on every floor, and each department presented theme-related merchandise. The Tea Room got involved too,

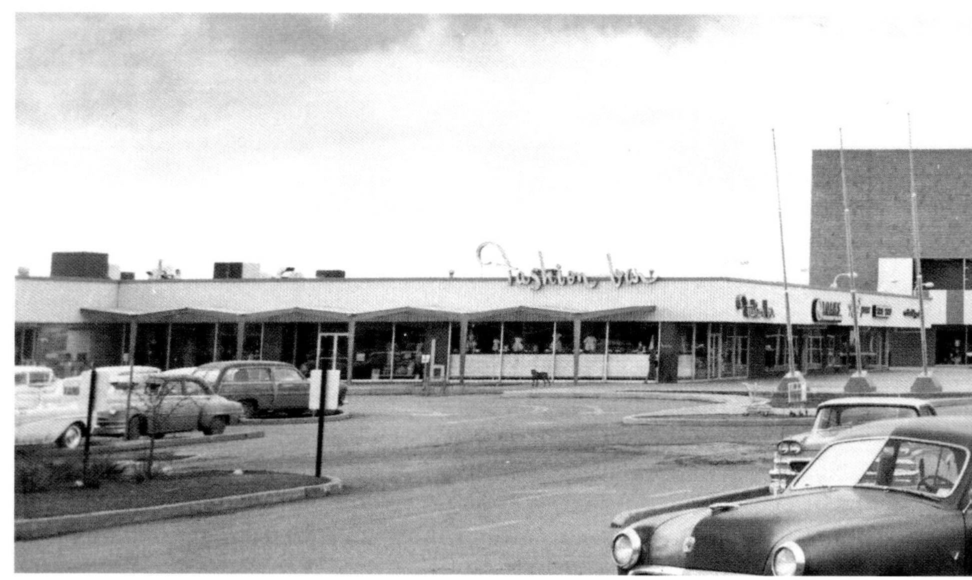

with cuisine from the featured country. The Denver's first fortnight, "Irish Awakening," centered on the Emerald Isle, birthplace of McNamara and Sheedy. In 1971, the store promoted its own state, with "Colorado—The Land of the Long Look." One year later, shortly after Palestinian terrorists murdered Israeli athletes at the 1972 Munich Olympics, The Denver hosted "Shalom Shalom," celebrating the twenty-fifth anniversary of modern Israel's founding. In 1973, it was Denmark's turn, with the Tea Room dressed up as Tivoli Gardens and Fontina and Havarti cheeses purveyed in the Epicure Shop. The store collaborated with Denver's local Greek community in celebrating all things Hellenic in 1974. There was then a break from fortnights for some years, but the idea returned in a late 1970s "Salute to Great Britain." In 1982, the store held its final fortnight—expenses were high, and the events had been less well attended over time—called "Voyage of Discovery: The Arts and Crafts of China."[144]

Even with significant energy spent boosting the old downtown emporium, Johns and his successors devoted even greater attention to opening suburban branches. Although early Joslin's branches predated The Denver's first non-downtown store, those were small, not full-line department stores like its Curtis

The Denver Dry Goods Company at Lakeside, 1959; Fashion Bar is visible at left. *Denver Public Library, Western History Collection, RMN 441-336.*

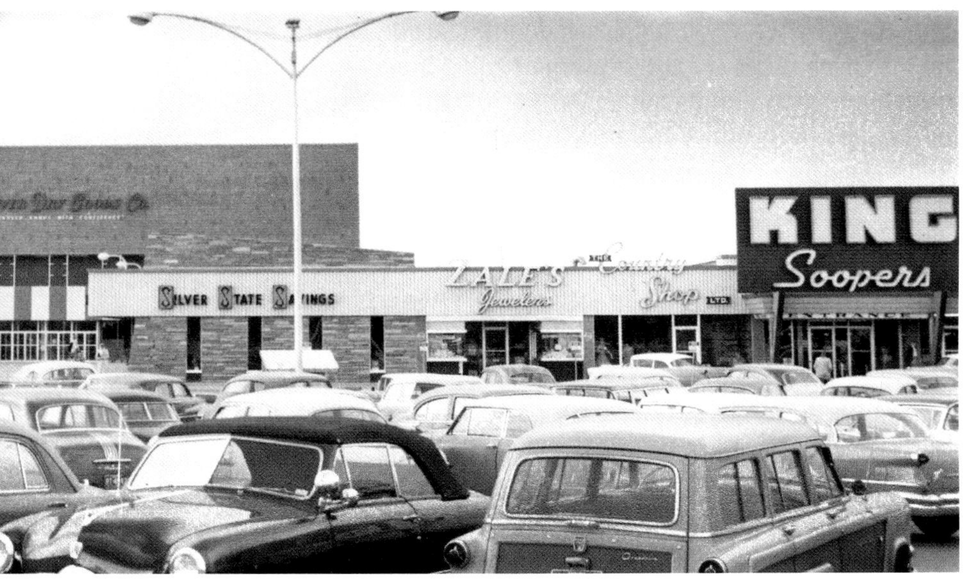

Street flagship. The Denver didn't take that route—following its peers in other cities, its first satellite store included, as all future ones would, smaller versions of nearly all of downtown's departments.

The first branch was not "suburban" at all, but inside city limits, just four miles southeast of downtown at East First Avenue and University Boulevard. Despite its proximity to downtown, the Cherry Creek store would prove the most lucrative, on a per-square-foot basis, of any, thanks to its location. Johns knew that he could not go wrong following money, and Cherry Creek had it, thanks to the nearby Country Club and Polo Grounds neighborhoods, along with easy access via University from Cherry Hills Village. Architect-developer Temple Hoyne Buell created the center on land he had owned since 1925, designing all of its buildings. Johns and Shinn traveled the country examining other suburban branches and brought back the best ideas they found. The ninety-five-thousand-square-foot, three-level store was fully air-conditioned and largely windowless, and its design, like modernized floors downtown, featured soft colors, dramatic lighting and wall-to-wall carpeting. Cherry Creek succeeded immediately, its sales surpassing Johns's most optimistic projections.[145]

Johns continued with a 1956 store at developer Gerri Von Frellick's Lakeside Center, a similar distance from downtown but in the opposite direction, at West 44th Avenue and Harlan Street. This three-level branch featured an outpost of the Stockmen's Store to cater to the "horsey set" living in then semi-rural Jefferson County. In 1962, booster organization Greeley Grows Greater enticed Johns to build in that northern Colorado college and meatpacking city's downtown, at 8th Avenue and 8th Street; the 48,000-square-foot, two-level outpost opened in 1963, with another Stockmen's Store for Weld County's farmers and ranchers. Johns then agreed to open in Von Frellick's Cinderella City in Englewood. This would be the largest branch to date, 151,000 square feet on three levels, when it opened in 1968. One week later, The Denver's new 139,000-square-foot Northglenn Mall store opened at Interstate 25 and 104th Avenue.[146]

The Denver continued to open locations through the 1970s and into the 1980s, beginning with a two-level, 110,000-square-foot store at a Colorado Springs mall, The Citadel, at Academy Boulevard and U.S. Highway 24, in 1972. The next year brought a single-level store at Foothills Fashion Mall in Fort Collins. A Southglenn Mall branch, at South University Boulevard and East Arapahoe Road, followed in 1974. This two-level, 123,000-square-foot facility, boasting a glass elevator, was the first in the chain to be managed by a woman (Marie Salman); it was also the first branch with food service, a tearoom known as the Greenhouse overlooking the mall's central court. An Aurora Mall store, with 120,000 square feet on two levels, followed in 1975, at Interstate 225 and East Alameda Avenue; it also featured the Greenhouse. The bicentennial year of 1976 brought a single-level branch, 52,000 square feet, at Boulder's Crossroads Mall, replacing an earlier boutique, the "Randall Shop," which had opened there in 1963. In 1978 and 1979, The Denver established small branches farther afield than ever before, at Rimrock Mall in Billings, Montana, and Pueblo Mall in Pueblo, Colorado. The final branch opened at Southwest Plaza in 1983. This elegant, two-level store featured a central escalator well adorned by a Frank Howell triptych painting, *Spirit of the West*, and aisles paved in elegant brown Mexican "Café Goleta" marble.[147]

FINAL DECADES

By the early 1960s, Scruggs, Vandervoort and Barney had allowed its Colorado operation to run itself for four decades. In 1964, it received an offer, never consummated, from Marshall-Wells Company to buy the store. Johns, an acute observer, knew that in order to survive and thrive in the coming era of competition from discount stores, The Denver needed to combine with a larger entity. He approached Associated Dry Goods of New York City, parent of Lord & Taylor and several well-regarded regional stores. He had long known its president, Lewis P. Seiler, and felt that The Denver would be a perfect fit; Seiler agreed. The companies announced the change in December 1964, with the transaction closing the following March. Now The Denver Dry Goods would have access to the deep corporate pockets its competitors May-D&F and Joslins had long enjoyed.[148]

Under the store's new ownership, the first change was dropping "Dry Goods Company" from the name in 1967. Henceforth, a nickname long used by Denver shoppers would prevail: "The Denver" made its official debut, with a new stylized cursive logo and a Columbine blue-and-white corporate identity. (Another customer-favored nickname was "The Denver Dry.") Downtown, the store covered its cream exterior paint with brilliant white, graced with blue awnings. This color scheme and logo lasted only seven years, replaced in 1974 by a dark-brown signature color and white cursive logo that resembled sketchy, rapid handwriting.[149]

The next change came at the top: in 1968, Frank Johns, who had worked for the store his entire adult life, retired as president to make way for an Associated man, forty-seven-year-old Walker Douglas Poole. Coming from Cincinnati, he was the first of many leaders in the store's final decades who had begun their careers elsewhere and served wherever Associated placed them. Carrick A. Hill succeeded Poole in 1975, coming from Los Angeles and helming The Denver for just two years before a promotion took him away. Samuel J. Gerson replaced Hill in 1978 but left to lead a Pittsburgh store in 1980. In a dozen years, The Denver had seen four leaders, and the rapid turnover had hurt profitability. Echoing Sheedy's replacement of McNamara with treasurer Owen in 1894, Associated management decided that fiscal discipline was needed, so it next awarded the presidency to F. Joseph Hayes, who had been the store's chief financial officer since coming in from Washington, D.C.'s Garfinckel's in 1975. He would not lead alone, however, as Associated decided to experiment with "tandem management," with a newly created chief executive officer responsible for merchandising and advertising. The new CEO was Thomas L. Roach, arriving from Florida. Together the two men transformed The Denver into Associated's most profitable division.[150]

It was difficult work, but the young men (Roach was thirty-six and Hayes thirty-seven) were up to it. Although The Denver now boasted thirteen locations, many appeared dated, and Colorado shoppers lacked a clear picture of what, exactly, The Denver represented, with various presidents implementing different fashion and merchandising plans. Roach and Hayes decided to go back to basics, emphasizing quality and value rather than enticing shoppers through too-frequent sales and other gimmicks. Their aim was convincing customers that while The Denver was not always the cheapest, its prices were always fair value for money. It was, in a sense, a return to the policies of Sheedy, Owen, Shinn and Johns—it worked.[151]

Their biggest headache was downtown, which had steadily lost traffic for years and was now busy only at lunchtime. Big-spending customers rarely came downtown anymore, preferring Cherry Creek and Southglenn; workers on lunch breaks, looking to pick up pantyhose or lipstick, were downtown's primary customers. By the time Roach and Hayes took over, the Regional Transportation District's plans for a Sixteenth Street Mall were already in motion, and the men were bullish on its prospects for improving business. They received funds from Associated to pay for remodeling and renovation, even as they both knew that the 400,000-square-foot facility was really too large. They partly solved their space problem in 1981, leasing the Sixteenth

Street basement to Denver-based sporting goods retailer Gart Brothers; this also helped Roach burnish the store's upscale fashion image by eliminating the bargain departments.[152]

As successful as Roach and Hayes were in remaking The Denver, in the end their efforts were for naught. In 1986, Associated promoted Roach to Los Angeles's J.W. Robinson and replaced him in Denver with Stanley Zweck-Bronner. Only sixteen days after that appointment came more significant news: Associated Dry Goods had been in merger talks with May Department Stores for nearly two years, and May had made an offer. Associated rejected this first offer as too low, but by July 16, 1986, the two companies had come to terms, with May buying Associated for $2.53 billion.[153]

What did this mean for Colorado? At first, May would not say, and into this information void local pundits leapt, predicting that May would keep both stores operating, with May-D&F positioned for the broad middle and The Denver catering to more affluent classes. This was pure speculation; May was not showing its hand, and if people believed the stores would continue competing with each other, so much the better for not arousing the Federal Trade Commission's ire (in addition to Colorado, May and Associated competed in Southern California and Pittsburgh). The stores continued operating separately through the holidays, but on January 30, 1987, the end came. May pulled the plug on The Denver, informing Hayes via telephone while he vacationed with his family. He flew home, and on January 30, he placed 5:30 a.m. calls to his managers, requesting their presence downtown by 7:00 a.m. Once assembled, he told them the news: after ninety-two years, The Denver, while still profitable, was no more. He wanted them to hear the news before a 10:00 a.m. press release. The story dominated that evening's newscasts and next morning's papers. The *Post* set its headline, "The Denver to Close," in extra-large type, normally reserved for wars and assassinations.[154]

Reactions were tearful—people could not believe that such a permanent-seeming institution could be shuttered just like that. Yet it was true, and liquidation sales began almost immediately. Four stores (Cherry Creek, Cinderella City, Northglenn and Aurora) were rebranded as May-D&F, but May sold the others off, to J.C. Penney or Mervyn's, or shut them down. Colorado leaders were not content to simply allow May to have its way. Governor Roy Romer and Denver mayor Federico Peña both castigated May as a poor corporate citizen, and the governor contacted Alex Dillard, executive vice-president of the Little Rock, Arkansas–based Dillard's chain, about buying The Denver's locations to preserve competition. Dillard was interested, but May was not, and nothing came of Romer's efforts. The stores closed, one by one, and the Tea Room enjoyed capacity crowds, with thousands paying their last respects before it ceased operations in March. Downtown closed its doors on April 10, one month shy of what would have been the ninety-third anniversary of Dennis Sheedy's founding of the store. By May 1, it was over, with liquidation sales and rebrandings completed. The Denver was gone.[155]

Chapter 7

A.T. LEWIS & SON

Colorado's Home Store

Life still is a joyful experience for Lewis because he has not lost his love for his work. To him the dry goods business is the greatest adventure in the world. It still finds him as enthusiastic as was young Dennie Lewis who wouldn't let the boss talk him out of a job.

—Rocky Mountain News, *1931*[156]

HE KNEW WHAT HE WANTED

The shortest-lived of Denver's great stores, A.T. Lewis & Son is not well remembered today, but in its time it ranked with Gano-Downs and Neusteter's as one of the city's most exclusive. A mild-mannered yet keenly ambitious, blond-haired and blue-eyed Illinois native, Aaron Dennison Lewis, "Dennie" to his close friends and family members, knew at an early age that he wanted a career in dry goods. Born in 1865 to Aaron Thompson Lewis and Amy Josephine (Russell) Lewis, young Aaron arrived in Denver in 1879 with his parents. His mother's family had been present in North America since 1620, her ancestor Edward Doty having been a *Mayflower* passenger. His father traced his ancestry to a 1732 Welsh migrant to New Jersey, Samuel Lewis. Aaron Dennison Lewis was always proud of his roots and close to his family.[157]

Having graduated from Denver schools, one day in 1883 Lewis paid a visit to a former classmate employed at Daniels and Fisher. As Lewis later recounted, as he looked around at the rich array of merchandise, he discovered in a flash what he wanted to do. His friend told him how to find William Bradley Daniels's office, and after being admitted, he approached the merchant prince and said, "Mr. Daniels, I'd like to get a job here." Daniels, paying him little attention, responded, "I don't want a boy." Lewis persisted, and growing annoyed, Daniels reiterated, "I tell you I don't want a boy." Finally seeing that Lewis would not be dissuaded, Daniels told him, "All right, go to work. But I won't pay you anything." Still living with his well-off parents, Lewis didn't mind the money, so eager was he to learn the trade, and was undoubtedly surprised when after three months the amused Daniels called him into his office and paid him his accumulated wages. Lewis laughed when he told an interviewer, "It wasn't a very big salary, but it looked big to me, especially when I thought I was working during all those weeks just for the experience." He remained at Daniels and Fisher for five years.[158]

The next chapter in Lewis's life began in 1888, when he and a friend, Dave Curtis (possibly his friend from Daniels and Fisher, but this is unknown), decided to venture, for fun, to the gold mining town of Breckenridge in Summit County. They arrived on horseback and stopped on Main Street in front of a two-story mercantile. A man Lewis later described as a "grizzled mountaineer," chewing tobacco, sat in front, and he struck up a conversation with the men. He owned the store but wanted a change, and he offered to sell it to them. Lewis had money saved, so he and Curtis paid the old man and hung a new sign, "Lewis and Curtis," above the door. His Daniels and Fisher years had taught Lewis the proper way to run a store. He first gave it a good cleaning—the old man had allowed dust to accumulate on the stock of men's clothing, heavy boots, miners' picks and women's stockings, and the windows were grimy. Stock was poorly displayed; Lewis and Curtis soon rearranged and marked down everything by 20 percent so they could clear it out and bring in better merchandise. More importantly, Lewis implemented the policy Daniels and Fisher used for pricing: everything was now clearly marked. The previous proprietor, with nothing marked, set prices on a sliding scale based on the customer; he charged higher prices to Breckenridge's successful citizens to cover credit he extended to those who sometimes could not pay. Lewis and Curtis thrived, earning a reputation as fair dealers. But after two years, Lewis felt constrained by the relatively small size of Breckenridge's population—he wanted a big store, more like Daniels and Fisher. He sold his share to Curtis and came down from the mountains with $5,000 in his pocket.[159]

FIFTY-THREE-FOLD

Aaron Thompson Lewis had lived a life not unlike that of Dennis Sheedy. Although native to the United States, as Sheedy was not, the elder Lewis's early years were similarly nomadic, and he had worked hard to reach his station in life. Born in New Brunswick, New Jersey, in 1830, Lewis had moved with his family to Galesburg, Illinois, where his father cleared land and began farming. As a young adult, he operated a small store in Monmouth, Illinois, about ten miles west of Galesburg that apparently was not lucrative. He then became a schoolteacher and then a banker. Like Sheedy, he "heard the call of the West" and moved to Wyoming, where he traded in cattle. It was with the proceeds of this career that he came to Denver and invested in real estate. By the time Aaron D. came down from Breckenridge, Aaron T. Lewis and his wife were comfortably ensconced at 1459 Lafayette Street. Although he was well known in business circles, he led a quiet life, preferring the company of his wife and sons (besides Aaron D., they included John Russell, Frederick Thompson and the adopted Charles Aaron Lewis).[160]

With his $5,000, Dennie approached his father with a proposition. He wanted to establish a store on Sixteenth Street. Not unlike the scene in Daniels's office seven years earlier, his enthusiasm and persistence, combined with his Breckenridge record, convinced his father that his investment would not be lost, and he agreed to match his son's funds, bringing in a business associate, Charles B. Barrow, who invested the same amount. Leasing a storefront at 819 Sixteenth Street, in the Barth Block at Stout Street, Lewis soon went to work, and on November 10, 1890, Lewis, Son & Barrow opened for business. The shop was small, just 37 feet wide and 90 feet deep (3,330 square feet), and although Lewis hired a few clerks, it was largely a one-man show: "he was his own buyer, advertising man, window trimmer, and, above all, an enthusiastic salesman," per a 1929 history. His idea was "dry goods only," rather than general merchandise such as he had sold in Breckenridge, and he wanted a deep selection. An 1896 description marveled at "roll after roll of the most exquisite patterns, embracing mohair frieze, mohair broche, mohair clellians, Priestley's cheviots, satin soleil, brocades, Endoras, Lupin's figured mohairs, Henriettas, serges, English canvas, burlaps, and sail cloths." Supplementing these yard goods were "linings, dress trimmings, domestics, linens, bedding, notions, stationery, leather goods, sterling silver, jewelry, veils, ribbons, handkerchiefs, laces, gloves, men's furnishings, ladies' knit underwear, ladies' hosiery, ladies' muslin underwear and corsets, ladies' ready-made suits, tailor-made suits and bicycle suits."[161]

Lewis, Son & Barrow survived the Panic of 1893, probably due to the father's conservative money management and the son's flexibility in merchandising—he soon began using the term "Inaugurators of Low Prices" in advertisements. By 1895, with Barrow having sold out to the Lewises, the firm, renamed A.T. Lewis & Son, needed larger quarters. There was a vacancy directly across Sixteenth in a four-story building designed by Robert Roeschlaub and built in 1891 for A.Z. Salomon and Company, which operated Salomon's Bazaar. After it closed, another concern, Holzman and Appel, briefly conducted business there. Although not on the corner, instead abutting the alley mid-block, its location was perfect, and it offered room for expansion. Soon after occupying the ground floor, Lewis added the second floor and then the third and fourth (housing dressmaking, a growing mail-order operation and a wholesale division). As the economy healed, Lewis began steering the store away from its Depression years' emphasis on low prices, and like other merchants of the day, he held elaborate seasonal "openings" for customers, events at which discriminating shoppers could peruse the latest fashions. The "Spring Opening" of 1900 offered a "bewildering scene of artistic beauty":

> *The first impression, on entering the store, was that of some Oriental bazaar on a gala occasion. The sweet perfume of the wood violet greeted the visitor, while strains of orchestral music put one in a holiday state of humor. The walls, from top to bottom, were covered with strands of brilliant-hued ribbons, the ceilings also were decorated with ribbons, arranged in artistic geometric patterns. Cerise and white was the color tone throughout, relieved at intervals with palm and fern verdure.*

One year later, Lewis added a millinery department, fitted with elegant glass and golden oak display cases containing a "fashionable and exclusive stock" of the "smartest specimens of New York millinery," including "great Gainsboroughs, Floradora hats, tailor hats, draped hats, felt walking hats, camel's-hair hats, chenille hats, feather hats, velvet hats, applique hats, and a hundred other hats which are just as fascinating and wholly indescribable," per a suitably impressed *Denver Times* reporter.[162]

In 1901, the building was proving too small, so Lewis got control of the adjacent Bancroft Block (built by Dr. Frederick J. Bancroft in 1882 in place of his former house), which held the Stout Street corner. He demolished it and commissioned Roeschlaub to extend the building. With this expansion, completed in August 1902, along with an abutting leased building on Stout

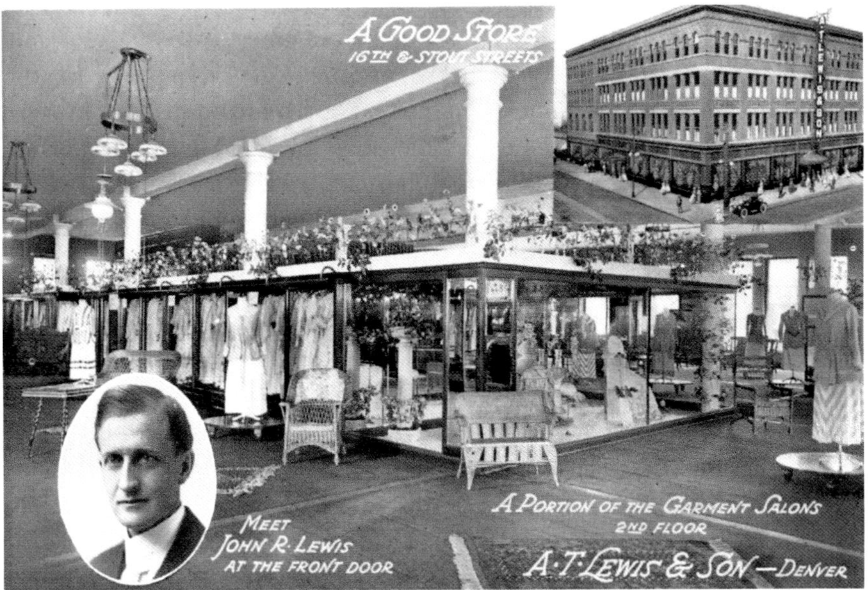

Postcard view of the interior of A.T. Lewis & Son, circa 1910. *Author's collection.*

Street, A.T. Lewis now occupied 100,000 square feet of space. Just twelve years since the store's founding, it had grown more than twenty-five-fold. As it grew, it became ever more exclusive, aspiring to Parisian levels of elegance. At the expansion's grand opening, a dress salon decorated "in Du Barry green" hosted a Mme. Coughlan, a "modiste well known in London and New York," supervising a staff of "New York assistants" capable of executing for Denver's well-dressed women styles that would not have been out of place in Manhattan.[163]

Aaron Thompson Lewis died in 1907, leaving his son in full ownership of the store. In his latter years, the elder Lewis had taken an active interest in the business, spending hours on the sales floor greeting customers. Denver's dominant newspapers eulogized Lewis, naturally, but so did the *Colorado Statesman*, an African American paper in which the store regularly advertised. The *Statesman* praised Lewis for seeking African American patronage, which set it apart from most other Denver stores, and for hiring from the community. It eulogized him as being "very kindly disposed and just with his help and not showing any partiality but treating each one according to his merit." After his death, his other sons also joined Dennie in the business, but it was Aaron D. who called the shots. Like his father, he was fundamentally decent; unlike his father, he participated actively in community life. He helped organize (and was the first chairman of) the Denver Tourist and Publicity Bureau and chaired the Denver Retail Merchants Association. Fascinated with Native American archaeology, he also funded expeditions to southwestern Colorado. He held memberships in the Denver Rotary, the Colorado State Historical and Natural History Society and various clubs.[164]

The store prospered through the 1900s and 1910s, and by 1916, Lewis once again concluded that the store was too small. He hired Harry W.J. Edbrooke, nephew of architect Frank Edbrooke, to design a six-story addition on Stout Street; costing $300,000, it doubled the store's size. By early 1918, the addition was ready. Sheathed in gleaming white terra cotta, with ornamentation that called to mind the great Louis J. Sullivan's work, the wing represented a fifty-three-fold increase over the size of the original 1890 Barth Block shop. Its décor radiated luxury, with various departments boasting mahogany, walnut or Flemish oak fixtures. After twenty-eight years in business, A.T. Lewis was now one of the largest stores in Denver.[165]

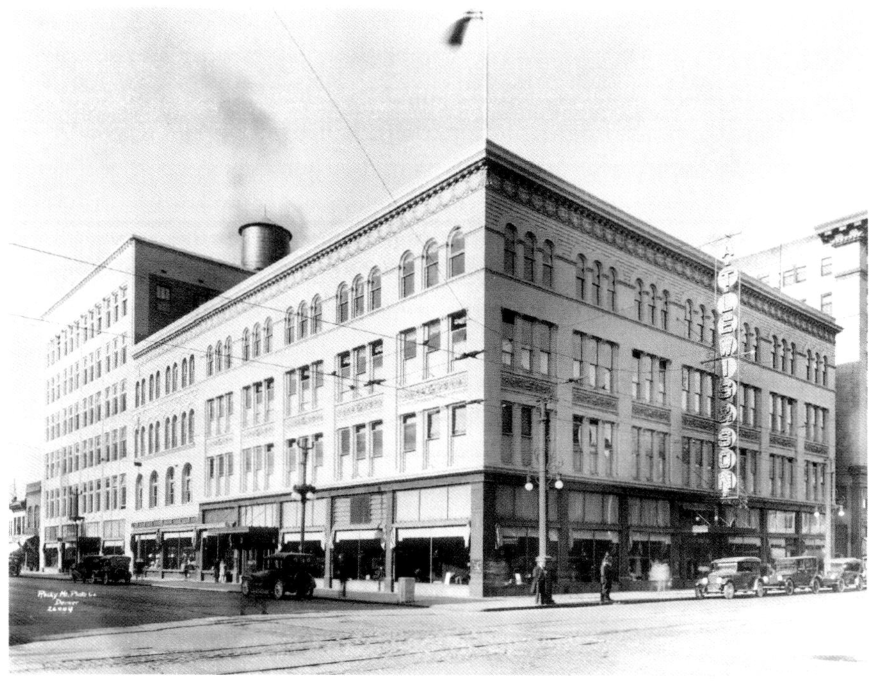

A.T. Lewis & Son on the western corner of Sixteenth and Stout Streets, circa 1925, showing the original building and later additions. *Denver Public Library, Western History Collection, X-24116.*

The addition housed a unique feature: a children's theater. Lewis held strong convictions about the importance of "honesty, fair play and courage" and wanted to inculcate in Denver's youth those qualities. Every Saturday, the theater staged short plays and screened short films highlighting the "sterling attributes of the pioneers which brought an empire into being and builded a monument of stone and steel on confidence." Performances were free, "a clean face" the only admission requirement. One year the theater hosted an exhibition of dolls, one of which, estimated to be more than one thousand years old, was discovered on a Lewis-funded archaeological expedition. In the show, it joined the A.T. Lewis and Son Doll Collection, an assemblage created over several years by Lewis and his toy buyers, comprising dolls from around the world. In conjunction, the store presented a lecture, "The Romance of Playthings," for the children and their mothers, along with a dance program, with children dressed as various "living dolls."[166]

In 1924, celebrating its thirty-sixth anniversary (the opening in Breckenridge being declared the store's nativity), A.T. Lewis sponsored a citywide essay contest for adults and children. "Denver in 1888" was open to anyone who had been resident for fifty years or more; "What Denver Needs for Its Future Development" allowed anyone seventeen or older to enter; and "What I Would Like Denver to Be When I Grow Up" was for anyone under seventeen. Simultaneously, the store celebrated its roots by filling its show windows with paintings illustrating Colorado's "progress and prosperity," along with displays of agricultural production (sugar beets, wheat), mining and industries.[167]

Through the 1920s, the store continued positioning itself as purveyor of the best goods, with prices to match, and this served the store well. Service levels were high, with a staff that numbered over seven hundred. It advertised on back covers of theater programs, with copy designed to appeal to the city's elite shoppers. It continued in this vein even after the October 1929 stock market crash and onset of the Great Depression—a September 1930 newspaper advertisement, decidedly out of step with increasingly austere times, asked, "Have You Decorated Your Maids?" "It's time," the ad continued, "the autumn social season is under way—Your home color schemes are being worked out—The maids in your employ should reflect the good taste of your establishment. Lewis' Shop of Correct Uniforms offers a complete selection in the new shades, gray and black—beautifully tailored, smartly cut, expertly finished—the right lines."[168]

It was therefore perhaps surprising to at least some customers when on January 10, 1933, the store placed a very different advertisement, announcing

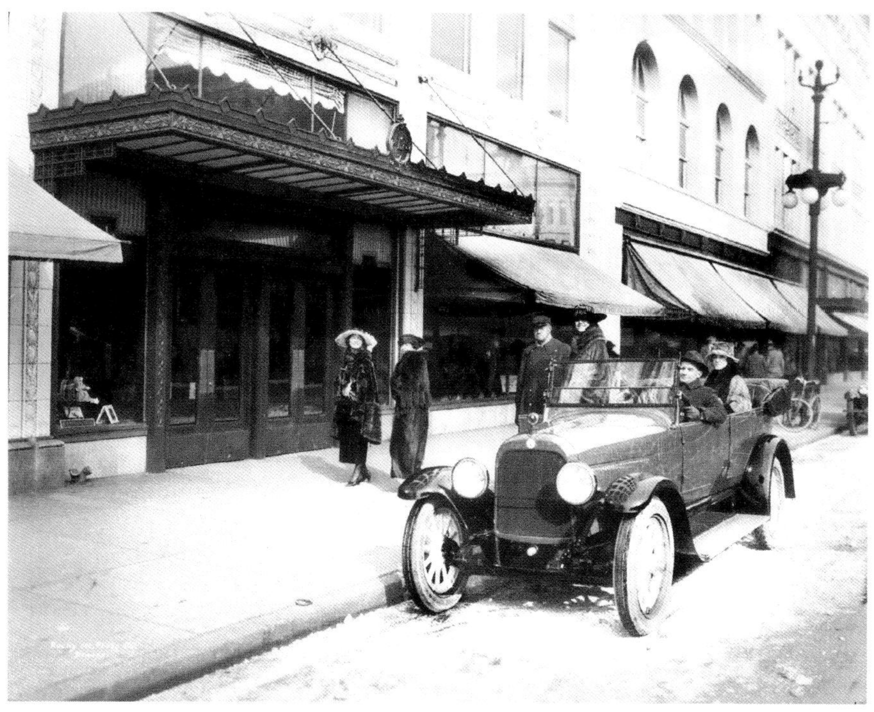

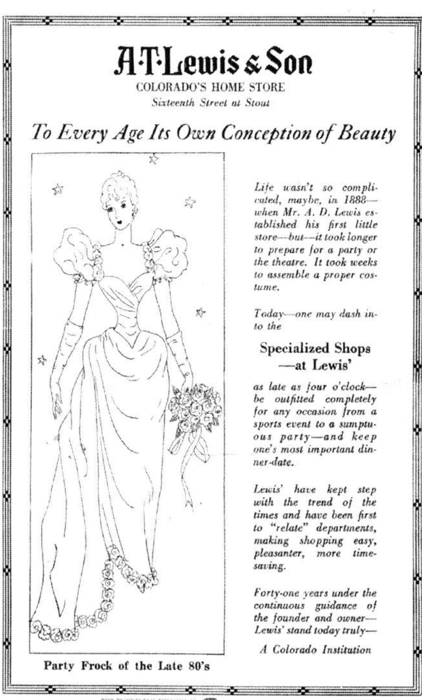

A·T·Lewis & Son

COLORADO'S HOME STORE

Sixteenth Street at Stout

To Every Age Its Own Conception of Beauty

Life wasn't so complicated, maybe, in 1888—when Mr. A. D. Lewis established his first little store—but—it took longer to prepare for a party or the theatre. It took weeks to assemble a proper costume.

Today—one may dash into the

Specialized Shops —at Lewis'

as late as four o'clock—be outfitted completely for any occasion from a sports event to a sumptuous party—and keep one's most important dinner-date.

Lewis' have kept step with the trend of the times and have been first to "relate" departments, making shopping easy, pleasanter, more timesaving.

Forty-one years under the continuous guidance of the founder and owner—Lewis' stand today truly—

A Colorado Institution

Party Frock of the Late 80's

Above: Likely a publicity shot commissioned by the store, circa 1925, showing well-dressed people in front of the canopied entrance to the six-story 1918 wing, mid-block on Stout Street. *Denver Public Library, Western History Collection, X-24117.*

Left: A.T. Lewis & Son advertisement from a 1929 theater program. *Author's collection.*

it was "retiring from business" and holding a complete liquidation sale. Like those dire advertisements taken out by McNamara Dry Goods forty years earlier, the copy was forthright: "We need cash." This came four days after a shift in the store's board of directors. To build his handsome 1918 addition, Lewis had sold shares, and two of the new 1933 board members "were chosen by the preferred stockholders to represent them on the board." Once elected, they moved to shut down, and Lewis acquiesced.

One week after the liquidation sale began, the store filed bankruptcy, listing liabilities of more than $165,000. Its assets, valued at more than $350,000, seemingly might have covered these, but for large sums, totaling $280,000, "which cannot be collected," likely due to many of its charge account customers' own financial difficulties. This was undoubtedly painful to the sixty-seven-year-old Aaron Dennison Lewis, having grown his store into a major Denver institution, only to watch it wither and die so rapidly. And there would be no comfortable retirement. Gano-Downs (then referring to itself as "Your Surest Store" in advertisements, a comforting idea in hard times) soon informed Denver's shoppers that "Mr. A.D. Lewis of A.T. Lewis & Son will join The Gano-Downs Co. in the capacity of manager of our Women's Departments." Lewis never published an autobiography, so we do not know his feelings ("manager" was not exactly an executive title), but they are not difficult to imagine. Yet despite the store's failure, this true merchant prince had succeeded in life, and Denver would miss him.[169]

Chapter 8

THE NEUSTETER COMPANY

Store of Quality and Fashion

Our [Denver] *ladies were quite aware of fashion. Our function was to supply it to them. We did it very well, for many, many years.*
—Myron Neusteter, 1987[170]

THREE BROTHERS

Like David May, Max Neusteter came to Colorado to heal his lungs, and also like him, he founded a great store. But unlike the May Company, the Neusteter Company would always be a strictly Colorado concern. Max was born in Cincinnati in 1874, son of Austrian immigrant Abraham Neusteter, a glasscutter. Young Max had moved to St. Louis, where he worked for Stix, Baer and Fuller, a leading store, before opening, with his brother Meyer, a ladies' clothing shop. Meyer also knew apparel, having worked as a traveling shirtwaist salesman. Ambitious and energetic, continuing to work for Stix as lead ready-to-wear buyer even after opening his store, Max developed tuberculosis in 1909. On doctors' orders to heal in a salutary climate, he ventured to Estes Park, Colorado, with his sister, Lillian; he returned again in 1910. That same year, Meyer honeymooned in Denver with his bride, Bernita, and was suitably impressed. In 1911, when Max heard of a dress store for sale, M. Philipsborn & Company, the brothers decided to buy it, forming a three-store chain (they also owned a shop in Lincoln, Nebraska).[171]

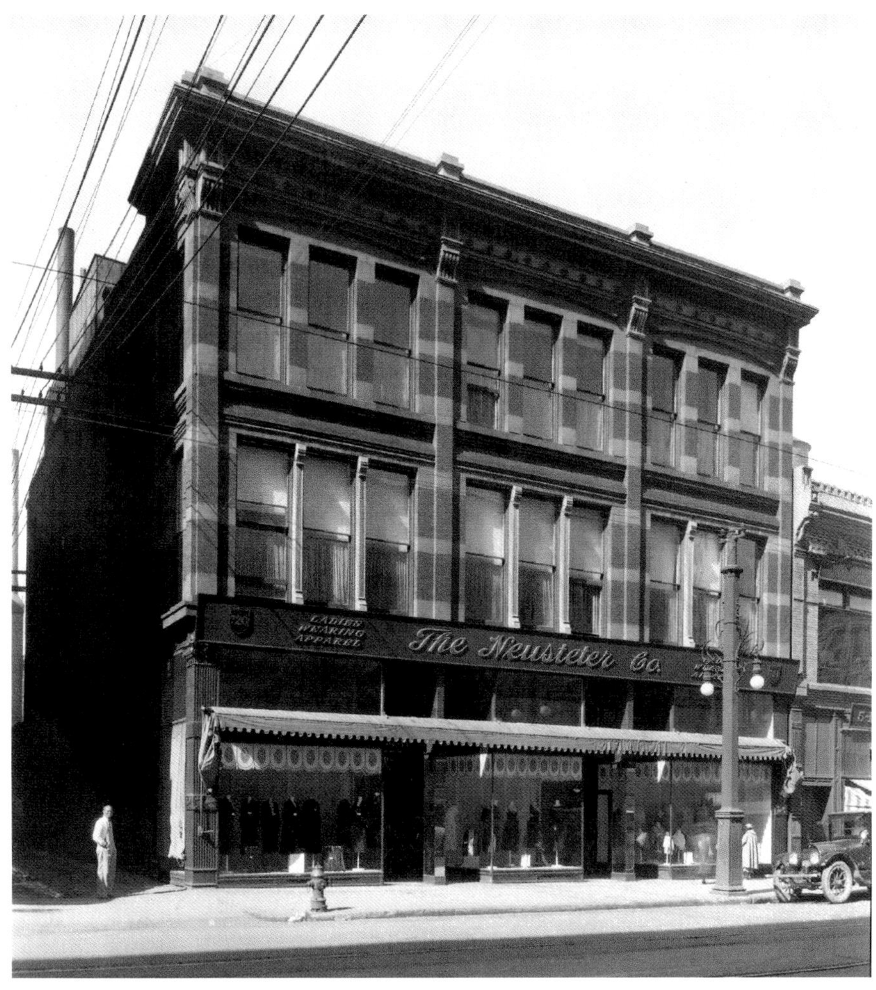

The Neusteter Company in its original building midblock on Sixteenth Street between Stout and California Streets, circa 1920. *History Colorado, Neusteter Collection, 10055028.*

The Neusteter Company opened on July 11, 1911, in a three-story building, midblock abutting the alley between Stout and California Streets; The Denver Dry Goods was next door, Gano-Downs was across Sixteenth and A.T. Lewis was nearby—it was an ideal location to capture the quality trade. Initially occupying the first floor, Neusteter's soon took over the other two and developed a reputation for quality. The brothers continued operating St. Louis and Lincoln but decided in 1916 or 1917 to concentrate on Denver, selling the other operations. Max and Meyer, later joined by younger brother Edward, bought homes in Denver. Emily Keene, one of

St. Louis's "arbiters of fashion," came out, helping to create Neusteter's reputation for high style. A 1920 opportunity turned into a near riot when E.I. du Pont de Nemours and Company, which had manufactured dresses, decided to get out of that business. Max bought du Pont's entire inventory of five thousand pieces and shipped them to Denver for a massive bargain sale, firmly establishing Neusteter's in the minds of Denver shoppers. After that sale, the brothers realized that they needed to expand.[172]

They bought their building in 1922, and Meyer approached Gerald Hughes, owner of the adjacent two-story, corner-holding building. This had housed the chain store S.H. Kress, which was relocating. Hughes agreed to lease the ground to Neusteter, stipulating that he had to build a new structure of at least four stories. Neusteter complied, employing Denver architects William E. and Arthur A. Fisher. The new five-story, granite and limestone building featured classical elements and "Chicago style" windows on upper floors. By June 1924, Neusteter's occupied it, while the original was remodeled and given two additional floors to match the new.[173]

The main entry was set back, steering shoppers through a glass-walled arcade that provided 360-degree views of mannequins. The Fishers commissioned murals illustrating the history of fashion from Denver artist Vance Kirkland. With additional space, Neusteter's added departments, including millinery, perfumes, jewelry, gloves and "toilet requisites." Spacious departments were fitted with elegant fixtures built of expensive woods, with wall-to-wall carpeting underfoot, still rare in 1924. Neusteter's was now one of the largest specialty stores in the country outside New York (Neusteter's never called itself a "department store," preferring the term "specialty shop").[174]

One year after the expansion, Max Neusteter died, aged fifty-two. His tuberculosis had never completely disappeared, and in the spring of 1925, he suffered what doctors termed a "nervous breakdown." In his final years, he raised money for the Jewish Consumptives' Relief Society (JCRS), a tuberculosis sanitarium west of Denver; a building there would later be named for him. With Max's death, Meyer became head of the store, with Edward manning a New York buying office.[175]

Through the 1920s and 1930s, Neusteter's continued to innovate, setting itself apart from other stores. It established a high school– and college-age department, with a mezzanine lounge (furnished with writing desks and easy chairs) above the first floor. It added infants' and toddlers' wear, bridal wear, gifts and accessories and gifts for men; a beauty salon and basement budget store completed the offering. Buyers in New York and Paris made deals with

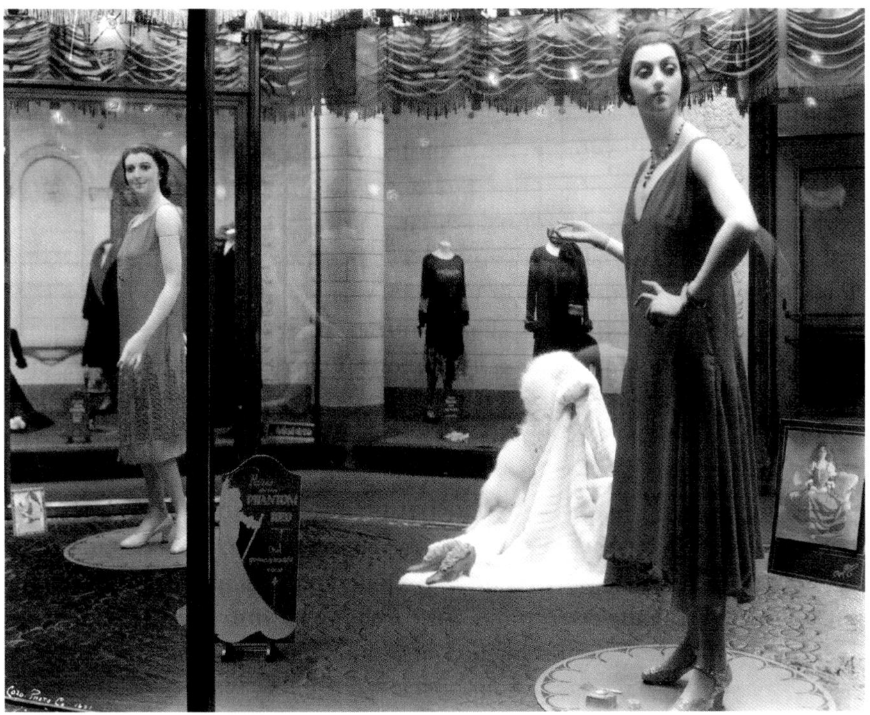

Arcade show windows at the Sixteenth Street entrance allowed shoppers to view apparel from all angles, circa 1925. *History Colorado, Neusteter Collection, 100550027.*

manufacturers guaranteeing Neusteter's exclusivity in Denver, cementing its reputation as the best high fashion store in Colorado. If a woman was unsure of what she wanted, or of just the right way to put together a look, Neusteter's employed personal shoppers to aid her. These women knew their customers' tastes, kept track of birthdays and anniversaries and contacted husbands to help select gifts for their wives. Even the lowest-level salesperson was expected to know the latest trends and be able to give good advice.[176]

Glory Days

Meyer steered Neusteter's safely through depression and war; things were touch-and-go in 1932 and 1933, but it survived through his management. In 1941, he bought the adjacent two-story Coronado Building on Stout, eventually moving some store departments to its ground floor. He also refreshed and remodeled the store until war made that impossible; bigger changes had to wait. In September 1946, he announced that Neusteter's would soon "double" in size with an addition on Stout Street, with part of the Coronado Building coming down for it. This announcement was premature—structural steel was still scarce until manufacturers retooled for peacetime. By early 1950, however, Meyer could announce an expansion that would add forty-six thousand square feet to the 1924 building's seventy-eight thousand. Fisher and Fisher again won the commission, but the new wing would not mimic the old. Instead, it would be thoroughly modern, largely windowless and would include new departments. The entire complex would be air-conditioned.[177]

By the fall of 1951, the addition, its façade sporting a new logo with a dramatic, attenuated "N," was ready (the store also dropped the apostrophe; for the rest of this narrative, it will be "Neusteters"). With additional space, Neusteters achieved a long hoped-for dream: a fine and fashionable men's

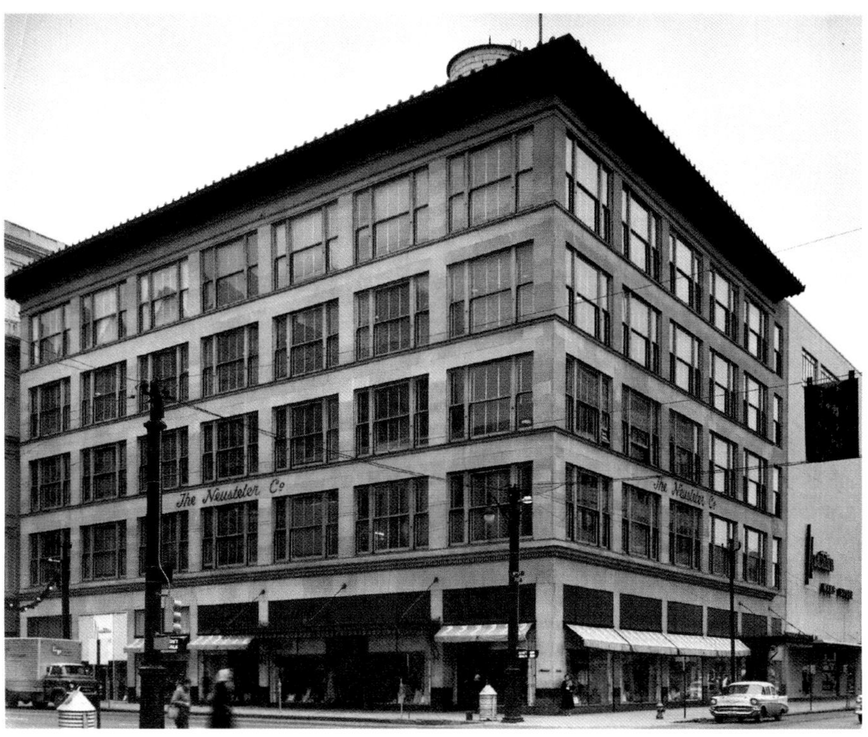

The Neusteter Company on the southern corner of Sixteenth and Stout Streets, circa 1960; the 1951 Man's Store wing is visible at far right. *History Colorado, Neusteter Collection, 10055029.*

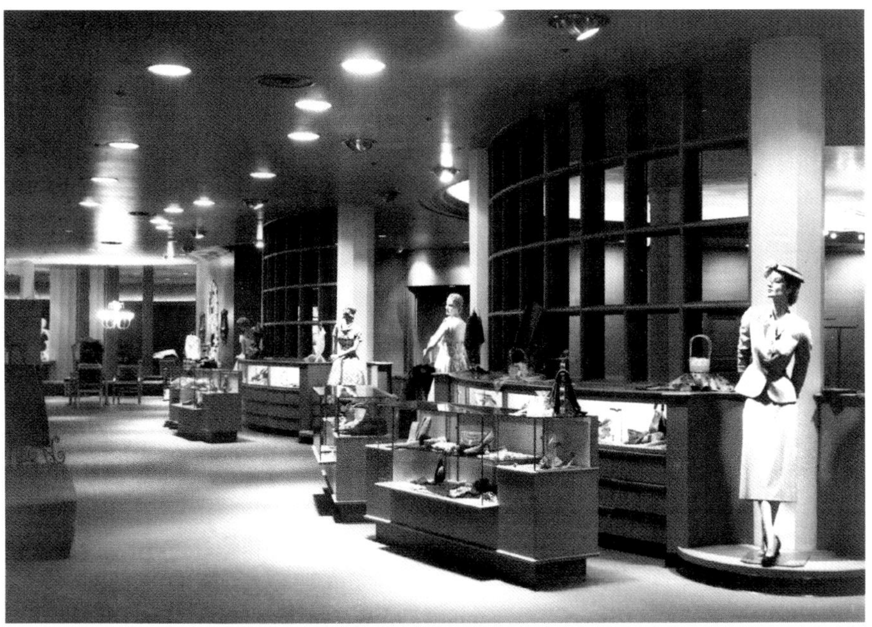

An upper floor downtown, circa 1955. *History Colorado, Neusteter Collection, 10055025.*

department. "The Man's Store," with its Colorado flagstone floor, featured the slogan "To guide the men who guide the west." Men would find lines previously unavailable in Denver, including Oxxford suits ("of Australian and New Zealand wool, loomed in England and hand-stitched in the United States with silk thread from Italy"), Cavanagh hats and ties by Christian Dior and Countess Mara. Denver's businessmen, or their wives, could pick up Scottish sweaters, handwoven socks from Holland and English pajamas. With the addition open, Neusteters then remodeled the old building, creating an even more luxurious environment. Moving more upscale meant closing the bargain basement, which was converted to a fur storage vault with a capacity to store twenty-five thousand coats for customers. The expansion proved successful, so the rest of the Coronado Building came down in 1953 for a 240-car parking lot.[178]

Edward Neusteter, still running the New York office, died suddenly in 1952 from a heart ailment; he had never married. By now, however, a new generation was coming up in the person of Meyer's son, Myron David Neusteter (nicknamed "Bud"). Born in Colorado in 1912, Myron grew up in east Denver, attending Aaron Gove Junior High and East High, and after a year at the University of Colorado, he completed his education at the

Wharton School at the University of Pennsylvania. After service in World War II as lieutenant commander in the navy, he became president of the Neusteter Company in 1946 (at which time Meyer became chairman). He was not inexperienced, having been "born in the blouse department" (as he later joked) and having worked in the store between college and the navy. His father initially assigned him as assistant to the handbags, jewelry and gloves buyer; he later apprenticed to one of the clothing buyers. He learned that training was less important than instinct—"you either had the talent or you didn't." Recognizing good fashion and being the first to present it, he felt, was key to Neusteters' success.[179]

In the 1950s, stores recognized that they needed to serve customers where shoppers wanted them to be. Myron heeded the call. In 1956, he opened the first Neusteters branch, in Boulder's Arapahoe Village, Arapahoe Avenue and Twenty-Eighth Street. The single-level, twenty-thousand-square-foot store included in miniature all of the departments found in downtown Denver, catering to Boulder residents and university students. Bigger news,

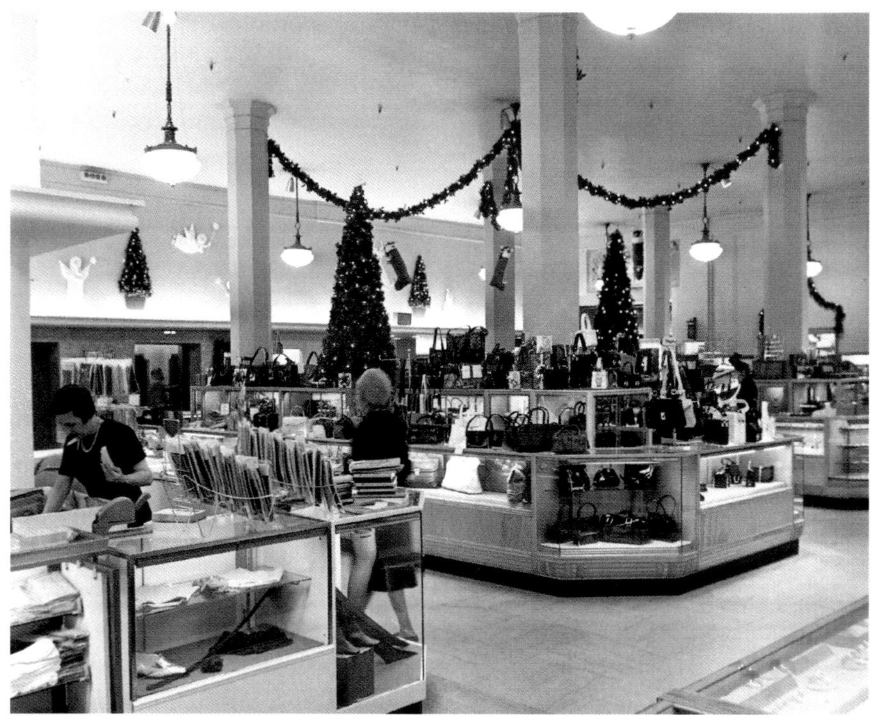

The first floor decorated for the Christmas season, circa 1960. *History Colorado, Neusteter Collection, 10055026.*

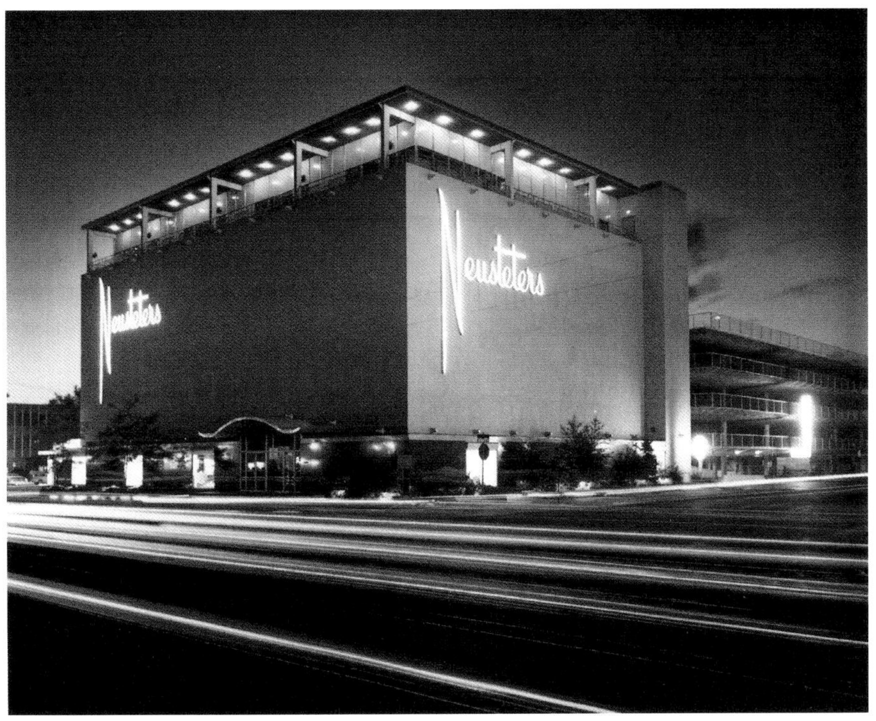

The Cherry Creek store at the northwest corner of East First Avenue and Milwaukee Street, circa 1960. *History Colorado, Neusteter Collection, 10027907.*

however, was Cherry Creek, which Neusteters announced in 1958. Planting a store just four miles southeast of downtown was risky, but The Denver Dry Goods and Sears, Roebuck had already pioneered the area and a Cherry Creek Neusteters would capture the country club trade. Built at East First Avenue and Milwaukee Street, the four-story branch was, at fifty thousand square feet, smaller than downtown but significantly larger than Boulder. The largely windowless façade, by architect Paul Reddy, was of crushed white marble, with black granite on the ground floor. A five-level, five-hundred-space parking structure included second- and third-floor store entrances. The fourth floor housed a first for Neusteters: a full-service restaurant and cocktail bar that, in addition to serving shoppers, would serve as setting for chic fashion shows. The building was designed so the restaurant could remain open after store hours.[180]

By August 29, 1960, Cherry Creek was ready to show itself. At its opening, eager shoppers poured in to marvel at its chic décor, with ash and mahogany paneling and murals by New York artist Richard West.

Equally they came to survey Neusteters' impressive merchandise. The first floor included accessories, cosmetics, millinery, sportswear, men's boutique and Van Cleef and Arpels jewelry. There were no escalators—not considered elegant—so patrons rode elevators to other floors. On two they encountered women's ready-to-wear and furs, and on three they found lingerie and foundations, better ladies' wear, ladies' shoes and infants' and children's departments. The "garden level" (basement) housed gifts, the same Mr. Mack beauty salon that also graced the downtown store and back-of-house areas. The white-tablecloth penthouse restaurant would not open until later; once it did, patrons enjoyed not only dramatic views but also its French-accented décor and French cuisine by longtime Denver restaurateur Joe Shaner.[181]

With Cherry Creek the new crown jewel, Myron did not rest. Colorado Springs, he felt, had a large enough concentration of the Neusteters sort of customer to justify a branch, and the city's Broadmoor Hotel, Colorado's finest resort, attracted well-heeled guests who would appreciate Neusteters. Unusually, considering national trends, Myron chose to build downtown, at Cascade Avenue and Kiowa Street near the Antlers Hotel; he had bought

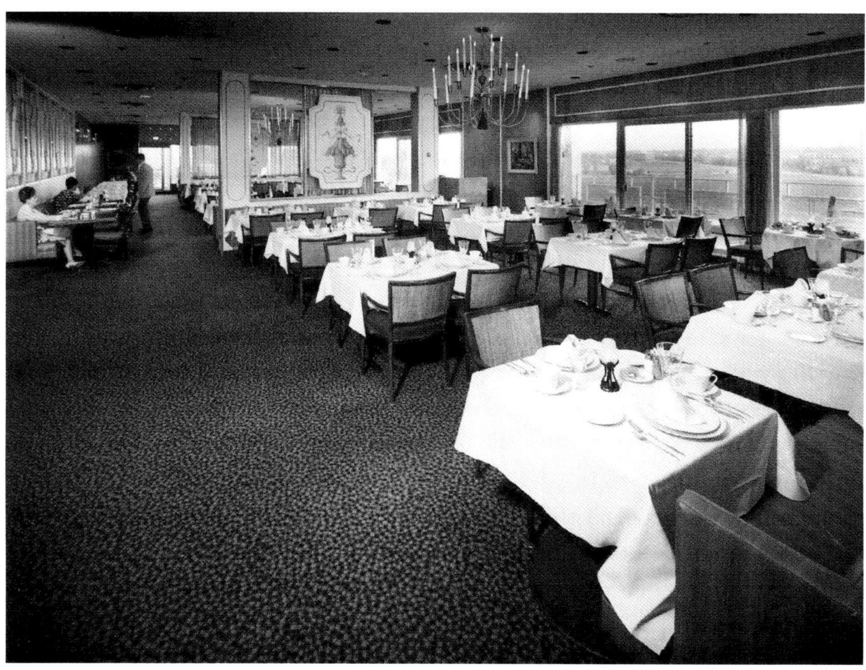

The fourth-story fine dining restaurant atop the Cherry Creek Neusteters, with views south to Pikes Peak, circa 1960. *History Colorado, Neusteter Collection, 10055021.*

the land in 1956, even before Cherry Creek gestated. The store featured three aboveground levels, topped by a one-hundred-seat, saucer-shaped penthouse restaurant with views of the United States Air Force Academy, Garden of the Gods, Cheyenne Mountain and Pikes Peak. Colorado Springs opened on October 26, 1964.[182]

Myron was acutely aware that new suburban centers were rapidly outpacing the old downtown emporia. Decades later, he maintained that he had gone into Cherry Creek because "everybody felt they had to be there." It had been a defensive move—it was necessary to be near the competition. "Ladies put convenience ahead of many other things," he said, and "we fell into the trap." With A.T. Lewis long gone and Gano-Downs a minor player, Neusteters' primary competitor was The Denver. When it announced that it would anchor Cinderella City, Myron had to follow, and Neusteters became its third anchor. He knew it would "chip away" at Cherry Creek, but he also knew that nearby Cherry Hills Village was home to big-spending customers. The forty-five-thousand-square-foot, three-level store opened in 1968, at the center's southwestern end.[183]

Neusteters' reputation supported expansion. Discriminating shoppers knew that it offered, for a price, the best in quality, fashion and service, its equal not to be found elsewhere in Colorado. Quality was paramount, even more than fashion. "People bought because it was Neusteters," Myron told a 1987 interviewer, explaining that each garment had to pass careful inspection, often by him personally, before it made its way to the floor. "I spent more time in our receiving room…if I didn't like what I saw, that buyer had to get rid of it one way or another—we wouldn't place it on sale."[184]

As for style, he did not consider Denver "a kind of backwoods," its ladies ignorant of what well-dressed women in New York, London or Paris were wearing. They knew fashion, and they trusted Neusteters to provide it. Over time, he felt, there had been a shift. Previously, the store itself was the trusted arbiter; by the 1970s, women bought based on designers' reputations, the label now more important than the store. Part of this was generational, and he recognized that some of Neusteters' best customers were aging or dying off. It needed to "develop a younger point of view," so he tasked his sons, Myron Jr. (called David or by his nickname, "Buzz") and William H., to experiment. In 1973, they opened "Savant" on the fourth floor downtown, featuring clothing from young designers chosen by Donna Douglas, whom David recruited from a Larimer Square boutique, to give Neusteters what Myron sought. Some older customers were not impressed, but younger women, those who were "active, highly traveled, vibrant" (per a *Denver Post* fashion

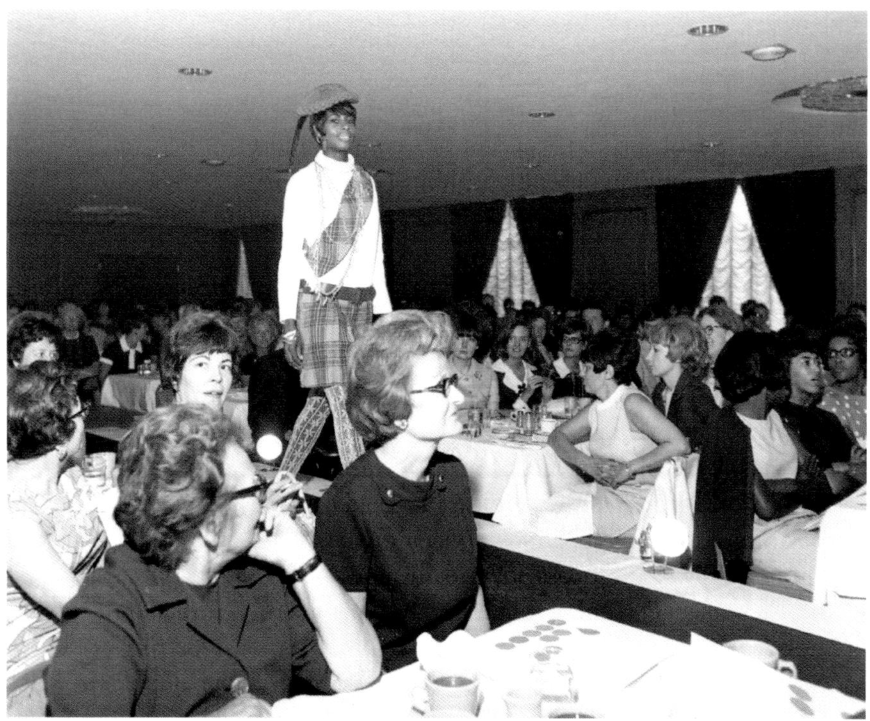

A 1960s Neusteters fashion show at the Albany Hotel. Myron Neusteter was proud that his store was the first major Denver store to feature African Americans in its advertising and the first to employ African American salespeople. *History Colorado, Neusteter Collection, 10043000.*

reporter) snapped up Diane von Furstenberg's tent dresses, Scott Barrie's "soft matte jersey and chiffon clothes" and his "famous clingy dresses." Two years later, William worked with another young buyer, Michele Whealen, to open "Dusty Rose" shops downtown and Cherry Creek, intimate boutiques where someone seeking the *avant garde* could find it without having to search an entire store. She could find everything for a look, from dresses and suits to accessories, jackets, scarves and costume jewelry, and in Cherry Creek she could even get her hair cut in the "chic new close-cropped fashion." Neusteters also continued to introduce exclusive lines to Denver, including England's popular Jaeger knitwear.[185]

Neusteters' commitment to the finest service set it apart from large department stores. Myron developed a program he called "Neusteter Professionals." To achieve "Professional" status, sales associates had to pass muster with him personally, possessing "qualities of personal excellence" in addition to the ability to reach and surpass sales quotas. He aimed to establish "standards of perfection in the art of selling," and once an associate was named "Professional," she or he not only received a certificate to frame and a pin to wear but also higher pay. It was all very formal, and it worked—customers knew they could expect nothing less than perfection.[186]

Another feature of Neusteters' fine service were women who modeled garments customers were interested in buying so they could see how it looked on a living person. A former employee remembers that in 1960, one of these was a "stunning blonde French model" named Marilene (possibly Marilyn). She modeled clothing for customers, posed for store artists creating drawings for newspaper advertisements and represented Neusteters in fashion shows and other events. Her dressing room was one of the fitting rooms on the fourth floor, and it had a large window. One day, the store took a call from a very irate woman whose husband, with an office across the street, had made it his business to keep an eye on that window. From then on, Marilene kept the draperies closed when she was changing outfits.[187]

During this period, Myron emerged as a leading arts patron. In 1960, he opened the Neusteter Gallery of Fine Arts on the second floor downtown, sponsoring an annual exhibition of Colorado artists and hosting others throughout the year. In 1962, Myron and his father focused on the Denver Art Museum, donating $30,000 to establish a fashion and textile department. When the museum announced plans for a seven-level tower facing Civic Center, Myron and his sister, Miriam Lackner, donated an undisclosed amount, described as a "magnificent contribution" by the museum's funding chairman, to sponsor a textile gallery, the Bernita and Meyer Neusteter Museum of Fashion, Costumes and Textiles, to occupy the sixth floor (later renumbered as the seventh) when the tower opened in 1971. In 1970, Myron assumed the presidency of the Central City Opera House Association at a difficult time for that organization, which operated a summer festival in the old mining town west of Denver. He assumed an active role managing its always-precarious finances and introduced money-raising ideas, including fashion shows and antique sales. More importantly, he brought a spirit of "testing" to the organization, which was losing its original high-society patrons to the march of time and needed to attract younger audiences (not unlike the situation at the store). Neusteter made a valiant effort, but Central City Opera would continue to struggle after his tenure. Also in the early 1970s, Myron began serving on the board of the State Historical Society of Colorado.[188]

KEEPING UP

Meyer died in 1965, his shares passing to Myron. As we have seen, Myron enjoyed his roles as fashion impresario and arts patron. Like Meyer, as he aged he delegated day-to-day operations to a new generation. His firstborn, Cynthia Sue, had married Eugene Richard Auer (who preferred his middle name) in 1958. Through the 1960s, Auer worked at Neusteters, rising through the menswear department. In 1967, as vice-president, he opened a new Cherry Creek menswear shop at 170 Fillmore Street, accessed from the main store across a courtyard. In 1971, now president, with Myron chairman, Auer introduced a new graphic identity for Neusteters, featuring a red-orange color scheme and a curvaceous, backward *N* logo. Auer also reinvigorated the menswear business, hiring Denver architect James Sudler to redesign the downtown and Cherry Creek men's stores. Downtown, Sudler installed a futuristic glass-walled elevator connecting the first and second floors. Per Sudler, the new décor, in brown and orange with wood-grain accents and "deep, cushy furniture," would engender a feeling of "male solidarity," arguably a retrograde concept when women were increasingly ready to assume their equal place in society. Auer told reporters that "a store is great only if every department is great," and he aimed "to create one of the most important menswear stores in the state."[189]

Had Auer stopped there, improving what earlier generations had built, this story might have turned out differently. But like Myron, Auer felt the need to compete, and like Myron, he thought more stores would allow him to reach more customers. In 1976, he opened a sixth branch at Aurora's Buckingham Square. Relatively small (10,165 square feet), this was not a full-line Neusteters, but instead the first "Neusteters II," offering "misses sportswear, moderately priced and better coats, designer sportswear, moderately priced and better ready to wear, designer ready to wear, and sophisticated junior clothing." Auer's idea, perfectly sensible, was to stock "only the most profitable, fastest moving merchandise." Sudler's firm designed the storefront, featuring beveled accordion glass; the nationally known Harry Hinson—who had worked for New York's Bonwit Teller, Bergdorf-Goodman and others—designed the interior. Auer followed up Buckingham with a second Neusteters II at Southglenn Mall later in 1976. Two more stores followed in 1977, at the Square on College Avenue in Fort Collins and in Northglenn Mall. Costing approximately $750,000 each to build and furnish, these gave Neusteters nine locations along the Colorado Front Range. Would this prove too many?[190]

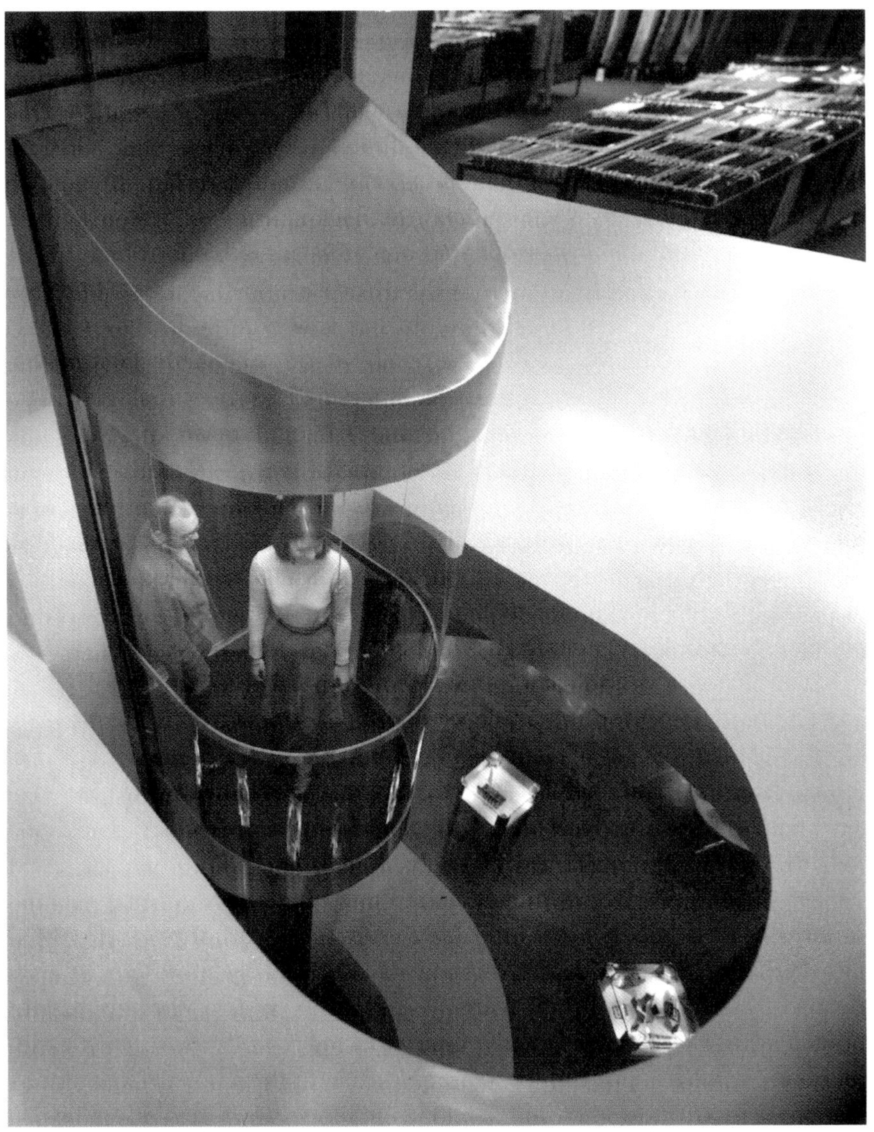

The men's department downtown after its 1973 remodeling by Denver architect James Sudler featured a futuristic, cylindrical glass-walled elevator linking the first and second floors to give shoppers a better idea of the range of menswear on offer. *History Colorado, Neusteter Collection, 10055022.*

UNRAVELING

Neusteters' demise was possibly the saddest of any Denver store, as it divided a family. It played out over several years, beginning in March 1979 with Auer's abrupt, unexplained resignation. Myron temporarily took back the presidency but soon handed over the reins to his younger son, thirty-two-year-old William. The company hired a retail-consulting firm to evaluate options, and rumors arose of a potential sale, which William strongly denied. Almost immediately, he began reversing course in an effort to right the ship. His store closings began with Northglenn in June, followed by Fort Collins in September and Colorado Springs in October, with Cinderella City and Buckingham Square shuttering a short time later. Yet William's moves were not entirely defensive. In March 1980, he announced an ambitious new, "unique merchandising concept" downtown, via an extensive remodeling that would restore it to its 1924 glory; he also slated Cherry Creek for renovation.[191]

Downtown certainly had its problems, one of which was parking. In 1974, family interests had spent $2.3 million to construct a seven-level, 560-space garage adjacent to the store, on the Coronado Building land. It matched the store's height; customer parking was free with validation, but otherwise it served office workers (The Denver and Neusteters soon collaborated on a bridge connecting the garage to The Denver's third floor). Myron was proud that the structure came "at no cost to the taxpayer," but he was unhappy that property valuations were so high. He called on city government to adjust property taxes to "take off the heavy burden with which downtown merchants are now saddled." He also opposed plans for a pedestrian mall on Sixteenth Street, first coming out against it in 1973. Once the mall concept was taken up by the Regional Transportation District (RTD) later in the 1970s to solve its downtown bus congestion problems, the long construction period, beginning in 1980 and lasting through 1982, would not aid Neusteters' efforts to revive its failing flagship. During the height of construction, customers entered via plywood walkways.[192]

In March 1980, William launched downtown's renovation. First he emptied the first floor and consolidated operations on two and four. Upon entering, instead of display counters, customers encountered a temporary corridor, built of plywood and given a colorful Art Deco treatment, leading to the elevators; signage promised a grand new store, but it was hard to imagine. Timing could not have been worse: on March 20, five minority stockholders, Myron's sister Miriam Lackner and her four children (Elaine N. Kohn, an attorney; Robert S. Kohn Jr.; Nancy K. Luby; and Janet L. Hollander) filed suit in Denver District Court against the majority stockholders, named as Myron; his wife, Shirley; and their children, Myron Jr., William and Cynthia N. Auer. The suit alleged "continuing mismanagement" resulting in lost income to minority shareholders and that the company was insolvent. Furthermore, the mismanagement, dating back to "sometime prior to 1977," had resulted in the store company borrowing assets from, and using the good credit of, the Neusteter Realty Company, of which Miriam and her children were also shareholders, in obtaining loans to keep the store afloat.[193]

Neusteter Realty Company dated from 1927, when Meyer, like many other merchant-entrepreneurs, established it partly as landlord to the store and partly to invest in real estate opportunities. It was legally separate from the store, and when Meyer died, he left shares in both companies to both children, in unequal measure. Meyer believed that men were better at business, and although he gave Miriam controlling interest in Neusteter Realty, he appointed Myron head of both it and the store. For years all was well, with both companies paying regular dividends. The realty company owned additional properties—including the former A.T. Lewis building across Stout Street from the store—and in its prime it even floated a 1974 proposal to the Denver Urban Renewal Authority for a multi-block development in DURA's Skyline Urban Renewal Plan, to include a forty-two-story tower with a hotel and office space. DURA's board approved it but later voted it down after Neusteter Realty could not come up with financing. It was the realty company, then headed by Miriam's son Robert Kohn, that built the parking garage adjacent to the downtown store.[194]

Myron was piqued by his sister's suit and countersued a week later, to recover approximately $45,000 in unpaid charge account balances from Miriam and her children (the parties settled out of court). Myron and his sons got some breathing room a day later when Denver district judge Clifton A. Flowers ruled that they were "experienced and well qualified" and had "acted in the best interests of the whole family." The courtroom scene was ugly, with the two branches sitting on opposite sides, studiously ignoring each other. Meanwhile, William's efforts downtown proceeded. In the summer of 1980, the company announced that the future Neusteters would occupy just the first and second floors, with upper floors leased as office space. Restoration work, mostly performed by an in-store team led by Duane Davis, uncovered the original 1924 cast plaster decorations in first-floor display windows and restored the Vance Kirkland murals to prominence. William announced that Neusteters would cater to three sorts of customers:

"the young, hip, often *avant-garde* woman, the woman desiring clean-cut, top-quality career clothing, and the designer and couture customer." The formerly impressive menswear department was reduced to just "the kind of things a woman might buy for a man." This marked a significant comedown from Neusteters' glory days.[195]

Legal battles continued. In 1983, Miriam's branch filed a new suit seeking to open the books (access to which Myron's branch would not allow), alleging that Myron had deceived her as far back as 1967, when Myron, as executor of Meyer's estate, convinced her to sell him 250 shares of Neusteter Realty common stock, giving him control. She did so, she said, because she "loved and trusted [her] brother" and because it was "not the way in our family for the women to question what the men were doing in the business." Myron's attorney countered that evidence would "show that there was no deceit…there was no secretiveness, [that] Myron Neusteter was always a loving, caring brother." He also pointed out that Lackner and her children had always had the ability, since 1967, to challenge the stock transfer but were only doing so when the store was on the ropes. Ultimately, the Colorado Supreme Court ruled that the Myron branch had to allow the Miriam branch, and its accountants, access to both companies' books. In some ways worse than Miriam's lawsuit, however, was a challenge on another front, when General Electric Credit Corporation (GECC), characterized by William as "godlike," sued Neusteters for continuing noncompliance with a 1982 loan agreement and refused further loans. Retailers are always mindful of cash flow, which can make or break them—this was a disaster.[196]

Beset on all sides, William shocked observers by announcing in November 1983 a shift in emphasis. Instead of catering to elite shoppers, as it had done since 1911, Neusteters would slash prices to compete with department stores and with "off price" retailers such as Loehmann's, Marshall's and T.J. Maxx, which were opening stores in Denver. This was meant to raise cash at any cost, not unlike Michael J. McNamara's efforts to save his store in 1893. It was not as though William's turnaround efforts had not been working—he told reporters that sales had increased by 40 percent in 1983 over 1982. But to anyone paying close attention, his awkwardly named "NeuValue" policy of not being undercut ran counter to everyone's expectations of what the Neusteter name meant. William told reporters that he expected to make more money with increased volume, despite a lower profit margin.[197]

Shoppers proved apathetic. The Neusteter Company filed Chapter 11 bankruptcy on October 11, 1985. Creditors included numerous fashion labels and Denver's two daily newspapers. William and Myron had done all they could to keep the companies viable, even agreeing in 1984 to sell their downtown half block to a developer for a one-thousand-room hotel (which never came to fruition). William shuttered Southglenn in June 1985, and in August, he announced Boulder's closure—only downtown and Cherry Creek would remain. The latter had been significantly remodeled since 1980, its original façade replaced with tan-colored, precast concrete panels; the leased restaurant enjoyed new popularity as the Chrysler, a glamorous spot with an Art Deco design. The long construction period, however, had hampered sales.[198]

The family feud roiled on. Another court date related to the 1980 suit came up less than two weeks after the bankruptcy, with "family members [sitting] in two camps on opposite sides of the courtroom…[huddling] during recesses with their separate attorneys."[199] So redolent of earlier court scenes, it was painful for both sides, and before the judge could rule, the two branches settled out of court. The following month, Neusteter Realty Company, now managed independently (one of Miriam's requirements in the 1983 suit settlement) filed Chapter 11, with unsecured debt of about $1.6 million, and secured debt, backed by the downtown store building and other property, of about $15 million. A few weeks after that, and just two weeks before Christmas, the Neusteter Company asked bankruptcy court for permission to close the downtown store.[200]

By this time, William was sick at heart. The previous spring, he and his wife had been badly injured in a car accident, and as he recovered over the summer, he reflected on the years-long series of family battles and the immense difficulties of keeping a local store going in an age when local stores were doomed. He told the *Denver Post*'s Penelope Purdy that "there's been too much pain, too much trauma, too much hurt, too much public airing of private gripes. And I don't want anything to do with that anymore. For better or worse, settle it, just get it over with." He explained that he "never really wanted to be president of Neusteters. My dream was to be in merchandising. But because of circumstances, I got pushed away from merchandising to being the guy to make tough decisions."[201]

In February 1986, the judge allowed the downtown closure, and the liquidation sale began. The final acts came quickly, with Neusteter Realty announcing in March that it would sell its assets, which included the land under the Cherry Creek store, the closed Colorado Springs store, the downtown store and the A.T. Lewis building. On May 28, William assembled the thirty-strong staff at Cherry Creek and told them it was over. With losses of $214,000 in April alone, the store was unable to pay $75,000 owed the realty company for back rent on the closed downtown location. Neusteters was left with no options. Liquidation followed, and the Neusteter Company, founded with such high hopes seventy-five years earlier, was gone. The family feud remains a family matter, and when Myron died in 2003, his son Myron Jr. would not comment on it. Dying at ninety-one, Myron had outlived Miriam.[202]

Chapter 9

FASHION BAR

A Family of Stores

The retail business can be the most exciting business in the world. You're a salesman, an artist, an actor, a gambler, and a pastor. Fashion is a very dangerous thing, and you have to be trusted.
—Jack Levy, 1971[203]

BROTHER AND SISTER

To some, including Fashion Bar in a history of Denver's *department* stores may not seem right. Most people remember it as a series of specialty shops rather than as a true department store. Instead of anchoring malls like May-D&F and The Denver, Fashion Bar occupied spaces in between the anchors, as what realtors call "inline" tenants. Despite this approach, which made business costs significantly cheaper than multi-level stores linked by escalators and bedecked with chandeliers, Fashion Bar belongs in this history as much as the others. It did boast a four-floor Sixteenth Street flagship (complete with escalators), but even in its suburban locations, one could get the department store experience by going from one Fashion Bar to another; some were linked internally. At various times, Fashion Bar's divisions included Fashion Bar Women, Fashion Bar Men, Stage, Stage Shoes, Hannah, Young Set, L'Uomo, FB Design, FB Limited, FB Career and FB Petites. Not every center included all of them, but most included some and customers were just as loyal and enthusiastic about

Fashion Bar as were those of the anchors. Most importantly, Fashion Bar was locally owned, with a distinctly Colorado personality; it thrived in an era increasingly dominated by national chains.

As with older stores, hardworking immigrants founded Fashion Bar. Unlike others, however, it was led not by one man, but by a brother-and-sister team. In later life, both credited each other as the primary reason for the store's success (and they were both right). Hannah Levy, daughter of cattle dealer Raphael Levy and Bertha Hilb Levy, was born in Haigerloch, Germany, southwest of Stuttgart, in 1905. Three years later, brother Jack came along; they had four other siblings, one of whom died in infancy. In 1923, Jack decided to immigrate to the United States; he had relatives who would help him survive and, eventually, thrive. One of his mother's relations, Leopold Weil, had arrived in the United States in 1851 at the age of eleven. Weil ventured to Central City, Colorado, in 1860, just two years after it was founded, to set up as a clothing merchant. He had settled in Denver by 1869 and helped found Temple Emanuel. Another relative, Isidore Hilb (Jack's mother's brother), had come to America after 1900, eventually landing in Denver, where he founded clothing wholesaler Hilb & Company. After disembarking at New York, Jack came to Denver, joining his uncle's firm. He began as a stock boy, and once his English was proficient, Hilb made him a traveling salesman. Levy soon developed a fine sense of how to make money.[204]

In 1926, three years after Jack came over, independent-minded Hannah decided to immigrate too. This was during Germany's Weimar Republic, a period of hyperinflation combined with political instability and increasing anti-Semitism, and Hannah sensed that she would not have much of a future if she stayed. Like Jack, she landed in New York but did not immediately join her brother. She remained in New York two years, taking menial jobs as cleaner, child minder, manicurist and delicatessen worker. Like Jack, she came over without English and was limited in the jobs she could take. Once she had saved enough for train fare, she came to Denver. Upon arrival, Hannah, like Jack, began attending services at Temple Emanuel, and it was good that she did. Seeking work, she applied at Neusteter's, but due to her still-sketchy English, she was rejected. Leaving the store, she ran into Meyer Neusteter, another Temple Emanuel congregant and likely acquaintance of her uncle Isidore. She told him she had not passed muster, but Meyer decided to override his manager and hired her. She started as a stock girl, but over time, her innate fashion sense began to shine, and she was promoted to saleswoman and, eventually, fashion coordinator.[205]

Jack and Hannah benefited greatly from their relatives' earlier immigration. Like them, they subsequently provided a conduit for their parents, Raphael and Bertha, and their other siblings to immigrate. Late in life, Hannah reflected how "our family was lucky to get out of Germany when we did, before Hitler came to power. With our values, I doubt if we would have lasted long under the Nazis." Jack and Hannah loved their adopted country—she wore a Liberty Bell charm on her necklace to show her love of American freedoms—and considered themselves "full and loyal Americans." They later grieved for relatives lost in the Holocaust.[206]

The year 1933 was not an auspicious one to launch a business (A.T. Lewis & Son had failed that January), but Jack and Hannah did not flinch. Jack, watching the rise of national chains that bought direct from manufacturers, realized there was little future in wholesaling. The siblings had worked hard and had saved money—they wanted their own shop. One of Jack's fellow salesmen, Emmett Heitler, also aspired to own a business and joined with the Levys to open a narrow storefront at 1534 Curtis Street. Abutting the Rialto Theater next to Joslin's, the new shop specialized in a product that had only recently become important: hosiery. As hemlines rose in the 1920s, old-style opaque leg coverings would not serve; modern women required sheer stockings. Later in life, Hannah remembered their luck at opening the shop just when nylon stockings came out, and they were the first in town to offer them. Nylons proved immediately popular, and when they ran out, they still had silk stockings to offer their mostly younger customers. Jack and Hannah named their venture "Hosiery Bar." Hannah quit Neusteter's to work full time as buyer and salesperson, but Jack continued to work at Hilb for another five years, until running the business became a full-time job. When they opened Hosiery Bar, Hannah was only twenty-eight years old and Jack twenty-five—some might have thought them wet behind the ears, but they had a plan. Beginning with nothing, they were building something for the rest of their lives.[207]

That same year, Jack married another recent immigrant, Alice Rosenthal; their families had been friendly in Germany, Alice having been born in a neighboring town. The *Denver Post* covered their wedding on its front page, describing how Alice had been Jack's "playmate and schoolday sweetheart" back in Germany. The *Post* further told of how she had managed to come to the United States through well-placed contacts formerly in the Franklin D. Roosevelt administration. She had stopped off

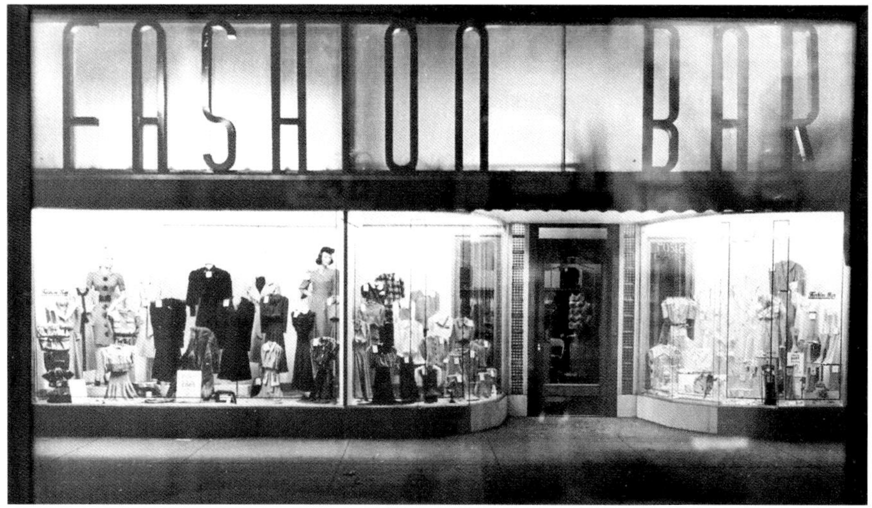

Fashion Bar's original Curtis Street location, midblock between Fifteenth and Sixteenth Streets, circa 1938. *Denver Public Library, Western History Collection, RMN 343-353.*

along the way in Princeton, New Jersey, visiting Albert Einstein, described as an "old friend of Miss Rosenthal's family." The great physicist was also a family friend to the Levys and Hilbs; he once visited them in Denver on his way to California. Alice and Jack would eventually have three children: Barbara, Robert (Bob) and John.[208]

With Jack's financial acumen and Hannah's quick grasp of her customers' desires, Hosiery Bar prospered despite the Depression. By 1936, they had saved enough to open a second Hosiery Bar at 707 Sixteenth Street, opposite The Denver Dry Goods Company. They also bought an adjoining business on Curtis Street, Black's Dress Shop, which they incorporated into Hosiery Bar. In 1937, the Levys and Heitler bought another clothing store, Green's Dress Shops, with locations in Colorado Springs, Pueblo and Greeley. With the two Hosiery Bars and the three Green's stores, they now had five locations and decided that they needed a common identity. Calling the dress shops "Hosiery Bar" would not do, so they held a contest, and the winning entry, by a young Greeley customer, combined the hosiery shops' "Bar" with the dress shops' offerings: Fashion Bar was born.[209]

A Family of Stores

In 1940, Heitler sold out to the Levys, giving them control of their growing operation, which now included another Fashion Bar at Sixteenth and California a few doors down from Hosiery Bar.[210] Jack and Hannah opened their first Western Slope store that same year in Grand Junction. The year 1941 brought a Boulder shop, as well as an important addition to their team: distant relative William Weil. Born in Cleveland and educated at Case Western Reserve, Weil started as a salesman and management trainee; Jack's "right-hand man," he would later serve as vice-president and finally president of Fashion Bar until his 1980 retirement. World War II came and went, with no significant impacts on Fashion Bar other than war-caused shortages. After it was over, as life returned to normalcy, Jack and Hannah began planning their future. In 1948, they moved their offices and warehouse to 1441 Wazee Street, from previous cramped quarters at 1648 Arapahoe Street.[211]

The first postwar Fashion Bar opened at 500 South Broadway, opposite a massive Montgomery Ward warehouse and store. In 1950, Jack opened in downtown Aurora, on East Colfax Avenue, and two years later, he opened

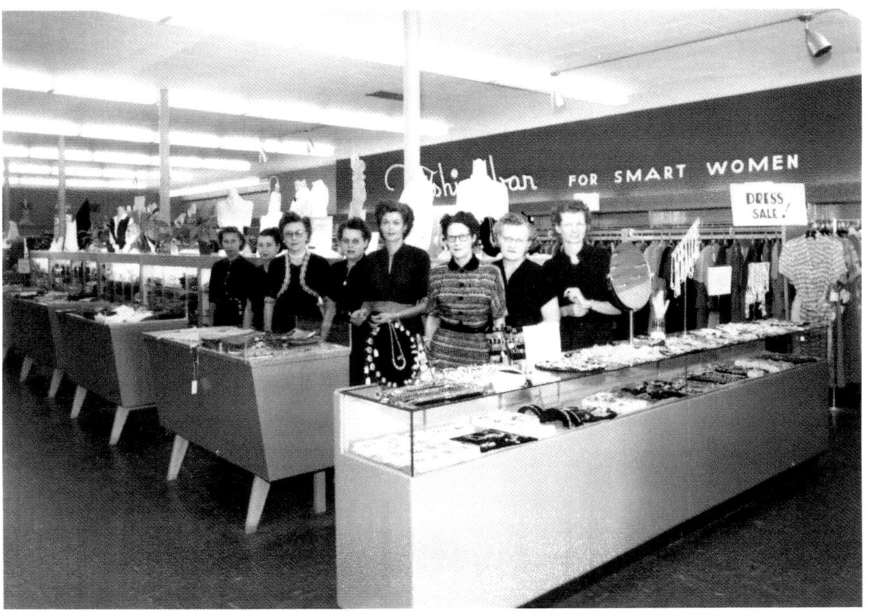

The downtown Aurora Fashion Bar, circa 1955. *Beck Archives, Special Collections, CJS and University Libraries, University of Denver.*

in downtown Englewood. The first Fashion Bar in a dedicated "shopping center" opened at University Hills in 1955, just across from May Company. In 1956, Fashion Bar joined The Denver Dry Goods at Lakeside, and in 1959, Jack moved Colorado Springs to a better spot. As business boomed and Fashion Bar's reputation for cutting-edge styles and attentive service grew, Jack augmented new stores by expanding and remodeling earlier ones; at Greeley, he built a new store, converting the old one into a budget shop.[212]

The 1960s did not slow down Jack. In 1958, he had bought three acres at 695 South Broadway, and in 1960, he opened a new warehouse, corporate headquarters and retail store (replacing 500 South Broadway) on the site, just south of Merchants' Park Shopping Center. In addition to the usual offerings, the "warehouse store" sold closeout merchandise, salesmen's samples and odd lots at bargain prices. In 1963, Jack opened the largest Fashion Bar yet, in Lakewood's Westland Center, and debuted another new store at Boulder's Crossroads Center.[213]

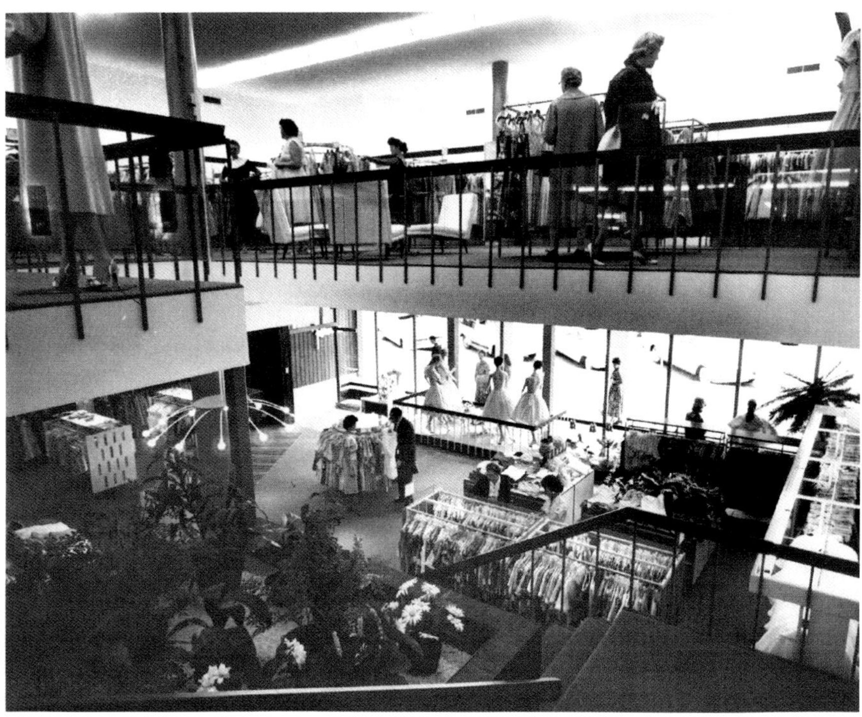

The downtown Colorado Springs Fashion Bar, circa 1965. *Beck Archives, Special Collections, CJS and University Libraries, University of Denver.*

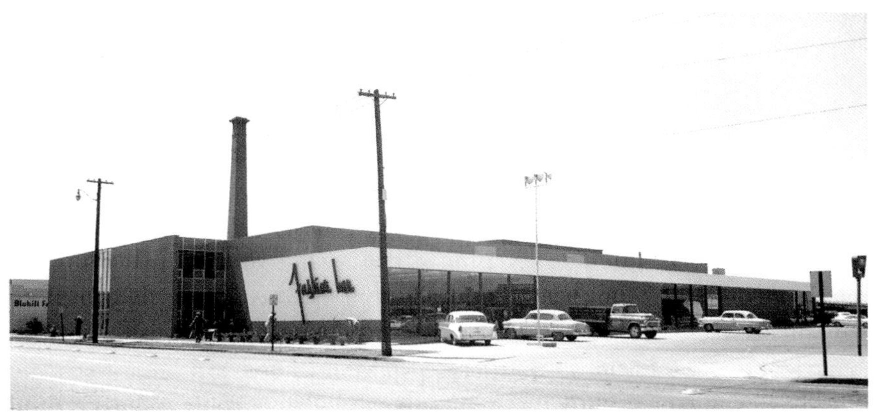

In 1960, Fashion Bar opened a new warehouse and store at 695 South Broadway next to the Merchants' Park Shopping Center, shown here shortly before opening. *Beck Archives, Special Collections, CJS and University Libraries, University of Denver.*

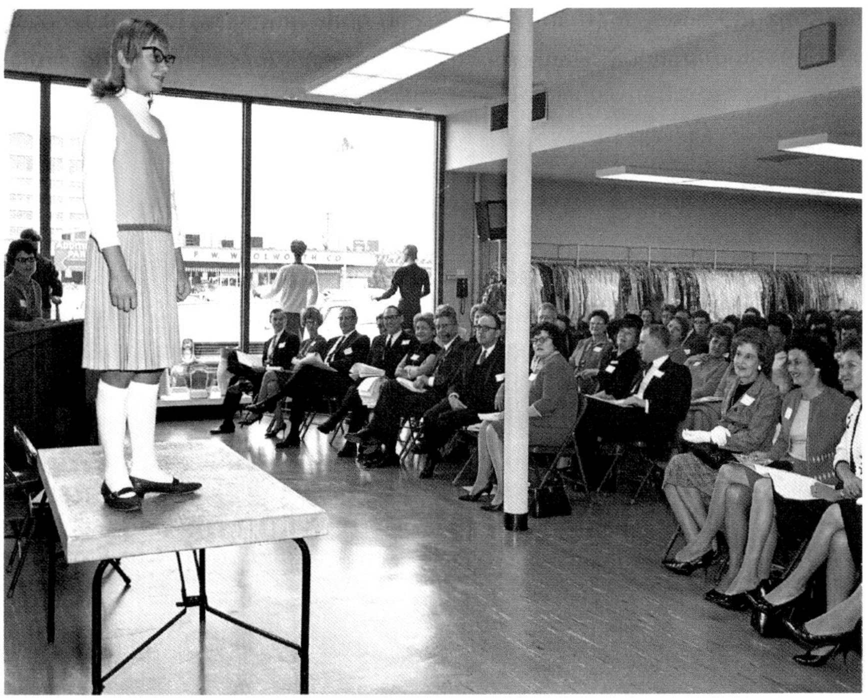

In this children's fashion show at 695 South Broadway, Jack Levy (*with pipe*) sits in the first row. His sister, Hannah, sits to his right, and to her right is later store president William Weil. Merchants' Park Shopping Center and the Montgomery Ward warehouse are visible through the window. *Beck Archives, Special Collections, CJS and University Libraries, University of Denver.*

At this time, Fashion Bar began branching out from women's apparel. It had added children's sections in the 1950s for younger shoppers starting families, but that was the extent of diversification. The Pueblo store had opened a menswear shop when it expanded in 1958, operated by an outside entity on a leased basis, but neither the Levys nor Weil was comfortable with having the company's name associated with something in which they were not fully involved. Jack's older son, Robert, was just starting out in the business, having completed his education at Boston College. Weil invited him in 1964 to launch menswear at Westland and Crossroads, and Bob, who was about the same age as Hannah when she and Jack founded Hosiery Bar, was willing. He considered himself a greenhorn, and despite the fact that his father was founder and president, he reported to Weil and was fully responsible for the venture's success. At first, he bought all menswear, from socks to suits, but as business grew, more buyers came on board. The initial men's departments were located inside the women's shops, but eventually the company established separate storefronts for them. This was the genesis of Fashion Bar's specialization: from a store that featured one product line (hosiery), it would find success in the 1960s through the 1980s by establishing a series of stores that each catered to different shoppers—a department store in essence, if not in name.[214]

Despite the suburbanization of American life, Jack also had his sights set on establishing a greater presence downtown. Neither the Curtis Street shop nor the Sixteenth and California branch reflected Fashion Bar's new personality. In 1961, Levy closed Curtis Street and opened a small storefront, the Little Shop, at 409 Sixteenth Street, selling better dresses, imported knits, sportswear and accessories. It was the precursor of a flagship store that would feature all Fashion Bar offerings. Levy wanted to be near May-D&F, so he bought the Tremont Hotel, diagonally opposite May-D&F at Sixteenth and Tremont, and leased the land underneath. In 1964, he announced plans for a multi-level store, capped by a twelve-story office tower, designed by Denver architect Richard L. Crowther, with whom Levy had already worked on several projects. Levy later realized that a twelve-story building would not produce sufficient revenue and expanded it to twenty-one floors (soon scaled back to sixteen). Here he ran afoul of his neighbors and the Denver zoning board. The 100- by 125-foot site was too small for such a tall structure without a zoning change (twelve stories was the maximum), and owners of the Security Life Building across the alley, as well as Hudson Moore Jr. of Cheesman Realty, owner of the Republic Building across Tremont, opposed the tower. Levy was forced to scale back to a three-story-plus-basement building housing just the store. However, by the time the zoning board ruled, construction had already begun, with a foundation engineered for a tower. Levy felt that income from the tower would have provided a hedge against the vagaries of downtown retailing, but he never got the chance to find out.[215]

The new flagship Fashion Bar, fourteenth in the chain, costing $2.25 million and containing fifty thousand square feet across four levels, opened on December 1, 1965, just in time for holiday shopping. Windowless upper floors were sheathed in brown precast pebbled concrete. On the main level, show windows lined Sixteenth Street, wrapping around to Tremont. A bronze canopy shielded windows and passersby from the elements and sun glare. Instead of doors, shoppers entered through an "air curtain," strong fans blowing air upward at such strength that outside air (hot or cold) could not enter. With escalators connecting all floors, department arrangement was unusual compared to traditional stores. The first floor was entirely devoted to menswear and shoe departments for both sexes. On two, the female shopper found sportswear, lingerie and hosiery, foundations, infant's

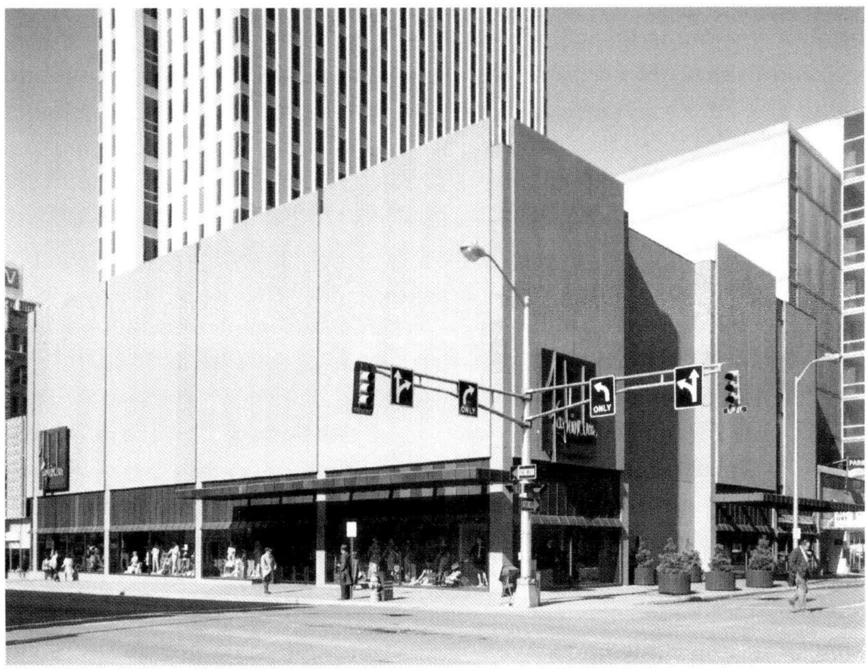

The downtown Denver flagship Fashion Bar, designed by architect Richard L. Crowther, at Sixteenth and Tremont Streets not long after its 1965 opening. *Beck Archives, Special Collections, CJS and University Libraries, University of Denver.*

wear and children's wear. Ascending to three, she found designer fashions, dresses, coats, bridal, jewelry and accessories. The basement featured large sizes and a bargain department.[216]

Downtown proved popular, but Jack remained busy. In 1966, Westland's men's department moved to its own storefront, and University Hills added menswear. Also in 1966, Jack opened at Bear Valley Shopping Center (five years later moving menswear to a separate storefront). Experimenting that year, Levy replaced the Sixteenth and California Fashion Bar with "Hipbone," an "elegant boutique" featuring "beat and mod looks and fashions and records from Northern California," designed to appeal to "Beatle-banged browsers" per a *Post* account. The shop, managed by twenty-seven-year-old Mickey Joelson, proved immediately successful, although a suggestive sign on the door that read "If you don't swing, don't ring" did not last long. The young (often teenage) shoppers responded not only Hipbone's vibe but also to its soundtrack music, programmed by twenty-two-year-old Michael O'Sullivan from his record shop in the shop's rear. No other Denver store went this far to court the youth market.[217]

With additional branches necessitating more logistical space, Levy closed the Broadway store in 1968 to expand the warehouse. Later that year, he

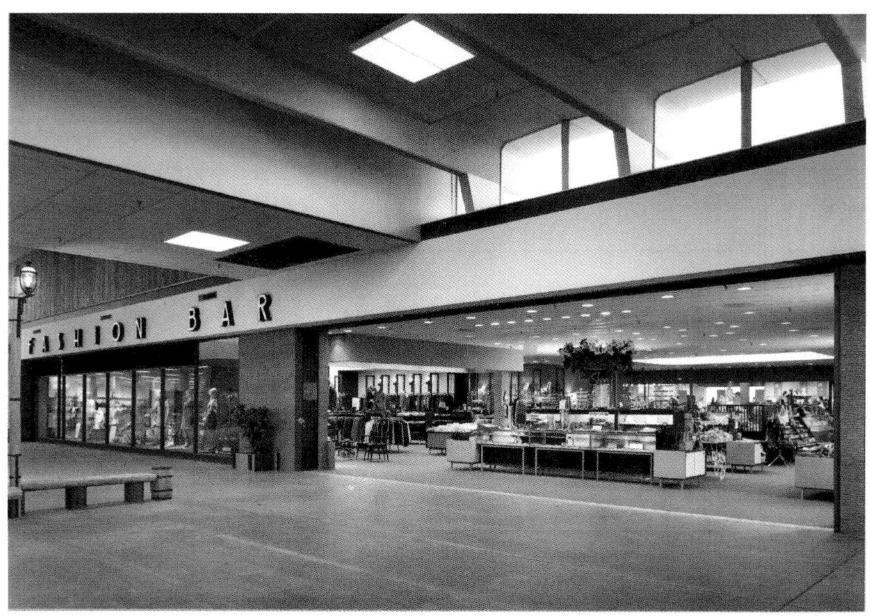

Fashion Bar's Bear Valley store included both men's and women's clothing when it opened in 1966. *Beck Archives, Special Collections, CJS and University Libraries, University of Denver.*

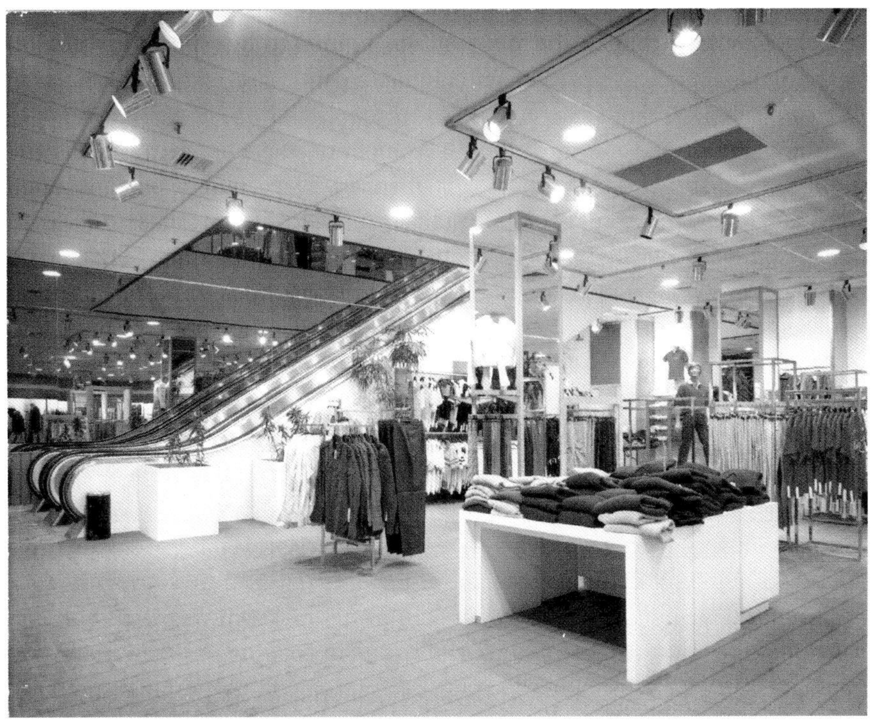

Fashion Bar's Aurora Mall store on the center's lower level was linked by escalator to women's departments on the upper level, circa 1975. The wall past the escalator was mirrored, making the store seem larger. *Beck Archives, Special Collections, CJS and University Libraries, University of Denver.*

opened stores at Northglenn Mall. In 1970, Jack bought the S.H. Kress store in Greeley for expansion (including a new concept for children, "Young Set") and opened a full-line men's store at University Hills. In 1971, Fashion Bar opened stores at Buckingham Square (the downtown Aurora store remaining open, for a time). That same year brought a new Colorado Springs store at The Citadel, the company keeping its downtown store (relocated to 115 North Tejon Street in 1960) open.[218]

Through the 1970s, Fashion Bar leased additional space to augment existing stores and took space in new malls. It also created new concepts: the first FB Design, offering items for the home, opened at Southglenn Mall in 1975, as did the first Hannah, a more upscale shop for mature women named for the co-founder. A third concept launched in 1975 was L'Uomo (Italian for "the man"), selling expensive European menswear not otherwise available in Denver; its first location was downtown. These joined Scene

II (later renamed Stage), chic fashions for juniors at budget prices that had started out as a department in a 1972 downtown remodeling. Fashion Bar opened stores on both levels of Aurora Mall (linked by an escalator) that same year, and in 1977, it opened shops at Westminster Mall. By 1981, when it ventured out of state to Cheyenne, Wyoming's Frontier Mall, Fashion Bar boasted sixty-five stores, occupying 650,000 square feet of space and employing 1,500.[219]

THE FASHION BAR DIFFERENCE

Although Jack and Hannah both gave each other full credit for Fashion Bar's success, it is fair to say that Hannah's instincts and drive gave the company the extra edge it needed to compete with Denver's department stores and national chains alike. "She is the inspiration," Jack told a reporter in 1977. "If it hadn't been for her, there would be no Fashion Bar." Her buying trips entailed an extraordinary amount of work and time, which she willingly gave for the sake of Fashion Bar's success (and which factored into her never marrying). In New York, her days started at 8:00 a.m. and ran to 6:00 p.m., with only ten minutes for breakfast and fifteen for lunch; in between, she would hit every manufacturer's showroom in the Garment District, and only after examining all of their lines and noticing what well-dressed New York women were wearing would she begin making deals. Her European trips, which she made several times annually, included visits to Italy (Fashion Bar maintained an office in Florence), France, Denmark, West Germany and Spain, and often she was so anxious for Denver women to discover what she found that she air-shipped goods to Denver at a time when air shipments were still rare. In 1947, she came across a checkerboard-patterned sweater that she just knew would sell. She had quantities flown to Denver and instructed managers to give them prominent display; they were such a smash that Fashion Bar ultimately sold twenty-five thousand of them. She was so concerned with speed that she had signs printed for junior buyers that read simply, "Do it now." Hannah knew that speed set Fashion Bar apart when she told a reporter, "We have built a tremendous acceptance by being the first with the newest."[220]

Hannah's choices were never faddish. She described herself as a "completely unorthodox buyer...I never follow trends [and] I buy on impulse" (meaning that she trusted her inner fashion sense enough to listen

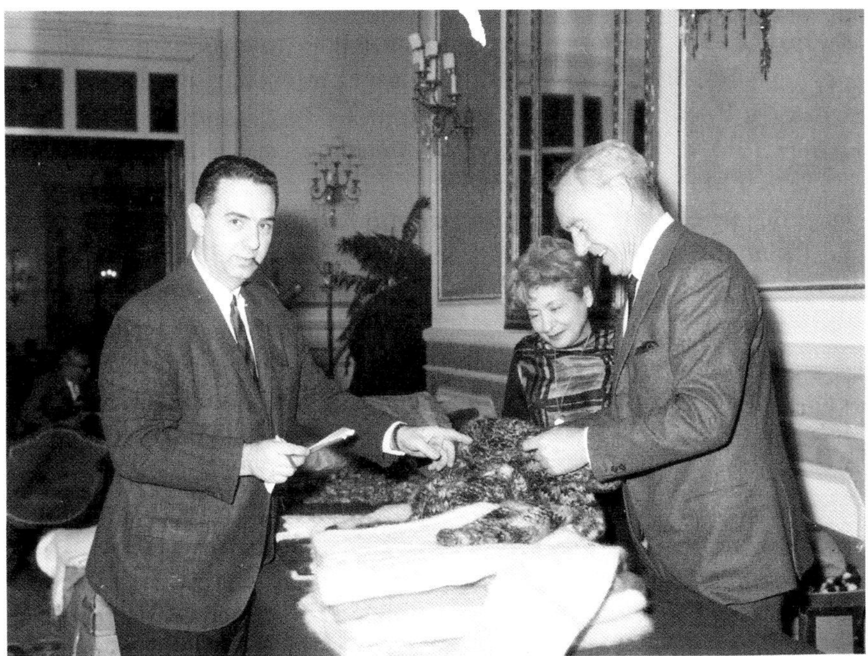

Hannah Levy inspects a sample sweater at a manufacturing expo in either Florence or Rome, Italy, circa 1965. *Beck Archives, Special Collections, CJS and University Libraries, University of Denver.*

to it). She spoke of how one "must learn to draw inspiration from a color, a line, a texture, a particular composition of design…sometimes you may seek without finding…[until] suddenly the whole picture falls into place." She believed that women need not spend great amounts of money to look chic and found manufacturers (often in Asia) that could interpret couture designs for women "with more taste than money." Hannah bought not just for the chain as a whole but for individual stores—she kept track of what sold best in each and gave instructions for which stores should get particular styles. The fashion press took notice of Hannah's brilliance; *Women's Wear Daily* considered her one of the nation's top dress buyers.[221]

Another aspect of Fashion Bar's philosophy that set it apart was listening closely to customers and actively soliciting their opinions. This often occurred on the sales floor, and if Jack or Hannah were not present, they expected those who were to tell them, because they truly cared about what customers had to say. Having utilized comment cards for years, in 1971 Jack commissioned an eight-page questionnaire, titled "Be a Board Member for a Day," and mailed it to eighty-one thousand charge account customers; a completed response would net a five-dollar gift card, to be used on anything (even if the purchase was only five dollars). The campaign yielded more than twenty-eight thousand responses and influenced Jack in numerous areas, including the hiring of additional sales clerks and eventually installing a state-of-the-art computer to speed up credit transactions. Most customers also applauded Fashion Bar's policy of remaining closed on Sundays at a time when more and more stores were open for both weekend days. Jack liked the feedback so well that surveys continued for several years.[222]

Strong customer service was another key aspect of Fashion Bar's business. In the 1960s, as national discount chains such as Kmart and Target began opening in Denver, Jack maintained his long-established policy of competing not just on price but on service. "People become tired of the 'serve yourself' atmosphere," he told a reporter, and "the first thing our employees learn is politeness." Staffing levels were high; Jack estimated that that Fashion Bar employed twice as many clerks as other stores. Their only job was to help customers find the right garments, and they were not on commission. Levy felt that his staffing levels created more of a "mom and pop" environment rather than that of a big chain, which he believed crucial. He cared about his employees, and he treated them as individuals, with respect, honoring achievements and longevity in annual banquets. Fashion Bar never saw its employees unionize, unlike some stores. From an early date, many store managers were women, when many shops, even those for women, had male managers.[223]

The design and visual appeal of Fashion Bar's stores and graphics also set it apart. Having been birthed in the 1930s, Fashion Bar was not saddled with tradition or ornate nineteenth-century buildings. From the beginning, its stores were designed in modern styles rather than harkening back to some earlier mode, and this emphasis on the "now" appealed to its mostly younger shopper base—as true in the 1930s as in the 1980s. As noted earlier, Levy worked closely with Richard L. Crowther on the downtown store, but Crowther had been working with him as early as the mid-1950s and would continue to do so for several years more. After Crowther, Fashion Bar worked with his former employee, Frank Kiszlowski, on stores in the 1970s and early 1980s. Fashion Bar employee Art Weymar created prizewinning fashion illustrations for advertisements beginning in the mid-1950s; in 1959, he won first prize in a national competition.[224]

Like Denver's earlier Jewish merchants, Jack and Hannah believed strongly in giving back to their community. In 1948, they honored their father, creating the Raphael Levy Memorial Foundation to support

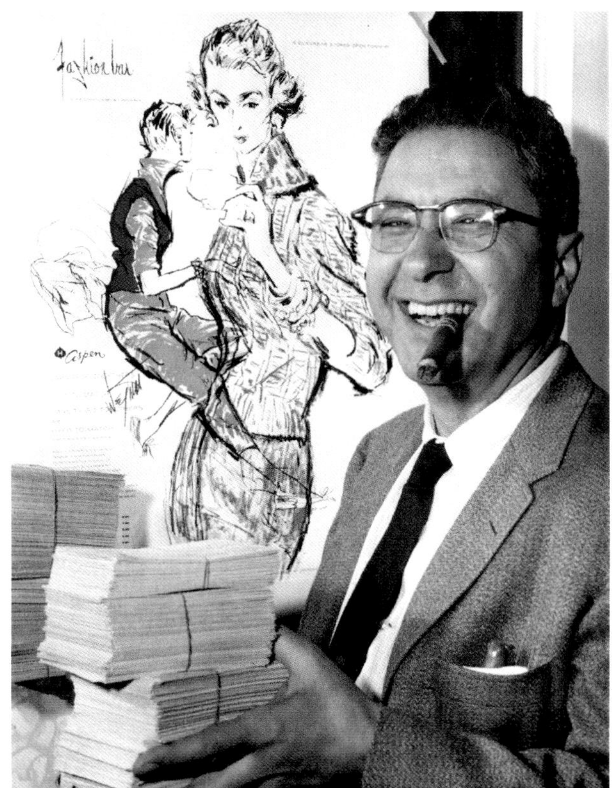

Right: Jack Levy in 1959, with cigar and stacks of customer postcards, in front of an Art Weymer–drawn advertisement. *Author's collection.*

Below: The Hannah store at Westland Mall, circa 1977. *Beck Archives, Special Collections, CJS and University Libraries, University of Denver.*

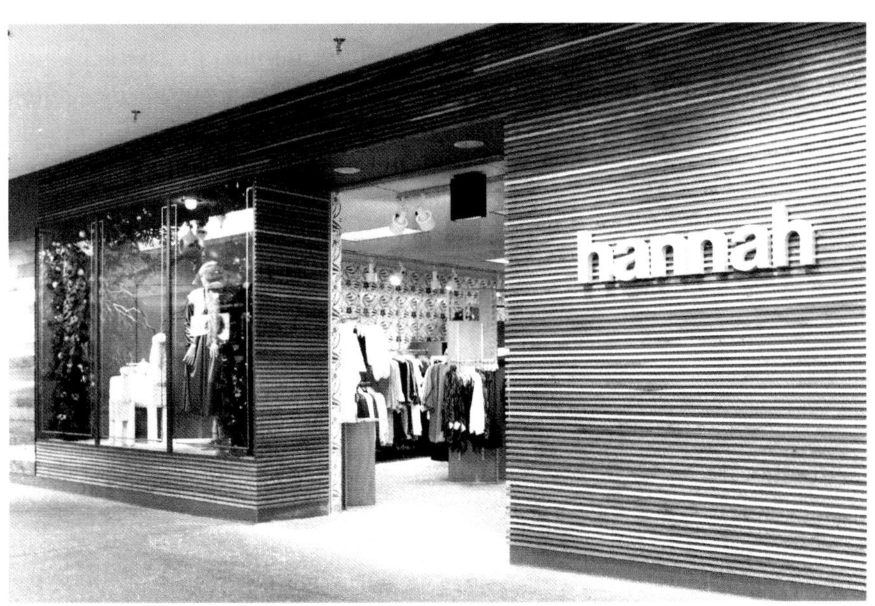

various charities. Jack and Hannah also devoted resources and time to General Rose Hospital. Jack was one of a number of Jewish leaders who founded it in 1945, sensing the need postwar Denver had for more hospital beds and for a facility where doctors of any faith could practice without discrimination. Levy was chairman of Rose's board from 1968 to 1970, and in 1982, the Rose Foundation named him "Humanitarian of the Year" for his longtime service to the hospital and community at large. Jack's wife, Alice, and daughter, Barbara Goldberg, were longtime volunteers at Rose, and after Alice died, the hospital named the Alice Levy Pavilion in her honor. Governor Richard D. Lamm declared "Jack Levy Day" on September 29, 1982, for his devotion to Rose and other work. In 1983, it was Hannah's turn for recognition, earning the Human Relations Award from the American Jewish Congress. Other organizations Jack and Hannah supported included the Jewish Community Center, the United Way, the University of Denver, the Denver Symphony Orchestra and the Denver Center for the Performing Arts.[225]

Second Generation

"We started as a family company. Now we're a company family, and all of our employees are members of that family," Jack told a reporter in 1967, and he no doubt meant it. But flesh-and-blood family remained paramount. In 1968, Jack reorganized, turning over the presidency to William Weil and creating a new title for himself, chairman of the board; this was mostly a cosmetic change, as Jack remained closely involved. In 1980, Weil retired, and Robert Levy became president, with brother John as treasurer. As Jack and Hannah had done before them, the siblings collaborated on important decisions, including relocating the headquarters and warehouse to an Aurora site on South Buckley Road. In 1985, Robert shifted over to the real estate side, turning over the presidency to John. Like Robert, John had begun working at Fashion Bar shortly after graduating college, concentrating on the women's stores.[226]

Witnessing John succeed Robert as president undoubtedly pleased Jack, who died a few months later, aged seventy-six. His last months were marked by sadness, as Hannah had passed the previous December, aged seventy-nine—they left the world about five months apart. Fashion Bar went on without them, as it had to do. In 1980, not long after Robert became president, Fashion Bar opened at Tamarac Square, a specialty mall in southeast Denver. When Chapel Hills Mall opened in Colorado Springs in 1982 and Southwest Plaza opened in 1983, both featured several Fashion Bar concepts. In 1985, John launched a new venture, FB Petites, having also created FB Careers for the white-collar woman. That same year, he took a chance on Tivoli Denver, a shopping center in a renovated brewery at the Auraria Higher Education Center near downtown, with Stage and Stage Shoes for college-age women. In 1985, he also shuttered FB Design, preferring to stick with Fashion Bar's core strengths in apparel. In 1986, John decided to enter a district Fashion Bar had long ignored, Cherry Creek North, opening Hannah and FB Petites at East Second Avenue and Milwaukee Street.[227]

Jack Levy and William Weil always maintained that Fashion Bar would never expand beyond Colorado. Robert broke that mold with Cheyenne in 1980, but in 1988, John went full-bore, announcing that Fashion Bar would enter the Phoenix, Tucson and San Diego markets with Stage (but no other nameplates) in multiple malls in each city. He also planned for Hannah stores in Los Angeles. When Jack expanded Fashion Bar, he never borrowed, funding strictly with profits. When Robert took over in 1980, he told a reporter that the company did "very little borrowing." John's move into Arizona and California necessitated more borrowing than had previously been Fashion Bar's practice, and thanks to the recession that hit Colorado in the mid-1980s, cash flow became tight. By 1991, with Colorado just beginning to recover, John decided to close eight unprofitable stores. The chain was losing money; for the first time since its founding, Fashion Bar's future was in doubt.[228]

The game was up in 1992. The previous year, the chain had achieved sales of $72 million but lost $3.4 million; this was far below a 1984 sales figure of $112.5 million. Fashion Bar had received many offers to be bought out over the years, but the Levys had never felt the need to merge with a larger organization, always preferring to remain family-operated. In 1992, unable to restore profitability, John signed an agreement with Specialty Retailers Inc. (SRI) of Houston, Texas, owner of other regional apparel chains, and spent several months in negotiation. On June 9, the firms consummated the deal, for $14.8 million, and the Levys were out. SRI's president, Bernard Fuchs, eliminated Fashion Bar's buying office, combining operations with his other chains. Instead of Denver-based buyers making choices for Colorado shoppers, it would be Houstonians deciding what Coloradoans wanted.[229]

Fuchs's plans to run Fashion Bar from Houston failed—he did not understand what he had. Rather than an undifferentiated merchant of middle-of-the-road merchandise (like SRI's other divisions), Fashion Bar was uniquely Colorado in its personality thanks to the decades Jack and Hannah had spent building it. Fashion was in its name, and Colorado shoppers knew they could find chic, trendy (but never faddish) fashions at affordable prices. The Hannah stores were the first to go: SRI closed them in 1994, unable to choose merchandise suitable to what Hannah herself had created. In early 1995, SRI announced thirty-seven closures: all Stages, as well as many FB Men's, FB Women's and FB Petites shops. Downtown, which was owned rather than leased, would remain, along with a clearance center at Westminster Mall (downtown would eventually close, in 2001). Oddly, after these closures, SRI decided to revive the Stage name, applying it to remaining Fashion Bars in Colorado as well as to SRI stores in other states. The Fashion Bar name disappeared entirely on January 31, 1997, when the Westminster clearance center shut its doors. After almost sixty-four years, the venture started by a brother and a sister, against all odds at the depths of the Great Depression, was gone for good. As of this writing, SRI survives as Stage Stores Incorporated.[230]

Chapter 10

MAY-D&F

Shopping Wonder of the West

This is a store keyed to the tempo of the Space Age, an architect's dream, a contemporary marvel….Denver is the heart of the West, a shining modern metropolis as inspiring as Paris, Rome or London. It is a city of culture, of symphony orchestras, museums, modern architecture, beautiful women and handsome men plus fine stores like May-D&F.
—Adele Simpson, 1960[231]

ZECKENDORF'S "SECOND RADIO CITY"

Before there was a City and County Building on Bannock Street, housing Denver's government and courts, there was a Denver County Courthouse occupying the block on Sixteenth Street between Tremont Street and Court Place. It was a typical domed, Neoclassical courthouse of its time (built in 1883 as the Arapahoe County Courthouse), but it was not beloved or praised by Denver boosters. It perhaps was not surprising, then, when in 1912 Leopold Guldman proposed demolishing it. The visionary Golden Eagle proprietor recognized that the shopping district was creeping southeastward, and he was prepared to offer $900,000 for the property. He would replace the courthouse with a twelve-story building housing a relocated Golden Eagle facing Sixteenth and a hotel fronting on Fifteenth. The city, wanting a new courthouse yet not ready to build one, declined his offer. Guldman would not live to see his idea reach fruition, but forty-six years later, a department store would indeed open at Courthouse Square, linked to a hotel.[232]

The City and County Building opened in 1932. Mayor Benjamin F. Stapleton lost his 1931 reelection bid to George Begole, a believer in fiscal conservatism. Begole wanted to sell the vacant courthouse but unrealistically expected pre-Depression fair market value, not accepting less than $1.25 million. There were no takers. He ordered demolition and directed the creation of a park in its place (never dedicated officially as parkland). When Stapleton became mayor again in 1935, it remained for sale. Finally, in 1945, Denver realtor and Stapleton crony B.B. (Burr Brett) Harding stepped in. In New York, he paid a call on developer William Zeckendorf, having a hunch that his reputation as progressive city-builder might translate into his buying the block.[233]

No stranger to big plans, Zeckendorf immediately warmed to the idea of a Denver project, and rumors soon flew of a New Yorker planning big things. New York developers are rarely known for their modesty, and Zeckendorf, president of Webb & Knapp, loved flashy public relations. He used press conferences to build excitement, which would then aid him with financing and political support. After winning the property with an offer of $818,600 (a bid was also submitted by Guldman's son-in-law, Lester Friedman), Zeckendorf announced plans for a "second Radio City," to perhaps include a department store, hotel, apartments, office space and radio and television broadcasting facilities. He adored New York's Rockefeller Center and wanted to build something like it. Denver citizens had other ideas, however, and before he could commence, he had to contend with multiple lawsuits filed by those who did not want public land sold for commercial purposes and who felt he was paying too little. By 1949, various courts had ruled in Zeckendorf's favor, and he gained control.[234]

Nothing happened immediately. Lacking concrete plans, he removed trees, lawn and reflecting pool, converting the block to parking to finance property taxes. By 1952, Mayor James Quigg Newton was "greatly disturbed" at the lack of progress, but Zeckendorf blamed Korean War–caused materials shortages. He announced plans in 1953 for a Statler Hotel, but it was too tall for Denver's height limit, enacted due to downtown's proximity to Stapleton Municipal Airport. Finally, Zeckendorf hit on the idea of buying a department store to anchor his project, and as recounted in the first chapter, he chose Daniels and Fisher. After obtaining a signed lease from the store, he further bought the Statler chain so he could include a hotel but soon realized that a department store and hotel could not both fit on the block; he began buying land across Court Place for the latter component. Denver voters granted him the right in November 1954 to build underneath Court Place, so that one vast (1,500-space) underground parking structure could support both store and hotel. Construction commenced in 1955.[235]

Suburbia in the City

As mentioned previously, Zeckendorf determined that Denver had too many downtown department stores and engineered Daniels and Fisher's sale to May Company, forming May-D&F. By summer 1958, May-D&F was nearly ready. Zeckendorf understood and appreciated the simple elegance of modern architecture, and for some years, he had employed I.M. Pei as his architect. Pei, who had previously designed Zeckendorf's Mile High Center at Seventeenth Avenue and Broadway, believed that reviving a city required harmony between business uses and spaces for relaxation and contemplation. To that end, for Courthouse Square he created a four-part assemblage embodying these principles. The Hilton Hotel, a block-long slab built of brown-pebbled precast concrete, stood across Court Place from the store. May-D&F occupied a four-story, mostly windowless box, sheathed in gold-tinted aluminum, set well back from Sixteenth. At the Sixteenth and Tremont corner, Pei designed a dramatic store entry in the form of a concrete-roofed, glass-walled hyperbolic paraboloid. To re-create the Rockefeller Center ambience so desired by his patron, Pei centered the complex on a sunken plaza (named for Zeckendorf) at Sixteenth and Court. In the winter, it would be used for ice skating and, in the summer, for whatever functions May-D&F could program. The rink opened in December 1957, nine months before the store itself, and Denverites immediately embraced it as their newest downtown landmark.[236]

On Monday August 4, 1958, May-D&F opened its doors to an excited public. Present to cut the ribbon were David May's son, Morton J.; his son, Morton D.; and two of David May's great-grandchildren. Daniels and Fisher doorman Carl Sandell, symbolizing continuity with Denver's pioneer store, was there too, although he would retire within a few years. May-D&F was helmed by David Saul Touff, who had taken over May's Colorado operations from Alfred Triefus. He knew that longtime Daniels and Fisher shoppers were skeptical that May-D&F could match the older store's reputation for quality and service, as many considered May Company a lesser store. Given wide

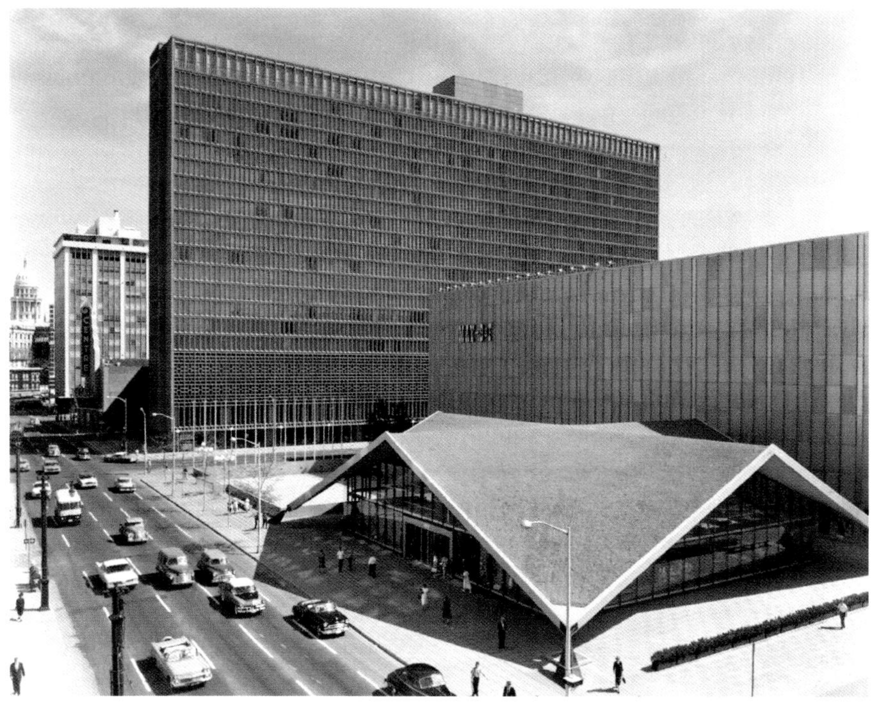

A new downtown landmark, May-D&F and the Denver Hilton Hotel, forming William Zeckendorf's Courthouse Square, circa 1960. *Denver Public Library, Western History Collection.*

latitude by St. Louis headquarters, Touff aimed to please both predecessor stores' loyal shoppers. Those looking for May's bargains would find them, particularly in the basement, with its bargain departments. People mourning Daniels and Fisher could gravitate to "Forecast Shops," special areas in several departments featuring top-quality fashions that would have been at home at Daniels and Fisher. Striving for continuity, May-D&F named the china, glassware, silver and linens departments the "Fisher Shops." Daniels and Fisher shoppers who had been used to top-notch hairstyling services at its Antoine Beauty Salon would find a new Antoine at May-D&F. Not everyone was convinced that this was a continuation of Daniels and Fisher, but it was certainly nicer than May Company. Best of all, parking was easy and convenient (free with validation), just as it was in suburbia.[237]

May-D&F had entrances on all four sides (and from parking garage elevators), but the most popular was on Sixteenth Street, through I.M. Pei's dramatic, soaring, hyperbolic paraboloid. Passing through heavy glass doors, shoppers' eyes immediately took in a vast, glass-walled space unlike any

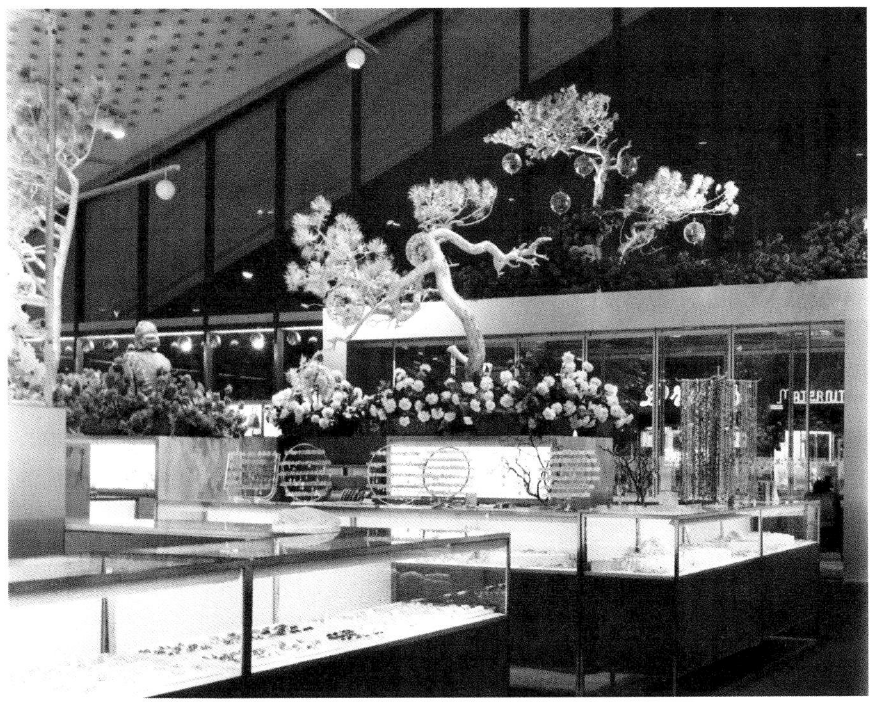

The Plaza Shops inside the I.M. Pei–designed hyperbolic paraboloid, circa 1959. *Bob Rhodes Collection.*

other store. Christened "Plaza Shops," it encompassed a series of accessories departments: handbags, jewelry, hosiery, hats and similar items. Passing into the main building, shoppers found cosmetics, clocks and watches, luggage, sporting goods and a gourmet shop. Men encountered a vast offering on the Court Place–facing side. The second level was filled with women's fashions, while on three shoppers found children's and teen apparel, toys, fabrics and notions and the aforementioned Fisher Shops and Antoine Beauty Salon. Four featured furniture (complemented by interior design service), appliances, radio and television and hi-fi (record players and records). The basement, along with bargain departments, also housed a postal substation. Not to be found anywhere, however, was a restaurant or snack bar, amenities that May and Daniels and Fisher shoppers were used to. For Hilton to sign a Courthouse Square lease, Zeckendorf had had to disallow foodservice by May-D&F so as not to compete. At the same time downtown premiered, May-D&F signage also went up at May Company at University Hills and Daniels and Fisher in Colorado Springs.[238]

DOWNTOWN FUN

With increasing suburbanization, enticing shoppers to venture downtown proved difficult, but it was crucial that the store succeed, even as May-D&F continued opening branches in the 1960s and later. Touff had to balance suburban growth with May's huge investment downtown, which offered far more than branches ever could thanks to its huge size. He determined that special events would entice customers. Fashion shows were perennial draws, and the store often booked a Hilton ballroom to stage them. But fashion shows were for an afternoon, hardly enough time to generate significant traffic. During Joseph Ross's tenure leading Daniels and Fisher, it had held a multi-day event celebrating Italian culture and design, and in 1960, Touff decided to feature American design in a "Salute to American Creativity" over a two-week period in fall—a fortnight, as described in The Denver's chapter. Two years later, he did it again, dedicating a festival to Italy. Every department took on an Italian theme, with special Italian merchandise and Italian culture highlighted in programs and events.[239]

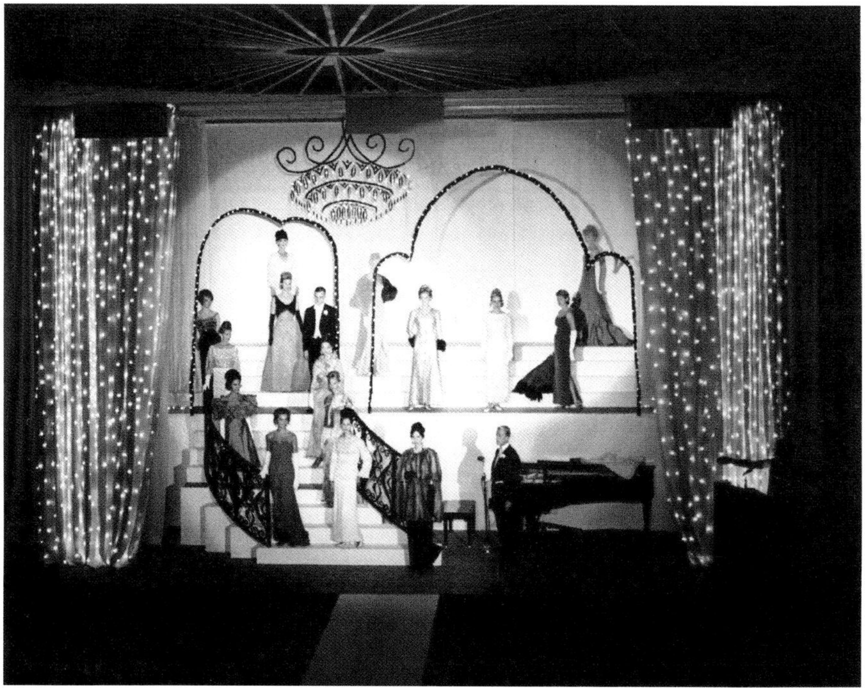

An elaborate May-D&F fashion show held in the Hilton Hotel's ballroom, circa 1965. *Bob Rhodes Collection.*

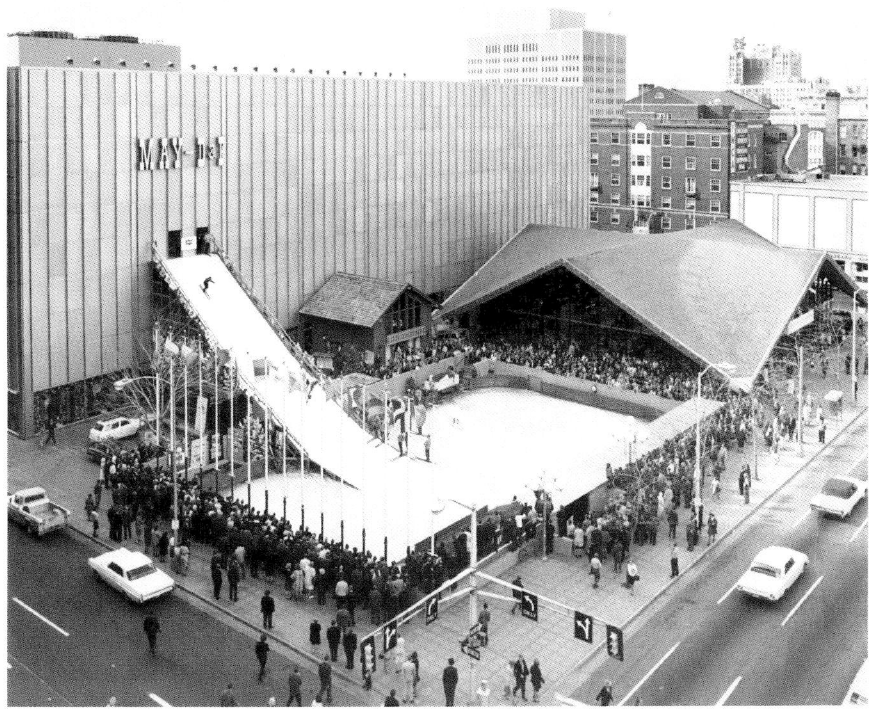

Above: A large crowd watches professional skiers emerge from the third floor and zoom down a nylon-carpeted ramp during 1964's Wonderful World of Winter fortnight. *Bob Rhodes Collection.*

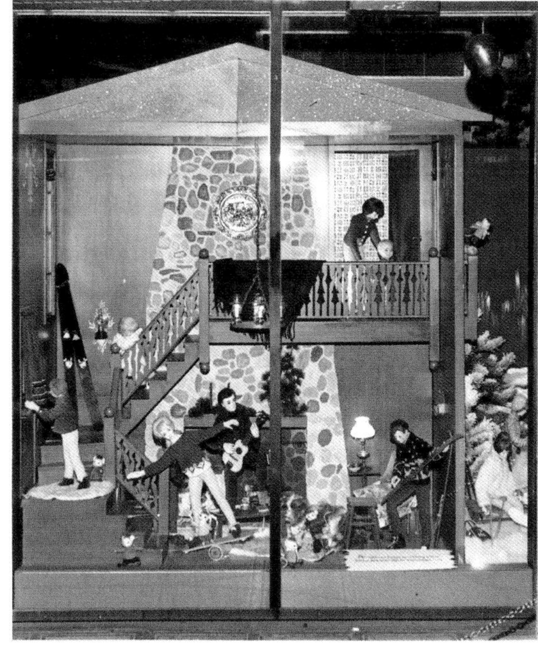

Right: A section of Bob Rhodes's animated windows for 1964's Wonderful World of Winter fortnight showing a family having fun in a ski lodge. *Bob Rhodes Collection.*

In creating May-D&F's "Salute Italia," Touff oversaw buyers (several of whom ventured to Italy), but he particularly relied on a young executive, Robert "Bob" Rhodes. He had department stores in his blood, his father having operated one in his hometown of Rome, Georgia. Rhodes had come west to work at an Estes Park dude ranch but soon found himself at May-D&F. Initially hired as display assistant, he rose to head that operation (later becoming vice-president of merchandising) and, arguably even more than Touff, became known as the creative spirit behind May-D&F's personality, designing its windows and finding dramatic ways to utilize the hyperbolic paraboloid's vast overhead space. For Salute Italia, Rhodes filled May-D&F with Italian artistry, including banners, artwork and a custom-built Venetian gondola in the Plaza Shops, created in-house by his "could build anything" assistant, Albert Gonzales. Italian sports cars decorated Zeckendorf Plaza.[240]

In 1964, May-D&F staged possibly its most elaborate fortnight, "The Wonderful World of Winter." It opened in November, a colder month,

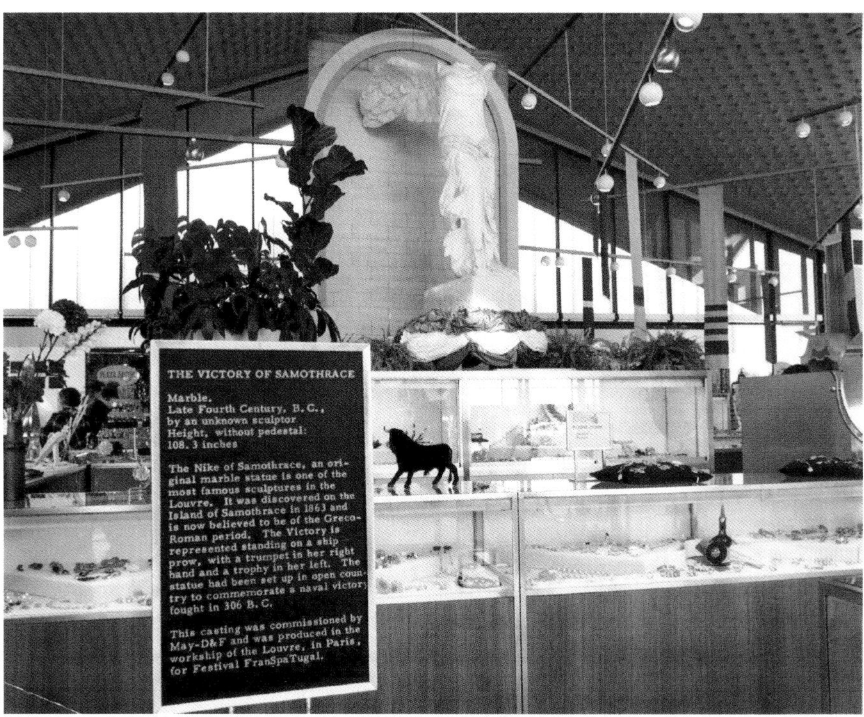

Visitors to Festival FranSpaTugal in 1966 encountered this Louvre Museum–built casting of the Winged Victory of Samothrace upon entering the Sixteenth Street entrance. Store architect I.M. Pei would go on to design the Louvre Pyramid, the grand entrance to the Parisian museum. *Bob Rhodes Collection.*

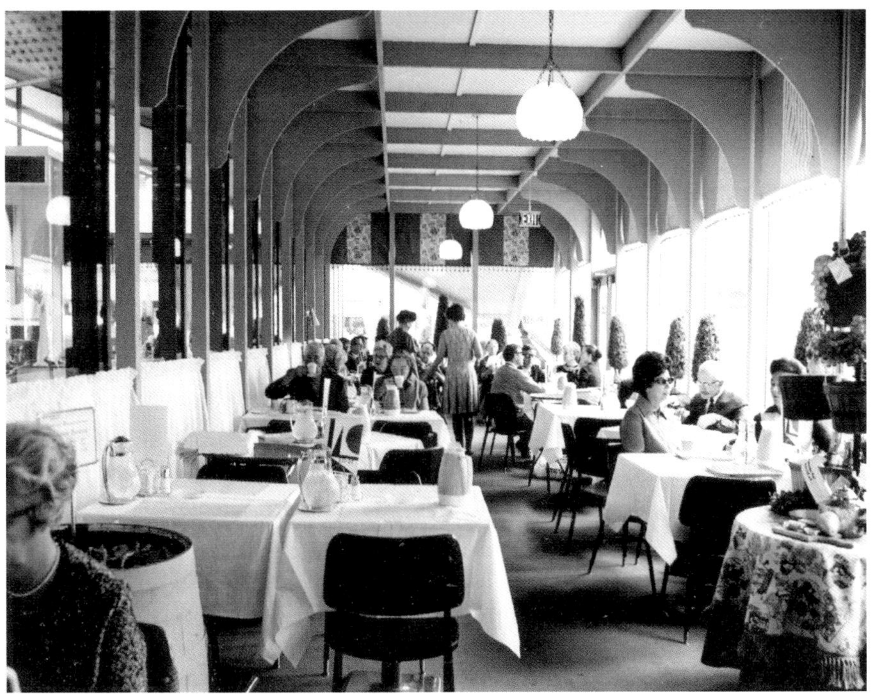

"A Little Bit of Copenhagen" was a temporary restaurant built on the plaza between the paraboloid and the ice skating rink for the 1968 Wonderful World of Scandinavia fortnight. *Bob Rhodes Collection.*

so that the ice skating rink could serve as focal point. Enlisting the trade group Colorado Ski Country USA as sponsor, May-D&F built a ski ramp covered in white nylon carpet that connected the store's third floor with the rink (removing two of Pei's aluminum panels for access), for Olympic athletes to give daily exhibitions of their prowess. After the skiers did their bit, workers folded up the ramp so that Olympic skaters could perform. Rhodes filled windows with scenes of winter fun, peopled by custom-designed figures from Chicago's Silvestri Animated Display Creators. After the festival was over, Rhodes augmented the windows with holiday trimmings, retaining the animations.[241]

"FranSpaTugal," celebrating France, Spain and Portugal, followed in 1966, and in 1968, May-D&F celebrated "The Wonderful World of Scandinavia": Sweden, Norway, Finland, Denmark and Iceland. This featured, among other items, Lego building blocks, designed in Denmark and distributed by Denver-based Samsonite, and Volvos on the plaza. Both events featured temporary restaurants in heated buildings abutting the paraboloid—the Hilton's lease allowed for this—with food from featured countries. FranSpaTugal's was called Plaza Bistro, charmingly decorated with copper kettles and French posters, while "A Taste of Copenhagen" purveyed Danish cuisine two years later.[242]

Two more fortnights followed, "Renaissance 2" in 1970 (France, Spain and Portugal, now combined with Israel) and the elaborate "Odyssey East" in 1972, celebrating China, Japan, Korea, Thailand, Taiwan and Hong Kong. Rhodes went all out, decorating the escalator with a Chinese dragon, transforming a Chinese junk into a gift shop and planting a Japanese garden in the paraboloid. A fourth-floor "Lantern Theater" hosted daily performances by Thai ballet dancers, Chinese folk dancers and Korean musicians. Odyssey East was the last fortnight for some time. Touff had resigned in 1969, and without his advocacy, there was little support from St. Louis to keep the expensive events going, as they provided only temporary traffic boosts. One last hurrah occurred in 1981, with "American Spirit." Over these two weeks, thousands came down to enjoy musical performances on all five floors, witnessing the setting up (and eventual toppling) of 125,000 dominos and partaking of Jelly Belly jellybeans in the new basement gourmet shop.[243]

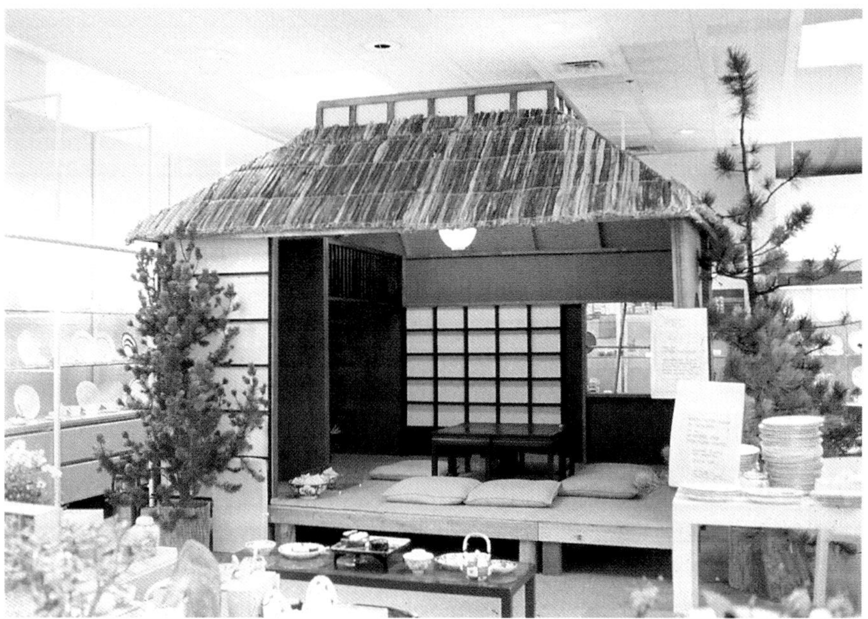

Among the exhibits for the 1972 fortnight, Odyssey East, was this Japanese teahouse in the third-floor china department, with daily tea ceremony demonstrations. *Bob Rhodes Collection.*

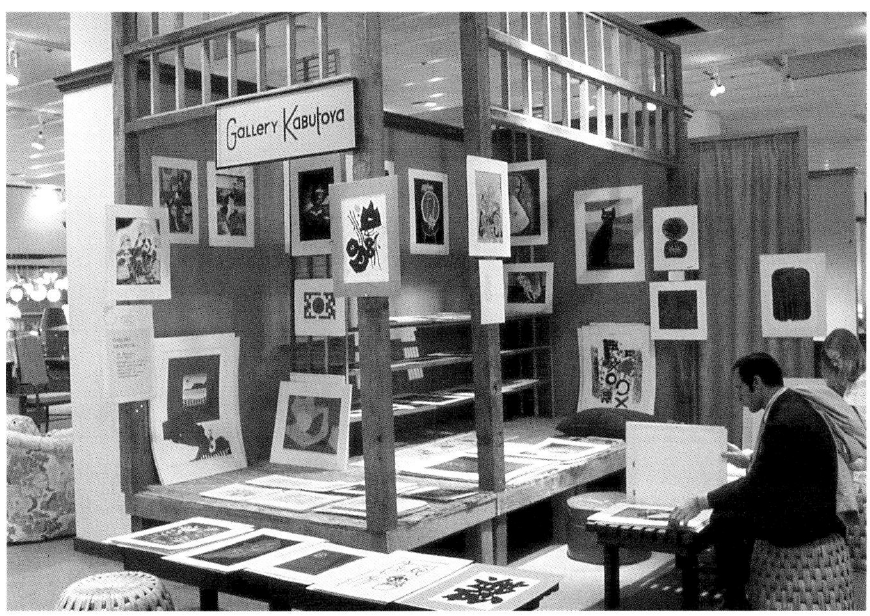

On the fourth floor, visitors to the 1972 Odyssey East fortnight could browse and buy contemporary Japanese art prints. *Bob Rhodes Collection.*

May-D&F also often staged short-term art exhibitions—New Mexican *santos*, Israeli artistry, Greco-Roman antiquities and Far Eastern art were some of these. Splashier was a series of fundraisers, called "Marathon," for the Denver Symphony Orchestra held each February from 1974 through 1983. Classical radio station KVOD set up a broadcasting studio in the paraboloid's display windows and for three days hosted mini-concerts by orchestra members and played recordings chosen by listeners who pledged money. Passersby could watch Gene Amole and other KVOD personalities hosting the fun and offering items for bidding. A huge, rainbow-striped canvas tent, designed by Denver architect Peter Dominick Jr. to fit the paraboloid's plaza-facing side, provided space for a gift shop. Certainly, May-D&F benefited from free publicity, but it also counted as philanthropy—the company was a big donor to numerous Denver institutions in its first decades after buying Daniels and Fisher.[244]

THINGS FALL APART

By the 1980s, the downtown store that in 1958 had seemed so exciting, so promising of a golden future, began to feel tarnished. May-D&F remodeled portions now and then, opening "Denver Louie's" restaurant on the fourth floor (named for Georgetown, Colorado's famed hotelier, Louis Dupuy) in 1977 after Hilton's lease expired and introducing a high-end men's clothing department christened "Daniels and Fisher" in 1982. May-D&F had aggressively pursued suburban expansion—the primary reason for downtown's unprofitability—averaging three or four new stores per decade. In the 1960s, it opened Westland (May's real estate arm developing the center) at West Colfax Avenue and Miller Street in Lakewood

This was followed by Bear Valley at South Sheridan Boulevard and U.S. Highway 285 and by Thornton's North Valley at Eighty-Fourth Avenue and Interstate 25. A Southglenn Mall store opened in 1974, as did a branch at Foothills Fashion Mall in Fort Collins. An Aurora Mall store followed in 1975. The 1980s saw openings at Southwest Plaza, Boulder's Crossroads Mall, Colorado Springs' The Citadel and Westminster Mall. This expansion was profitable for May-D&F as a whole but not for downtown, and plans were afoot for a large mall just four miles away at Cherry Creek—management knew downtown could not survive without drastic changes.[245]

In 1984, May began talks with the city to lease two floors, as it needed more office space and the store was convenient to the City and County Building. Downtown boosters worried, but store president Joseph K. Davis insisted that downsizing was necessary, as it had 150,000 square feet more than it could profitably use. Davis also negotiated with the State of Colorado. Nothing came of the talks, but two years later, it mattered less when news broke of May Department Stores' effort to acquire Associated Dry Goods, The Denver's parent. By mid-July 1986, the two companies, with combined annual sales of $9.4 billion, agreed to merge, with May the acquirer. With this purchase, David May's tiny Leadville shop had grown to become America's fourth-largest department store chain, behind Sears, Kmart and JCPenney. As we have seen (see chapter 6), May at first did not announce its plans for The Denver but decided in January 1987 to close the chain, creating four new May-D&F locations in the process (the Cherry Creek store would relocate to the new Cherry Creek mall in 1990); May-D&F signage also went up at a Goldwater's (former Associated division) store in Albuquerque, New Mexico. Yet closing the flagship Denver Dry Goods store did not improve the fortunes

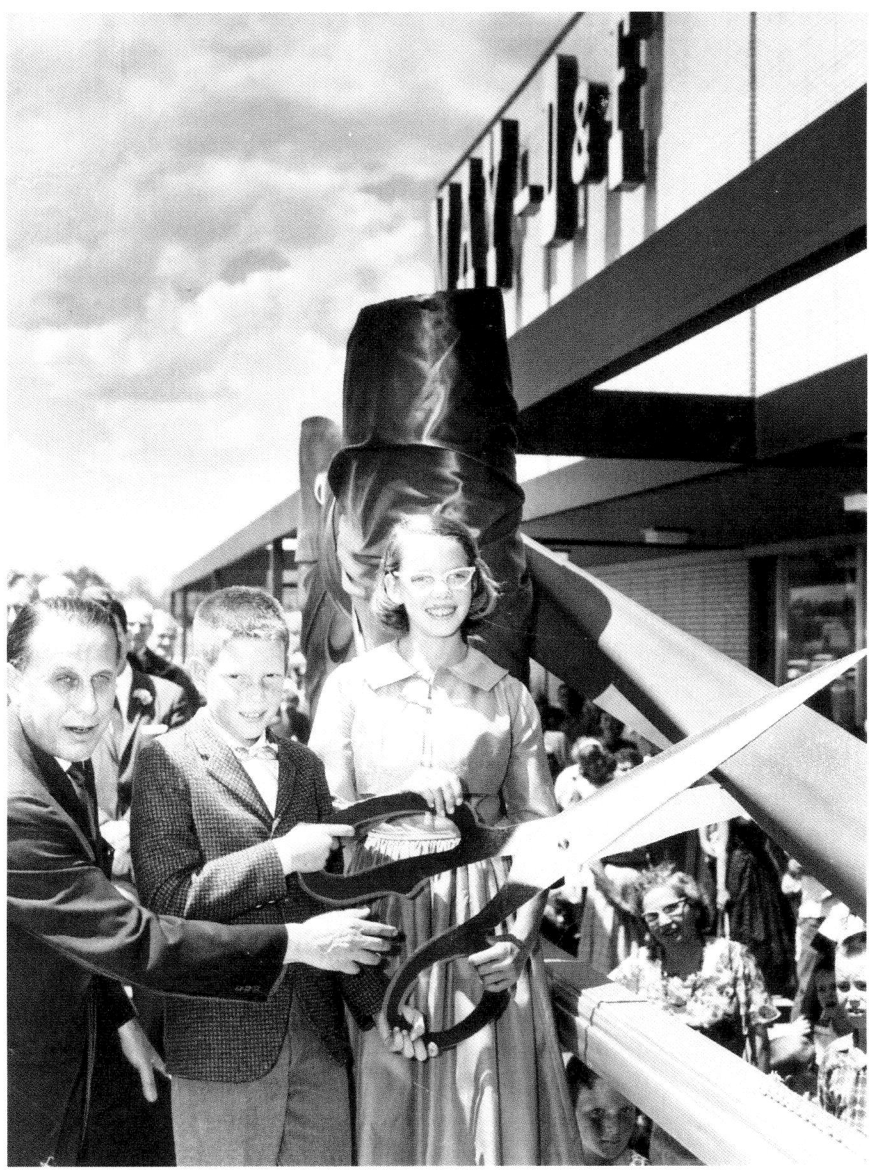

David May's grandson Morton D. May (*left*) and two of his great-great-grandchildren cut the ribbon for May-D&F at the May Company–developed Westland Shopping Center in 1960. *Denver Public Library, Western History Collection, RMN 441-344.*

of the downtown May-D&F; with one less major store downtown, there was one less reason to venture there to shop.[246]

In 1993, downtown closed. It was also the end for the May-D&F name—May Department Stores decided that local names and local management did not matter as much as cutting costs, and it consolidated May-D&F with another division (acquired through another merger), Houston-based Foley's. May had announced in 1991 that it would not renew the downtown lease, set to expire in 1994, but decided to close a year early rather than spend money on new signage. Management assumed that Colorado shoppers would not mind the change, and they were basically correct—people still patronized Foley's. It was clear to industry observers, however, that David May's company was no longer "a chain run by buyers" but was now run by bean counters—gone were the merchants, replaced by accountants. Downtown began its liquidation sale on April 13 and closed its doors two weeks later. How saddened and surprised William Zeckendorf and David Touff, by then long gone, would have been.[247]

Foley's, with its frequent "Red Apple" sales, was fated to last only thirteen years. May continued its acquisition binge through the 1990s and into the new century, notably landing Target's department store division, which included Marshall Field's. Yet these consolidations were not enough to insulate May from rapid changes buffeting department stores, including the advent of online retailing. In 2005, May announced a merger with Federated Department Stores, parent of Macy's and Bloomingdale's. After the merger's completion in 2006, May's various regional nameplates were replaced by the Macy's name, now affixed to more than eight hundred stores across America. In subsequent years, Macy's has closed numerous locations as e-commerce has become ever more popular; no one knows where this will end.[248]

Chapter 11

HOLIDAYS

For many longtime Denverites, whenever the subject of department stores comes up, talk turns quickly to memories of coming downtown between Thanksgiving and Christmas to not just shop, but to experience the most magical time of the year. Nowhere else was it possible to see so many colorful holiday displays, lights, animated windows and huge crowds. Even after stores branched out, coming downtown to see the windows and buy those special gifts they could not find in suburbia was a Christmas season highlight for many.

While merchants have long known that the holiday season meant the difference between a break-even year and a profitable one (hence the term "Black Friday"), the traditions that many remember were first developed in the 1920s, the golden age of department stores. Prior to that decade, all stores decorated for Christmas and featured gift ideas (especially toys) in December newspaper advertisements, but it was in the 1920s that they began trying to outdo each other in ornate displays. This was the national trend, and Denver's stores were on board. To make Christmas even more festive and cement Sixteenth Street as "the place to be" during the holidays, as early as the 1910s the Denver Retail Merchants Association spent great sums to decorate Sixteenth Street, festooning it with evergreen garlands, trees, lights, wreaths and bells. In the 1950s, religious themes were especially popular, with angels and nativity scenes in windows. Stores largely moved away from sacred subjects in the 1960s, but all continued to allocate a large portion of their annual display budgets to holiday decorating. Uniquely in

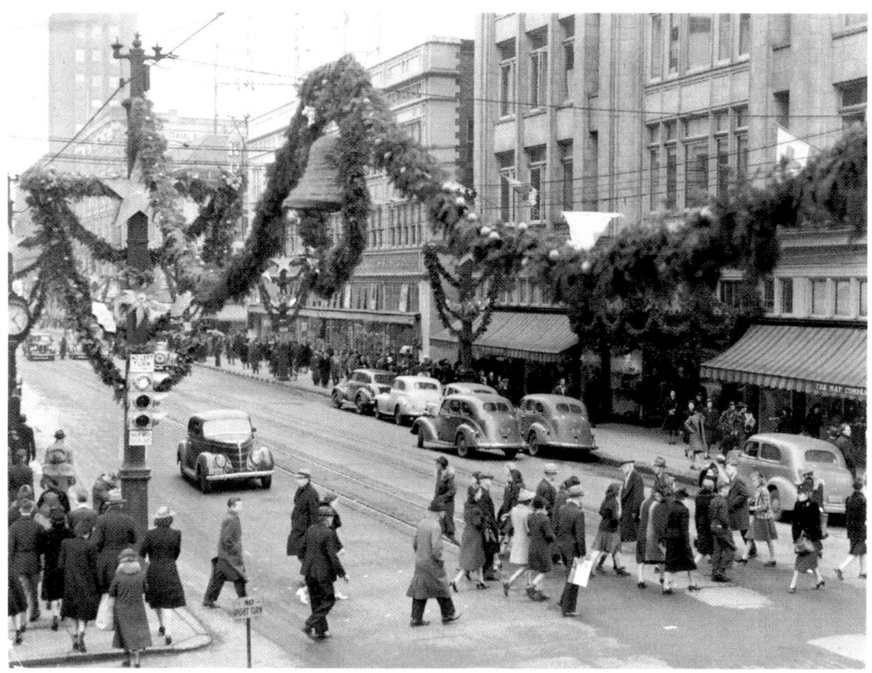

Holiday shoppers cross Sixteenth Street at Champa Street in 1940, the street decorated for the season. The Daniels and Fisher Tower is visible at far left, while the May Company is on the right. S.H. Kress, a national chain variety store, is next to May. *Author's collection.*

Denver, stores kept Christmas displays in place after the holidays, so that National Western Stock Show visitors could enjoy them in mid-January.

The Denver Dry Goods was arguably the best store to visit at Christmas. Windows were always spectacular, of course, even during the store's last decade, when director of visual merchandising Gerald J. Greenwood crafted a series of memorable themes, including one illustrating Dickens's *A Christmas Carol.* The first floor was especially festive, its four-hundred-foot aisle festooned with a long row of spectacular decorated chandeliers, kept in storage all year and displayed only at Christmas. Each year, the chandeliers' trimmings changed to match that year's theme and color scheme, and the effect always overwhelmed. The Tea Room offered holiday cuisine, and on Saturday mornings it hosted "Breakfast with Santa," two hours before the store opened, a buffet meal followed by fun activities for hundreds of children in attendance. In the 1970s, when Tom Roach and F. Joseph Hayes led the store, it offered free giftwrapping, with snow-white paper and red velvet bows. Behind the scenes, male executives and managers, especially those

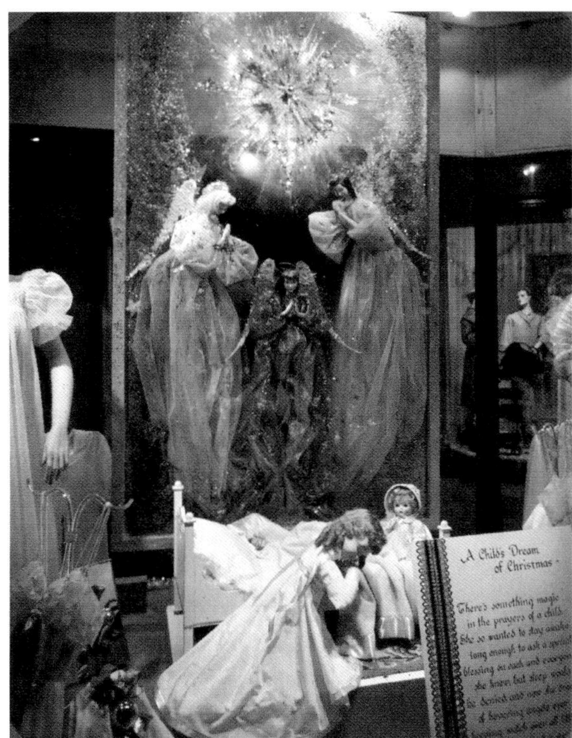

Right: Neusteters' downtown arcade windows took on a religious theme during the 1953 Christmas season. *History Colorado, Neusteter Collection, 10055024.*

Below: In the mid-1960s, the Neusteters window designer created a peaceful, frosty wonderland for the holidays. *History Colorado, Neusteter Collection, 10055023.*

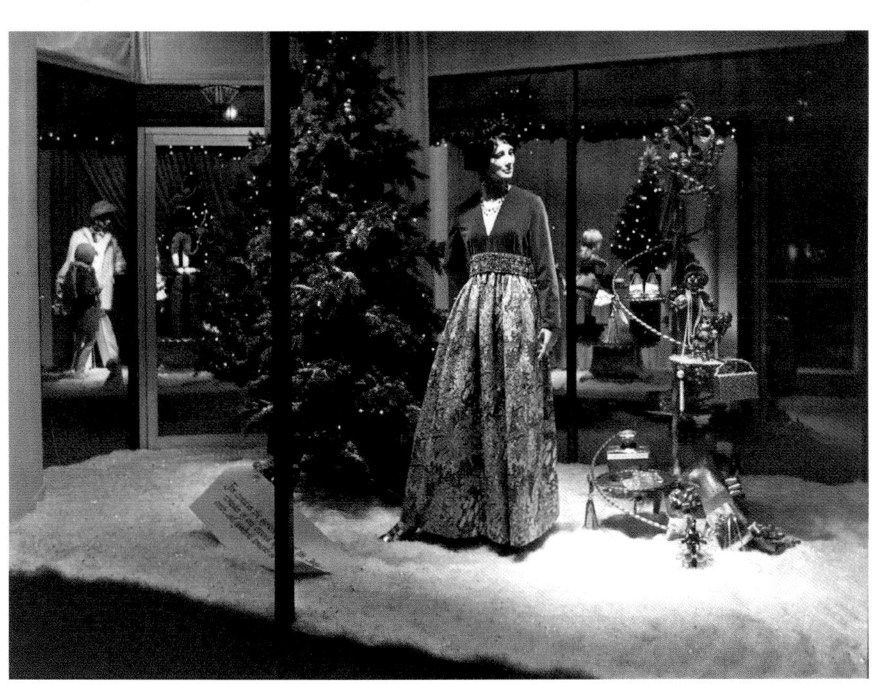

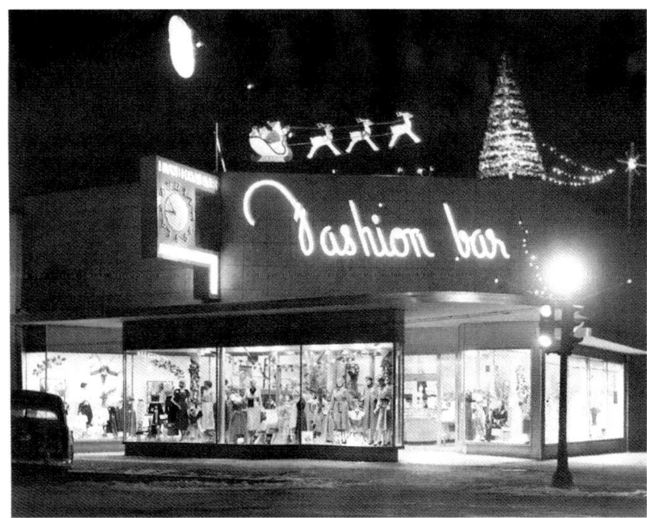

Fashion Bar's Grand Junction store decorated for Christmas 1951. *Beck Archives, Special Collections, CJS and University Libraries, University of Denver.*

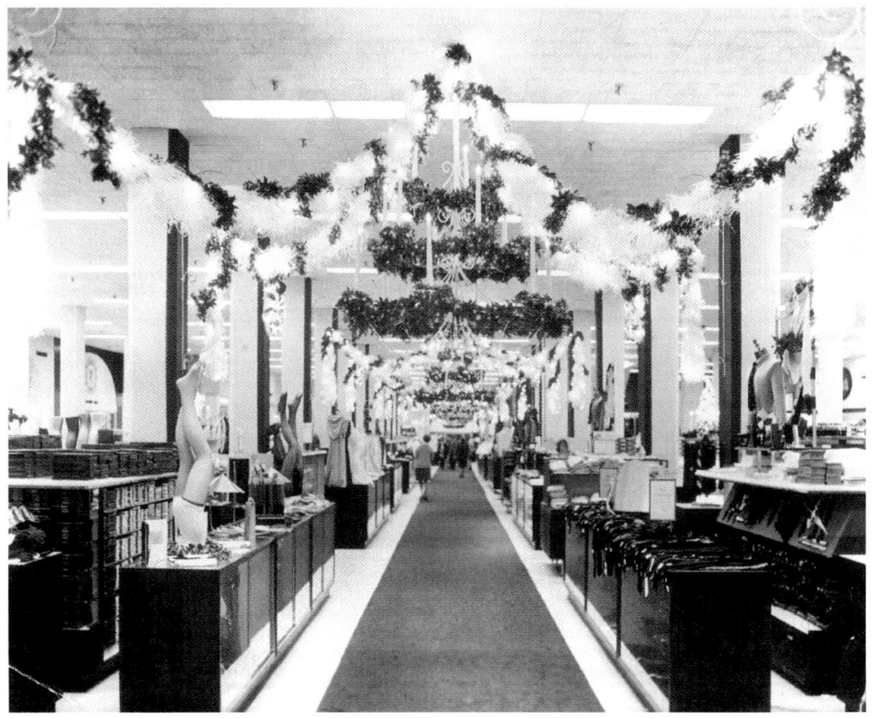

The Denver Dry Goods' first floor main aisle during the holidays in the late 1960s or early 1970s, with red carpet on the floor and lavishly decorated chandeliers, hung only at Christmastime. *History Colorado, 10040050.*

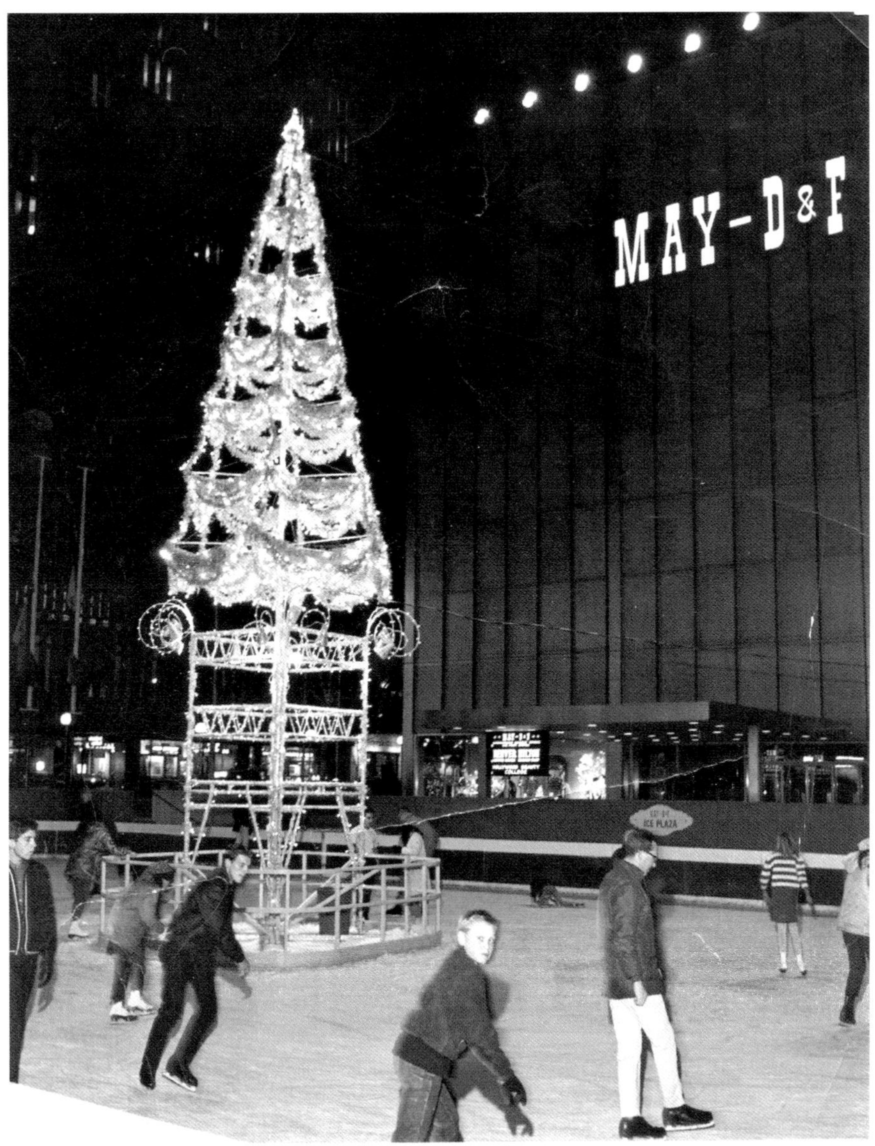

Thousands of Denverites have warm memories of skating at Zeckendorf Plaza in front of May-D&F. In this 1960s scene, a decorated metal Christmas tree, used inside the paraboloid during a previous season, gives the architectural ensemble the "Rockefeller Center look" that Zeckendorf had promised. *Bob Rhodes Collection.*

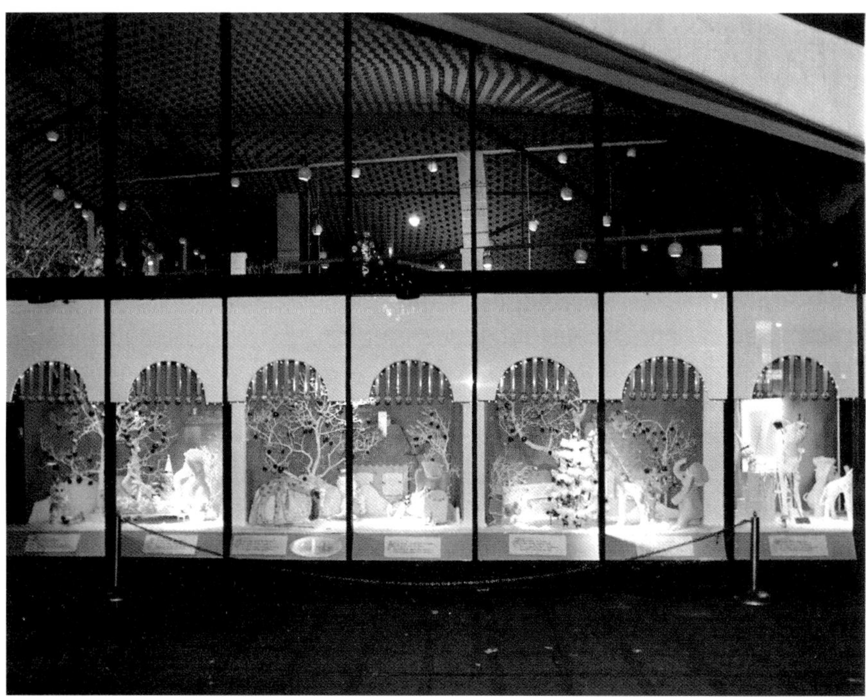

Bob Rhodes created animated circus-themed windows for the May-D&F paraboloid in this 1960s holiday scene. *Bob Rhodes Collection.*

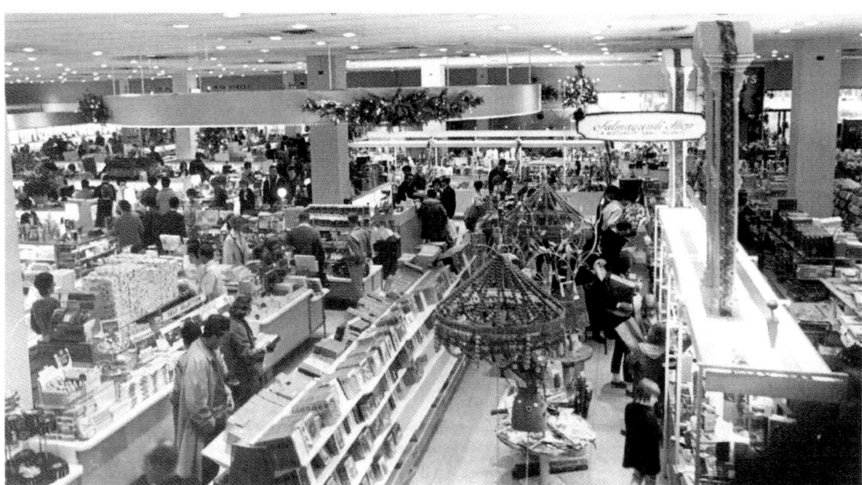

Holiday shoppers crowd the first floor of the downtown May-D&F in this 1967 scene viewed from an escalator; the store's popular gourmet food counter is at left. *Denver Public Library, Western History Collection.*

with older-sounding voices, manned a phone bank on Sunday evenings. Parents dialed in, and children spoke to "Santa Claus." The men who took these calls had a great time and remember them fondly.[249]

The Denver had its fans, but so did May-D&F, home to Zeckendorf Plaza's ice skating. Coming down to this rink during December was great fun for young and old, gliding, or just scooting, around the ice on rented skates, followed by hot cocoa. In the store's heyday of the 1960s and early 1970s, it was visual merchandiser Bob Rhodes who gave May-D&F the holiday spirit through his spectacular windows and interior decorations.[250]

Although suburban branches all got into the holiday spirit too, with decorations and Santa Claus in residence to listen to children's wish lists, they never compared with coming to the vast downtown department stores during the holidays.

Epilogue
GONE BUT NOT FORGOTTEN

When you think about it, department stores are kind of like museums.
—Andy Warhol[251]

LANDMARKS EXTANT, LANDMARKS LOST

We still have the campanile built by William Cooke Daniels. The Daniels and Fisher Tower, for forty years the tallest element in Denver's small-city skyline, has miraculously survived, even though the department store is long gone. After the store consolidated with May Company in 1958 and moved uptown, Boulder financier Allen J. Lefferdink attempted to create the "Tower Merchandise Mart," where wholesale firms could display their wares.

Lefferdink, a classic real estate schemer, was never as wealthy as he claimed, and eventually his creditors (and a grand jury) caught up with him.[252] In 1967, voters passed the Skyline Urban Renewal Plan, calling for demolition of twenty-seven "blighted" downtown blocks, including the now-vacant store. Denver Urban Renewal Authority (DURA) would administer the plan, and there was much anguish at the thought that the tower would meet the wrecking ball. Ultimately, it did not: DURA, although no friend of historic preservation at that time, saw wisdom in retaining the tower, even incorporating its stylized image into its logo.[253]

DURA demolished the store in 1971 and through the 1970s entertained several plans to renovate the tower. After the fourth plan failed to materialize, in

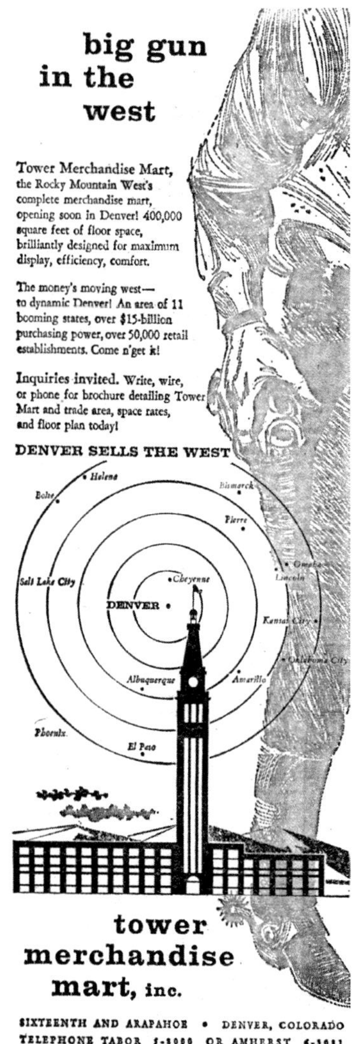

A 1959 newspaper advertisement for Allen Lefferdink's Tower Merchandise Mart, his ill-fated repurposing of the Daniels and Fisher building. *Author's collection.*

1980 DURA awarded redevelopment rights to David C. French, who transformed the building into an "office condominium," each floor individually owned. Work commenced that year and was completed in 1982.[254] In subsequent years, the Daniels and Fisher Condominium Association improved on French's work, and today the tower reigns as one of downtown's greatest ornaments.

At Sixteenth and California Streets, The Denver Dry Goods Building stands proudly, its many layers of paint stripped to reveal Frank Edbrooke's lively brick and limestone design. Here again DURA was involved, but in a very different way. Instead of demolishing the building, DURA, under Susan Powers's leadership in the late 1980s and early 1990s, recognized its importance to the city's history and built environment. After DURA entertained numerous proposals, the building reentered the city's daily life in 1993 with affordable rental apartments developed by New Yorker Jonathan F.P. Rose filling upper floors of the Fifteenth Street building, new retailers on the ground level and second floor and, later, condominiums filling upper floors (including the subdivided Tea Room) of the Sixteenth Street building.[255]

Across the alley, the Neusteter building was reborn after the store closed when Cambridge Development Company, headed by Jeff Selby and Allen Gerstenberger, transformed it in 1987–88 into apartments, with retailer Eddie Bauer occupying the street floor in 1989; in 1993, the building was converted to condominiums. Cambridge donated the Vance Kirkland murals to the Denver Art Museum, which later gave them to the Vance Kirkland Museum of Fine and Decorative Arts, which has them on loan to the condominium association as of this writing.

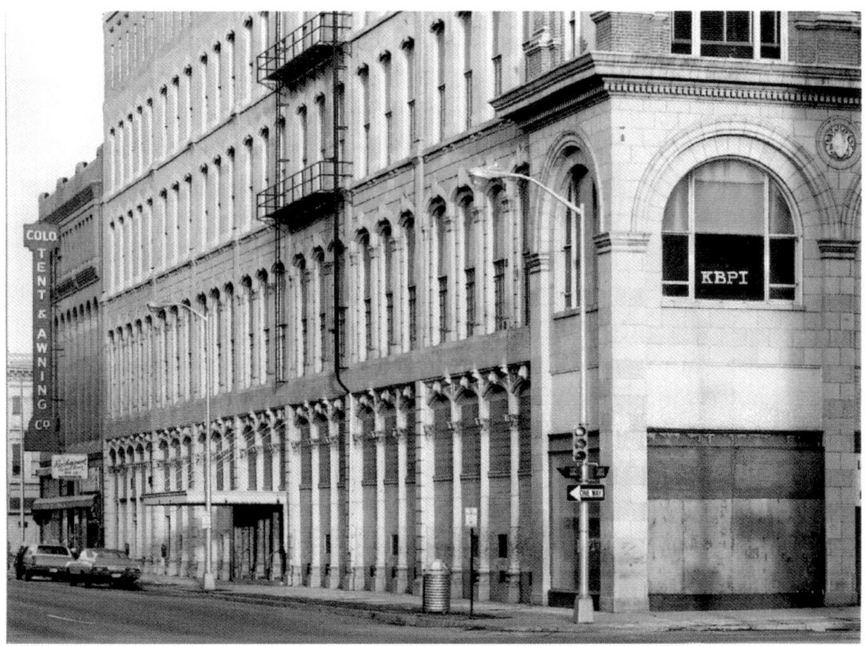

Daniels and Fisher not long before its 1971 demolition, its windows boarded up. *Author's collection.*

Sadly, in 2018, a new retail tenant destroyed the 1924 cast plaster window decorations that William Neusteter's team had restored in 1980. In Cherry Creek, the vacant Neusteters did not remain empty for long after the August 16, 1986 completion of its liquidation sale. Joyce Meskis, co-owner with her then-husband, Rudy Knauer, of the nearby Tattered Cover Bookstore, leased the entire building, minus the fourth-floor restaurant. The Tattered Cover had opened in 1971 and, since 1983, had occupied a portion of the Second Avenue retail space attached to the Neusteter garage. The new forty-thousand-square-foot bookstore made national headlines when it opened in late November; its 130 employees and 120 customer-volunteers helped move books, and Denver embraced its new literary landmark. In 1995, Meskis opened the Fourth Story Restaurant and Bar on the top floor. Although the Tattered Cover was forced to move in 2006 after a steep rent increase, the building still stands, now sheathed in glass, occupied by a spa and a furniture store.[256]

The A.T. Lewis & Son building also still stands. Half-ownership passed to Neusteter Realty in 1935, with the other half owned by the J.K. Mullen Company; national chain W.T. Grant occupied part of the main floor. The balance of the ground floor went to other retailers; at some point, the building received coats of white paint. In 1942, the Denver & Rio Grande Western Railroad bought the 1918 addition at 1541 Stout and made it its headquarters and ticket office; it remained there until the early 1970s. The buildings languished and might have been demolished but for the collapse of Denver's 1970s and 1980s oil boom. In 1995, inspired by the success of the Denver Dry Goods and Neusteter apartments, the Lewis buildings' then owner, the Boettcher Foundation, partnered with Downtown Denver Partnership and developer BCORP/HRT to transform the complex into residential apartments (45 percent reserved for people making no more than 60 percent of Denver's median income). Renovation stripped off the original building's paint, revealing its handsome design and ornamentation; a national off-price clothier occupied the street floor and basement.[257]

When Joslins closed downtown in 1995, retail "experts" predicted that it would be demolished, but Denver is blessed with creative redevelopers. Brokers Charles Woolley and David Friedman of St. Charles Town Company listed it in March 1996 and shortly landed a team to buy and renovate it into a 160-room Courtyard by Marriott hotel. Hiring Denver architect C.W. Fentress J.W. Bradburn and Associates for the renovation, Denver-based National Properties and McBroom Company brought on Denver-based Sage Hospitality Resources to operate the hotel, which opened in 1997. The handsome old George Tritch Block is now revealed, its red brick gleaming and its Victorian details re-exposed. While most of Joslins' suburban buildings have been demolished along with their malls, one branch, at J.C.R.S. Shopping Center in Lakewood, deserves special mention. In 1974, an Oklahoman named Bill Waugh brought his Mexican "eatertainment" concept to Denver, opening the legendary Casa Bonita in the former Joslins. Still in operation as of this writing, the vast, multi-level eatery seating approximately one thousand, features an eighty-five-foot pink stucco tower in front and, inside, a thirty-foot waterfall (next to which Acapulco-style divers regularly plunge into a pool), winding ramps to secluded dining rooms, strolling mariachis, a pirate cave, gunfights and fake palm trees. Depicted in several *South Park* episodes, Casa Bonita was named a landmark by the Lakewood Historical Society in 2015.[258]

While the "box" portion of the downtown May-D&F still technically exists, now with additional floors and sheathed in reflective glass and filled with hotel rooms, I.M. Pei's elegant hyperbolic paraboloid and Zeckendorf Plaza are lost, their 1996 demolition the result of a hotelier with limited imagination and no taste and a city administration desperate for more hotel rooms to serve its struggling convention center. Both conspired to destroy an early, important work of a world-class architect in service of their plans (after his Denver works, Pei designed the National Center for Atmospheric Research in Boulder, the John F. Kennedy Presidential Library and Museum in Boston, Dallas City Hall, the National Gallery of Art East Building in Washington and the glass pyramid at Paris's Musée du Louvre). Right-thinking Denverites valiantly tried to save the structures, with journalists Michael Paglia (*Westword*) and Mary Voelz Chandler (*Rocky Mountain News*) penning numerous columns and architect Alan Golin Gass (who had interned with Pei during Courthouse Square's construction) testifying at city council's landmark designation hearing. It was to no avail, and longtime residents still mourn its loss.[259]

The only other extant department store building on Sixteenth Street is Fashion Bar's, but it is nearly unrecognizable. After Stage Stores Inc. closed it in 2001, it sat empty until a developer remodeled it, installing windows and stucco façade on upper floors and subdividing the first floor into retail spaces. Traces of Crowther's design remain, chiefly the bronze panels and entrance canopies above first-floor windows.

Sixteenth Street's other department store buildings are gone. May Company at Sixteenth and Lawrence served as longtime home to American Furniture before its demolition by DURA in 1972; across Sixteenth, the former Golden Eagle met the same fate. May's Champa and Curtis Street properties remained empty after May-D&F opened in 1958; defense contractor The Martin Company leased the Curtis annex for two years to house 1,500 employees. Nearby Colorado National Bank eventually bought and demolished all of the properties on its block; May's buildings came down in 1965. Today, a parking garage occupies the site. At Stout Street, the Gano-Downs/Joseph Magnin building, still owned by the heirs of Dr. Henry K. Steele after Magnin closed, sold in 1980 to Hudson's Bay Company, which demolished it for an office building.[260]

Then there are the houses. Dennis Sheedy's vast Queen Anne pile of red brick and sandstone dominates Grant Street at Eleventh Avenue, while William Garrett Fisher's stately Neoclassical mansion graces Logan Street at Sixteenth Avenue. John J. Joslin's two-story Italianate home still stands, in fine shape, at 2915 Champa Street. While his 2546 Champa Street house remains, David May's East Colfax and Logan Street (at Thirteenth Avenue) mansions are gone, as are Leopold Guldman's at Tenth Avenue and Humboldt Street and Thirteenth Avenue and Williams Street. William Bradley Daniels's house at 1422 Curtis Street had a fascinating afterlife after his 1890 death when Denver's gambling kingpin, Ed Chase, bought

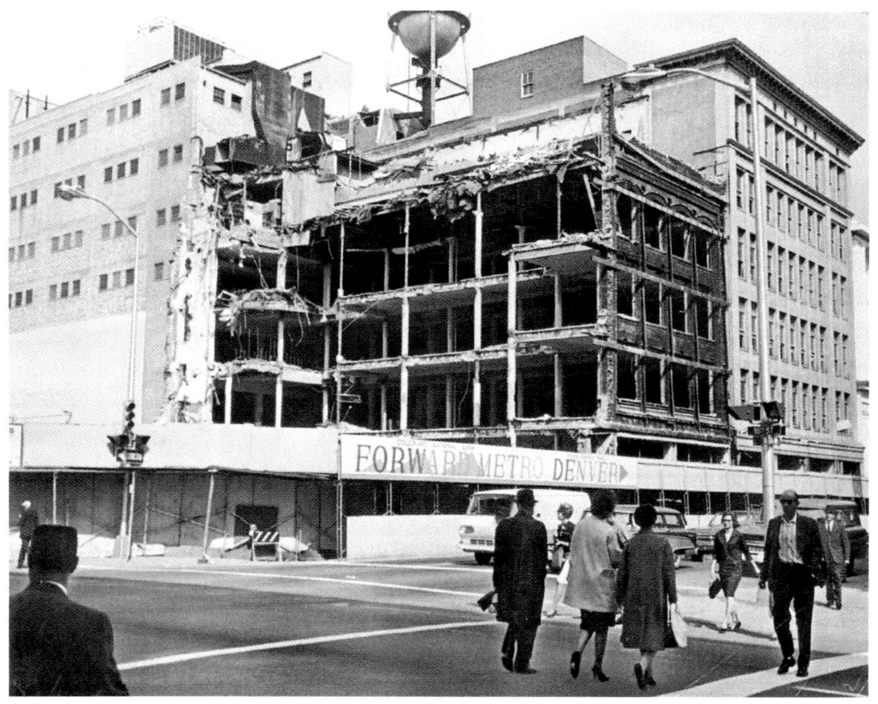

Demolition of the May Company at Sixteenth and Champa Streets, 1965. *Denver Public Library, Western History Collection, X-23282, photograph by Ed Maker.*

it and opened the Inter-Ocean Club, filling parlors with slot machines and poker tables. After becoming a rooming house in 1907, it was demolished in the mid-1920s to make way for the Mountain States Telephone Building. Homes lived in by various members of the Neusteter family are still extant, as are those lived in by Jack or Hannah Levy (in her later years, Hannah lived in apartment 10I at 888 Logan Street, one of Denver's more elegant midcentury residential high-rises).[261]

A VANISHED WORLD

At the time when Andy Warhol compared department stores to museums, most Americans took them for granted, even if some might have been puzzled by his analogy. Every major city, and most minor ones, boasted local department stores, and while many were owned by non-local entities,

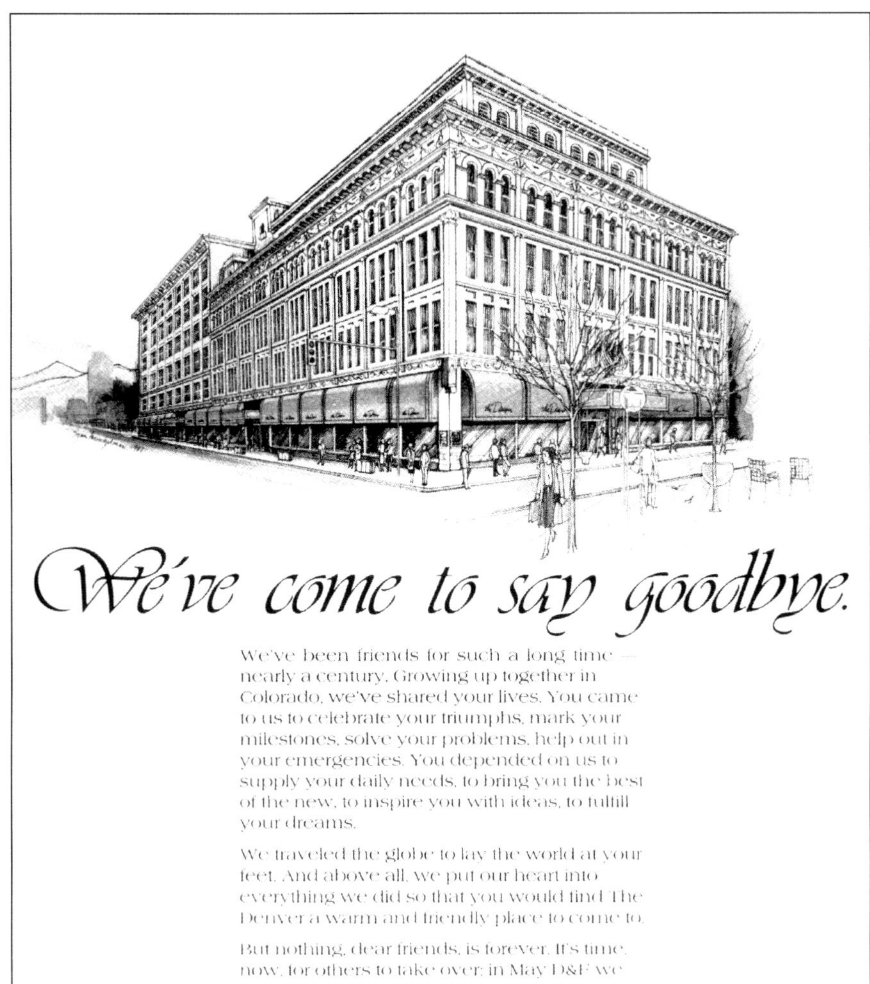

The Denver's advertising department prepared this farewell message to run in the *Denver Post*, but May Department Stores Company executives would not permit its publication, fearing customer backlash. *Jim O'Hagan Collection.*

they still carried hometown names, with local executives and buyers still calling shots and participating in community life. Denver's great names are all gone, replaced by retailers originally local to New York City (Macy's) and Little Rock, Arkansas (Dillard's). No one really knows if those chains will around in another fifty years; Macy's has been closing stores ever since its 2006 acquisition of May Department Stores. Journalists covering the American department store industry write frequently of its "death," predicting that online retail will be the final nail in its coffin. One hopes these pundits are wrong, even if local flavor is gone—there's still something about shopping in a department store that feels different from, and in some ways better than, going through the self-scan lane at Target or clicking the "buy" button on Amazon.

This book has recounted the stories of ten of Denver's great stores. There were others. The Fair, Salomon's Bazaar, Preis Clothing Company, Appel & Company, Ballin & Ransohoff, J.S. Appel, Colorado Dry Goods, Flanders Dry Goods—these are names even less well remembered than A.T. Lewis or Golden Eagle, and unfortunately, there is no room to tell their stories here. Steel's, Broadway Southwest and Printemps, names imported from elsewhere, also enticed Denver shoppers, however briefly. Denver hosted national chains too: Montgomery Ward, with its huge warehouse and store on South Broadway; JCPenney, with its founder's Joslin's connection; and Sears, Roebuck. So-called "junior" department stores, such as W.T. Grant and Colorado's own Eaker's and Howell's chains, had their fans too, as did the Montaldo's, a high-fashion women's chain with an elegant multi-level, mansard-roofed store on California Street. Small Denver retailers such as Amter's (women's fashion), Hedgcock & Jones (laces and millinery, founded by former Daniels and Fisher men), Cottrell's (menswear) and Fontius Shoes, the latter two birthed during the Panic of 1893, deserve to have their stories told too. It is immensely difficult in the twenty-first century to comprehend and appreciate the breadth and depth Denver's stores once offered its citizens and visitors, when the city served as "the *entrepôt* of the West."

NOTES

Introduction

1. Longstreth, *American Department Store Transformed*, 250.

Chapter 1

2. *Denver Republican*, December 25, 1890.
3. Marguerite Riordan Papers, "Daniels and Fishers" [*sic*], 9–10.
4. Ibid., 11, 14, 17; ibid., "Material Furnished by Mrs. Pierpont Fuller, Letters of Wm. G. Fisher to His Mother"; *Denver Post*, October 6, 1907; *Republican*, October 6, 1907.
5. Leonard and Noel, *Denver*, 36, 54.
6. Daniels and Fisher Stores Company, *From Prairie Days*, 10; *News*, January 1, 1878; *Republican*, January 1, 1889; September 28, 1892.
7. In the early 1880s, one of Daniels, Fisher and Smith's employees was Margaret Tobin, hired to work in the carpet and drapery department. She later married local miner J.J. Brown, moved to Denver, survived the sinking of the RMS *Titanic* in 1912 and, after her death, was immortalized as "the unsinkable Molly Brown" on stage and screen. Iversen, *Molly Brown*, 85–86.
8. *Post*, October 6, 1907; *Republican*, October 6, 1907.
9. "Condensed Store Directory," undated but between 1893 and 1911, collection of Ron and Judy Proctor.

10. Marguerite Riordan Papers, "Daniels and Fishers," 95; *Denver Times*, May 26, 1901.
11. *Republican*; December 25, 1890; *Times*, December 25, 1890. For a fuller account of the Donna Madixxa saga, see chapter 3 of the author's *Daniels and Fisher: Denver's Best Place to Shop* and Forbes Parkhill's lively *Donna Madixxa Goes West: The Biography of a Witch.*
12. *Post*, January 14, 1907; *Republican*, September 29, 1892; *Rocky Mountain Herald*, November 7, 1896.
13. *Times*, February 3, 1899.
14. *Post*, April 28, 1901; *Republican*, September 24, 1901. In addition to the photographs in this book, the Denver Public Library website has the full collection of the 1902 images: www.digital.denverlibrary.org.
15. *Post*, April 28, 1901; *Times*, April 28, 1901.
16. *News*, April 25, 1897.
17. *Post*, January 20, 1907; April 3, 1907; February 1, 1909; *News*, February 28, 1909; *Times*, April 3, 1907; Jean-Pierre Chardeaux, e-mails to author, September 14, 15 and 21, 2017.
18. *The Hitchhiker's Guide to the Galaxy: Earth Edition*, "World's Tallest Buildings—A Timeline for the 20th Century," http://h2g2.com/edited_entry/A32873871; *Post*, February 16, 1910; *Republican*, February 13, 1910; *Times*, November 13, 1910.
19. *Post*, February 16, 1910; *Republican*, February 13, 1910; *Times*, November 6, 1910; November 13, 1910.
20. *Post*, July 13, 1910; March 29, 1911.
21. *News*, August 22, 1950; *Post*, July 30, 1911; June 10, 1954; May 7, 1965; Mary Alice Fitzgerald Papers; Oral history recorded January 1997, transcript dated December 10, 1997, interviewed by Jodi Blakeley and Maggie Postlethwaite; Judith Stalnaker, "Denver's Most Beautiful Model: Maraget Gessing Bona," https://www.historycolorado.org/story/preservation/2017/10/05/denvers-most-beautiful-model-margaret-gessing-bona. Some accounts give Sandell's height as seven feet, three inches.
22. *News*, March 19, 1918; October 27, 1918; *Post*, March 19, 1918; October 27, 1918; *Republican*, September 29, 1912.
23. *Post*, April 1, 1918; December 31, 1918; September 26, 1955.
24. Charles MacAllister Willcox and the Willcox Family Papers, letters from Orlando B. Willcox to Charles MacAllister Willcox, August 7, 1928; January 22, 1929; February 13, 1929; and March 9, 1929; telegram from Eugene Greenhut to Charles MacAllister Willcox, February 25, 1929; *News*, March 3, 1929; *Post*, March 3, 1929.

25. *News*, August 24, 1930.
26. *Cervi's*, July 30, 1953; *News*, January 30, 1940; January 30, 1945; *Post*, October 18, 1939; December 23, 1944.
27. *Post*, February 13, 1946; October 18, 1946.
28. Ibid., August 1, 1950.
29. Zeckendorf, *Autobiography*, 122; *News*, July 19, 1953; September 16, 1953; May 23, 1954; May 30, 1954; *Post*, December 28, 1946; January 8, 1952; July 19, 1953; May 23, 1954; May 30, 1954.
30. *Cervi's*, May 26, 1955; *News*, September 29, 1954; November 16, 1954; January 23, 1955; *Post*, September 28, 1954; November 15, 1954; January 16, 1955.
31. Zeckendorf, *Autobiography*, 125; *Cervi's*, October 10, 1957.
32. Zeckendorf, *Autobiography*, 125; *Cervi's*, October 10, 1957; *News*, August 20, 1957; August 21, 1957.
33. *News*, October 8, 1957; October 29, 1957; October 31, 1957; November 18, 1957; July 22, 1958; *Post*, November 18, 1957; December 12, 1966.

Chapter 2

34. *News*, May 11, 1924.
35. Ibid.
36. Ibid., January 8, 1926; *Post*, January 8, 1926; January 9, 1926.
37. *News*, April 23, 1934.
38. Vickers, *History of the City*, 481; *Herald*, April 13, 1873; *News*, April 23, 1934; *Post*, May 31, 1973; Wilbur Fisk stone, ed., "History of Colorado," vol. 2, published by the S.J. Clarke Publishing Company, 1918, http://files.usgwarchives.net/co/denver/bios/joslinjj.txt.
39. Vickers, *History of the City*, 481; *Herald*, April 13, 1873; *News*, April 23, 1939.
40. *News*, June 6, 1873; August 8, 1873; January 8, 1874; January 1, 1878; May 6, 1880; *Times*, June 17, 1903.
41. Hall, *History of the State of Colorado*, 486; *News*, June 24, 1874; February 9, 1879, March 20, 1879, May 4, 1879; May 22, 1879.
42. *News*, February 8, 1879 (advertisement); May 4, 1879 (advertisement); July 8, 1879 (advertisement); October 7, 1879; *Times*, September 22, 1879.
43. *News*, July 11, 1887; April 29, 1888 (advertisement); *Times*, September 20, 1899; January 10, 1902.
44. *Times*, January 28, 1900; May 4, 1902.

45. *Post*, June 28, 1939; Hendrickson, *Grand Emporiums*, 143; Wikipedia, "James Cash Penney," https://en.wikipedia.org/wiki/James_Cash_Penney; Wikipedia, "Garfinckel's," https://en.wikipedia.org/wiki/Garfinckel%27s.
46. *American Cloak and Suit Review* (July 1914); *Dry Goods Economist*, June 27, 1914; Howard, *From Main Street to Mall*, 14–15; Funding Universe, "Mercantile Stores Company Inc. History," http://www.fundinguniverse.com/company-histories/mercantile-stores-company-inc-history.
47. *News*, May 12, 1916.
48. *Post*, September 29, 1911; *Times*, September 29, 1911.
49. *Post*, July 10, 1922; *Times*, July 10, 1922.
50. *News*, January 8, 1926; January 10, 1926; *Post*, January 8, 1926; January 10, 1926.
51. *News*, July 14, 1929; May 21, 1933; June 29, 1939; September 7, 1948; *Post*, May 21, 1933; June 28, 1939. The façade remodeling is seen in photograph Rh-83, by Harry Mellon Rhoads, Denver Public Library Western History Collection, showing a parade on September 27, 1927, to honor aviator Charles A. Lindbergh.
52. *News*, May 21, 1933; *Post*, May 21, 1933; January 16, 1938.
53. *News*, April 30, 1948; *Post*, October 19, 1944; January 29, 1946; April 30, 1948; July 29, 1951; October 22, 1953; May 31, 1973.
54. *News*; January 3, 1960; *Post*, August 11, 1952; September 7, 1952.
55. *Cervi's*, October 1, 1953; *Post*, October 22, 1953; September 2, 1954; October 13, 1954; October 14, 1954.
56. *Boulder Daily Camera*, November 2, 1956; February 15, 2014; November 1, 2014; *Post*, November 17, 1954.
57. *Post*, July 28, 1957 (supplement: "Denver: A Progress Report of the Greater Denver Area, 1957").
58. Howard, *From Main Street to Mall*, 110–13; *Post*, November 5, 1954; March 22, 1955.
59. *News*, December 3, 1955.
60. *Post*, May 29, 1959, March 22, 1970.
61. *News*, June 3, 1973.
62. Ibid., August 17, 1963; August 19, 1963; June 14, 1965; August 23, 1965; *Post*, August 16, 1963; June 11, 1965.
63. *News*, November 8, 1964; February 27, 1966; *Post*, November 8, 1964; March 2, 1966.
64. *News*, November 19, 1967; *Post*, November 19, 1967; September 18, 1968.
65. *Cervi's*, December 23, 1965; *News*, December 10, 1964; December 20, 1970; *Post*, May 10, 1970, August 4, 1971.

66. *News*, February 8, 1977.
67. Ibid., July 20, 1986; October 5, 1986.
68. Ibid., May 13, 1993; April 8, 1994; May 29, 1994; *Post*, April 8, 1994.
69. *News*, October 23, 1994; January 12, 1995; *Post*, October 7, 1994; October 10, 1994.
70. *News*, March 17, 1989; August 4, 1995; April 25, 1996; *Post*, May 15, 1994; August 20, 1994; October 3, 1995; April 25, 1996.
71. *Post*, September 12, 1995; July 30, 1997.
72. *Cincinnati Enquirer*, May 19, 1998; *Denver Business Journal*, May 22, 1998; *Post*, May 21, 1998; July 29, 1998; Dillard's Inc. press release, "Dillard's, Inc., Announces Definitive Agreement."

Chapter 3

73. May Company, "The May Story," 5.
74. Biographical details derive from *Fortune* (December 1948): 109; *The Mayfare*, special edition, "The May Co. Celebrates Seventy-Five Years of Progress, 1877–1952"; *News*, September 13, 1925; July 23, 1927; April 23, 1939; *Post*, July 23, 1927; Clamme and Castelo, *Strangers Among Us*, 81; Forbes Parkhill, "The May Story," appearing in six installments in the *Post*, September 23–28, 1952.
75. May's meeting Field on this trip may be apocryphal, but it was mentioned in more than one account of May's life; *News*, April 23, 1939; *Post*, July 23, 1927.
76. *Times*, January 12, 1900.
77. *Post*, September 27, 1952.
78. Gravenhorst, *Famous-Barr*, 32.
79. *Republican*, January 7, 1906, 2.
80. *Post*, December 2, 1906 (includes photographs of the bronze fixtures).
81. Ibid.; December 4, 1906.
82. *Fortune* (December 1948): 152.
83. *News*, October 9, 1924; September 13, 1925.
84. Lisicky, *Baltimore's Bygone Department Stores*, 67.
85. *Fortune* (December 1948): 153.
86. Longstreth, *City Center to Regional Mall*, 139.
87. *News*, November 19, 1940; March 5, 1945; July 23, 1946; *Post*, November 18, 1940.
88. The strike received extensive coverage: *News*, August 21, 1946; November 22, 1946; November 27, 1946; December 13, 1946; December 15, 1946;

March 31, 1947; April 2, 1947; *Post*, August 30, 1946; September 6, 1946; September 26, 1946; November 21, 1946; November 22, 1946; December 11, 1946; December 12, 1946; December 12, 1946; January 7, 1947; March 31, 1947; April 2, 1947.

89. *Fortune* (December 1948): 109–12.

90. *News*, April 3, 1949; *Post*, January 13, 1954.

91. *News*, November 29, 1953; *Post*, November 29, 1953; June 19, 1955; September 23, 1955; September 27, 1955.

92. Mall Hall of Fame, "Westland Center," http://mall-hall-of-fame.blogspot.com/2008/01/westland-towne-center-west-colfax.html.

93. *Cervi's*, November 17, 1949.

Chapter 4

94. Abrams, "Leopold Henry Guldman"; Lee, "Patriarch of Denver Merchants"; *Post*, June 3, 1936.

95. Abrams, "Leopold Henry Guldman"; Lee, "Patriarch of Denver Merchants"; *News*, March 22, 1879 (advertisement); March 25, 1879. Most references to Guldman's first partner refer to him as "Wineman," but the March 22 advertisement includes the correct spelling of his name, Winneman.

96. *News*, January 1, 1881; July 14, 1883.

97. Ibid., April 9, 1882; *Times*, July 30, 1898; March 24, 1899; June 23, 1901; May 2, 1916.

98. Smiley, *History of Denver*, 471–72; Leslie Davis interview by Dr. Jeanne Abrams and Michael Lee, cited in Lee, "Patriarch of Denver Merchants," note 5; *Times*, June 23, 1901.

99. Abrams, "Leopold Henry Guldman"; *News*, February 3, 1923; *Post*, February 11, 1923; September 19, 1932; June 8, 1936; May 6, 1937; *Times*, October 13, 1899; February 6, 1902; Colorado Gives, "Robert E. Loup Jewish Community Center," https://www.coloradogives.org/jccdenver/overview#profile-details.

100. *Post*, December 22, 1935; June 3, 1936; *Times*, June 13, 1899.

101. *Times*, July 3, 1902; Lee, "Patriarch of Denver Merchants."

102. *News*, August 6, 1914; August 15, 1914; *Post*, July 27, 1930; December 7, 1933; December 14, 1934; *Republican*, December 31, 1905.

103. *Post*, May 11, 1931; May 12, 1931; July 16, 1931.

104. *News*, June 3, 1936; Abrams, "Leopold Henry Guldman"; Lee, "Patriarch of Denver Merchants"; Zimmer, *Denver's Historic Homes*, 35.

105. *News*, June 3, 1936; *Post*, June 3, 1936; June 8, 1936; Measuring Worth, measuringworth.com.
106. *News*, April 4, 1937; April 26, 1959; *Post*, November 20, 1936; February 15, 1937; July 1, 1937; May 10, 1938; August 8, 1970.

Chapter 5

107. *News*, December 18, 1972.
108. Noel, *Denver's Larimer Street*, 142–44.
109. *News*, June 27, 1937; city directories, 1885, 1887, 1889, 1890, 1893, 1896.
110. City directories, 1874, 1893, 1894, 1896.
111. *Republican*, December 30, 1906; *Times*, December 17, 1898.
112. *News*, April 19, 1959 (Gano-Downs advertisement).
113. Ibid.; *Post*, December 24, 1971.
114. *News*, February 13, 1926; July 7, 1937; *Post*, June 27, 1937.
115. *Post*, August 31, 1951; November 20, 1952; July 28, 1957.
116. *News*, April 19, 1959 (Gano-Downs advertisement); November 22, 1960; *Post*, undated 1957 clipping; January 26, 1960.
117. *News*, November 29, 1960; January 2, 1961; *Post*, November 28, 1960; December 14, 1960; January 2, 1961; January 18, 1961; February 19, 1970.
118. *News*, May 10, 1964; *Post*, September 8, 1963; April 13, 1966; May 2, 1966.
119. *News*, February 12, 1967; *Post*, July 21, 1968; August 31, 1969.
120. *News*, February 20, 1970; March 29, 1970; March 5, 1972; *Post*, February 19, 1970; December 24, 1971; October 24, 1972; Wikipedia, "Amfac, Inc.," https://en.wikipedia.org/wiki/Amfac,_Inc. Cyril Magnin had a Denver connection already: he was on the board of National Jewish Hospital.
121. *News*, April 2, 1972; May 2, 1972; December 18, 1972; *Post*, February 1, 1972; June 16, 1972; January 21, 1973.
122. *News*, December 11, 1976; June 5, 1982; *Post*, December 12, 1976; February 17, 1980. As for Joseph Magnin, it too would not last. Amfac closed downtown in 1979; Cinderella City and Cherry Creek shuttered in 1984, along with the remaining stores in the chain.

Chapter 6

123. *News*, April 17, 1986.
124. Hall, *History of the State of Colorado*, 4:509; Vickers, *History of the City*, 534.
125. *You and Your Store*, "Denver Dry Goods Company."
126. *News*, January 1, 1880; March 17, 1880; April 2, 1880; July 4, 1880; January 1, 1881; *Republican*, July 3, 1883; Doner, "Denver's Merchant Princes," 29.
127. *Post*, April 15, 1953.
128. Noel, *Denver Landmarks and Historic Districts*, 26–27; *Ballenger & Richards' Seventeenth Annual Denver City Directory*, 56.
129. Leonard and Noel, *Denver*, 103–5; *Colorado Sun*, July 16, 1893; September 7, 1893.
130. *News*, August 16, 1918; *Sun*, September 10, 1893; September 11, 1893; *Times*, May 22, 1894; Byers, *Encyclopedia of Biography of Colorado*, 1:381–82; Sheedy, *Autobiography*, 56.
131. *Denver Catholic Register* (October 22, 1953): 1–3; *Times*, April 22, 1899; December 8, 1901.
132. *Times*, October 16, 1923; Sheedy, *Autobiography*, 32–44.
133. Sheedy, *Autobiography*, 57; Doner, "Denver's Merchant Princes," 56–57.
134. *Herald*, November 7, 1896; *Republican*, January 1, 1899; *Times*, October 3, 1898; minutes of Denver Dry Goods Company Stockholders' Meeting, May 26, 1896, quoted in Doner, "Denver's Merchant Princes," 46–47.
135. *Denver Catholic Register* (December 1, 1919); *News*, June 2, 1923; *Republican*, January 1, 1907; *Times*, August 2, 1902; *You and Your Store*, "Denver Dry Goods Company."
136. *Post*, March 4, 1899; April 15, 1953; *Times*, July 26, 1902.
137. *News*, October 16, 1923; February 15, 1924; February 25, 1924; December 26, 1958; *Post*, February 14, 1924; *Times*, October 26, 1923; October 27, 1923; minutes of Denver Dry Goods Board Meeting, December 27, 1923, quoted in Doner, "Denver's Merchant Princes," 76–76.
138. *News*, November 29, 1924; *Post*, November 28, 1924; April 15, 1953.
139. *News*, May 7, 1971; April 19, 1987; *Post*, February 6, 1977; author's personal recollection, circa 1970.
140. *Cervi's*, July 27, 1950; *News*, November 14, 1937; November 20, 1945; *Post*, November 19, 1945; July 17, 1947; Thomas J. Noel, conversation with author, February 28, 2018.

141. This description of departments is based on a house telephone directory from the period immediately after World War II; the basic layout of the departments had been set during the mid-1920s reconfiguration that followed the 1924 addition.
142. *Post*, November 30, 1944; July 27, 1948.
143. Ibid., November 9, 1947; September 26, 1950; October 1, 1950; October 7, 1950; June 24, 1955; May 25, 1958; September 18, 1960; November 22, 1962; May 16, 1965; April 13, 1966; August 30, 1966.
144. *News*, September 6, 1970; September 14, 1970; September 12, 1971; October 9, 1982; *Post*, September 11, 1970; April 4, 1971; September 4, 1972; September 24, 1972; September 16, 1973; September 17, 1973; September 16, 1974; Denver Dry Goods newspaper advertisement (both papers), September 14, 1970, and store-printed brochure.
145. *Cervi's*, April 17, 1952; *News*, November 23, 1950; October 11, 1953; October 8, 1954; October 5, 1955; *Post*, November 22, 1950.
146. Candelario, *Northglenn*, 7; *Cervi's*, June 13, 1962; *News*, August 23, 1956; August 24, 1956; November 15, 1964; *Post*, March 6, 1955; February 4, 1968; July 2, 1962; November 16, 1964; February 27, 1966; March 7, 1968; March 13, 1968; March 14, 1968; Denver Dry Goods Telephone Directory, March 1, 1957.
147. *Cervi's*, September 11, 1972; *News*, August 10, 1973; August 14, 1975; March 9, 1976; May 4, 1978; *Post*, May 20, 1968; February 3, 1972; July 6, 1972; July 16, 1974; August 13, 1974; May 29, 1977; January 18, 1978; October 5, 1979; March 3, 1983.
148. *Post*, April 21, 1964; December 14, 1964; Doner, "Denver's Merchant Princes," 83–84 (Johns's decision to approach Seiler is per an interview she conducted with him on April 4, 1984).
149. *Post*, May 24, 1967.
150. *News*, December 8, 1974; March 28, 1975; January 18, 1978; January 25, 1979; April 26, 1979; February 3, 1980; *Post*, July 9, 1968; September 27, 1977; December 27, 1977; *Rocky Mountain Journal*, August 27, 1975; author's conversation with F. Joseph Hayes, February 20, 2016.
151. *News*, April 26, 1979; February 3, 1980; author's conversation with F. Joseph Hayes, February 20, 2016.
152. *News*, February 3, 1980; March 21, 1981.
153. *New York Times*, July 16, 1985; *News*, March 27, 1986; June 7, 1986; June 23, 1986; July 2, 1986.
154. *News*, July 17, 1986; *Post*, July 17, 1986; January 31, 1987; author's conversation with F. Joseph Hayes, February 20, 2016.

155. *News*, February 12, 1987; February 18, 1987; February 19, 1987; February 20, 1987; March 4, 1987; March 16, 1987; April 10, 1987; May 1, 1987.

Chapter 7

156. *News*, June 7, 1931.
157. Ibid., November 3, 1927; June 7, 1931; *Post*, January 20, 1907; Baker and Hafen, *History of Colorado*, vol. 4 (Denver, CO: Linderman Company Inc.), 130–33.
158. *News*, June 7, 1931.
159. Ibid., November 8, 1924; November 3, 1929; *History of Colorado*, 133.
160. *Post*, January 20, 1907.
161. *Herald*, November 7, 1896; *News*, November 3, 1929; June 7, 1931; *Times*, October 1, 1898.
162. Haber, Fuller and Wetzel, *Robert S. Roeschlaub*, 126; *Republican*, July 24, 1898 (advertisement); *Times*, October 1, 1898; April 11, 1900; September 22, 1901.
163. *Republican*, November 10, 1901; *Times*, August 2, 1902; September 10, 1902.
164. *Post*, January 20, 1907; *Colorado Statesman*, January 26, 1907; *History of Colorado*, 134.
165. *Post*, August 15, 1916; April 1, 1918.
166. *News*, October 17, 1924; November 3, 1929.
167. Ibid., November 8, 1924.
168. Ibid., September 15, 1930 (advertisement).
169. *Post*, August 15, 1916; January 6, 1933; January 10, 1933 (advertisement); January 15, 1933 (advertisement); January 18, 1933.

Chapter 8

170. Neusteter, oral interview.
171. Ibid.; *News*, June 22, 1961; Meyer Neusteter, typescript of a speech given at the fiftieth anniversary employee dinner, 1961, in Neusteter Company Collection (MSS #1281), History Colorado, Denver, CO.
172. Meyer Neusteter, typescript of speech; *News*, April 23, 1939. Keene lived at Fourth Avenue and Dexter Street in what later became Denver's Hilltop neighborhood and raised horses. In 1924 or 1925, she was thrown from a horse and died.

173. Some accounts say that the original building was completely demolished, but a June 29, 1924 *Denver Post* advertisement shows a drawing of the original building with steel girders being erected on top of it. The copy reads, "The building we have just now vacated will be abandoned and rebuilt to conform with the first unit." Also, when the building was being renovated decades later, construction manager Jill Morelli alluded to the original building as being "encapsulated" by the five-story expansion (*Post*, November 18, 1987).
174. Meyer Neusteter, typescript of speech; *Post*, June 29, 1924; Noel and Norgren, *Denver*, 122.
175. Meyer Neusteter, typescript of speech; *News*, August 24, 1925.
176. *News*, September 23, 1924; October 25, 1936; April 23, 1939.
177. Ibid., May 9, 1941; March 4, 1942; January 8, 1950; *Post*, September 4, 1946.
178. *News*, October 28, 1951; February 8, 1952; *Post*, October 25, 1951; October 28, 1951; February 4, 1952; January 20, 1953.
179. Neusteter, oral interview; *News*, September 7, 1952; *Post*, September 7, 1952; October 22, 2003.
180. *News*, July 30, 1956; April 30, 1959; July 28, 1960; *Post*, August 7, 1958; November 23, 1958.
181. *News*, July 28, 1960; *Post*, August 21, 1960; August 28, 1960.
182. *Cervi's*, August 30, 1956; *News*, October 25, 1964; *Post*, October 11, 1964.
183. Neusteter, oral interview; *Post*, Marcy 27, 1966; March 7, 1968.
184. Neusteter, oral interview.
185. Ibid.; *News*, January 3, 1973; *Rocky Mountain Journal*, August 13, 1975.
186. "Neusteter Professionals," company document in Neusteter Company collection, 1939–83, manuscript, MSS #1281, Stephen H. Hart Library and Research Center, History Colorado Center.
187. Sandra Dallas, e-mail to author, May 31, 2018. Dallas worked in the store's advertising department at the time.
188. *News*, July 15, 1962; May 1, 1966; October 16, 1966; February 6, 1970; June 14, 1970; *Post*, July 25, 1971; April 16, 1972; Johnson, *Opera in the Rockies*, 63–66. The Neusteter galleries at the Denver Art Museum were not a solo effort; Morton D. May donated a pre-Columbian gauze hanging and Fashion Bar sent employees to the museum to assist in setting up displays. Per his 1987 oral interview, as a young man Myron had been present at the 1932 reopening of the Central City Opera, when Lillian Gish starred in *Camille*.

189. *News*, January 28, 1966; October 29, 1973; *Post*, October 1, 1958; November 19, 1967; October 31, 1971.
190. *News*, December 20, 1975; July 19, 1976; October 12, 1976; October 16, 1976; *Post*, March 14, 1976; July 18, 1976; *Rocky Mountain Journal*, December 31, 1975.
191. *News*, September 2, 1979; March 12, 1980; *Post*, August 21, 1979; September 10, 1970; *Rocky Mountain Journal*, March 21, 1979. For his part, Auer was back in the retail game a year later, when he opened an upscale women's store called Auer's, located a block from the Cherry Creek Neusteters at Second Avenue and St. Paul Street.
192. *Post*, October 28, 1973; March 3, 1974; September 1, 1974.
193. *News*, March 12, 1980; March 21, 1980; *Post*, March 21, 1980.
194. *Post*, March 3, 1974; May 16, 1974; February 7, 1975; February 23, 1986.
195. *News*, March 27, 1980; March 28, 1980; June 27, 1980; August 17, 1980.
196. Ibid., August 19, 1983; *Rocky Mountain Business Journal*, September 19, 1983; *Neusteter v. DIST.CT. In & FOR CITY, ETC.*, http://law.justia.com/cases/colorado/supreme-court/1984/83sa151-0.html.
197. *News*, November 23, 1983; *Post*, November 23, 1983.
198. *News*, January 10, 1984; August 30, 1985; October 12, 1985; *Post*, November 22, 1984; October 21, 1985.
199. *News*, October 24, 1985.
200. Ibid., November 19, 1985; *Post*, December 13, 1985; February 23, 1986.
201. *Post*, February 23, 1986.
202. Ibid., April 1, 1986; May 29, 1986; October 22, 2003.

Chapter 9

203. *News*, September 27, 1971.
204. Abrams, "Hannah Levy."
205. *News*, September 6, 1983; Abrams, "Hannah Levy"; Hannah and Jack Levy, oral interview, 1983. Hannah remembered that the encounter was with Max Neusteter, but he was dead by this time, which makes it more likely that it was Meyer Neusteter that hired her.
206. *News*, September 6, 1983; Abrams, "Hannah Levy"; Hannah and Jack Levy, oral interview.
207. *Post*, September 23, 1969; Abrams, "Hannah Levy;" Hannah and Jack Levy, oral interview.

208. *Post*, December 12, 1933; Abrams, "Hannah Levy."
209. *News*, September 28, 1958; Abrams, "Hannah Levy."
210. Heitler went on to become a vice-president at Denver-based Samsonite Corporation, his wife being a Schwayder, the family who had founded that company, as Schwayder Brothers Trunk and Bag Manufacturing in 1910. He remained good friends with the Levys.
211. *News*, January 3, 1968; Abrams, "Hannah Levy."
212. *News*, March 3, 1963.
213. Ibid., August 25, 1960; August 17, 1962; September 26, 1962; March 7, 1963; *Post*, December 14, 1958.
214. *News*, March 7, 1963; February 10, 1980; author's conversation with Robert Levy, November 9, 2017.
215. *News*, November 7, 1961; February 26, 1964; November 1, 1964; March 27, 1965; April 7, 1965; *Post*, February 26, 1964; March 27, 1965.
216. *News*, September 23, 1965; November 28, 1966; December 1, 1965; December 2, 1965; *Post*, November 21, 1965.
217. *News*, June 12, 1966; August 12, 1966; July 16, 1971; *Post*, July 24, 1966; August 25, 1966 (*Contemporary* magazine).
218. *News*, September 12, 1966; August 29, 1968; August 5, 1970; October 19, 1970; December 30, 1970; August 15, 1971; *Post*, March 1, 1970; May 31, 1971.
219. *News*, September 19, 1973; October 17, 1977; October 2, 1980; *Post*, June 28, 1972; July 3, 1972; May 4, 1975 (*Contemporary* magazine); May 7, 1975; May 2, 1980; *Rocky Mountain Journal*, August 27, 1975; December 31, 1975.
220. *News*, August 19, 1958; September 23, 1964; October 17, 1977; *Post*, May 18, 1972; Abrams, "Hannah Levy."
221. *News*, August 19, 1958; March 7, 1963; September 23, 1965; September 6, 1983; *Post*, August 24, 1956; September 23, 1969; May 18, 1972.
222. *News*, September 27, 1971; September 19, 1973; November 28, 1976.
223. Ibid., September 22, 1966; November 28, 1976.
224. Ibid., August 25, 1960; March 7, 1963; February 26, 1964; August 29, 1968; August 15, 1970; December 30, 1970; May 31, 1971; August 15, 1971; *Post*, August 24, 1958; November 21, 1965; February 26, 1966; June 12, 1966; July 24, 1966; May 21, 1967; *Journal*, December 31, 1975; author's conversations with Frank Kiszlowski in 1981 and 1982.
225. *News*, November 28, 1982; December 2, 1984; April 8, 1985; Abrams, "Hannah Levy"; ProPublica, "Raphael Levy Memorial Foundation Inc.," https://projects.propublica.org/nonprofits/organizations/846022586;

Rose Community Foundation, "Our History: Major General Maurice Rose," https://rcfdenver.org/about-us/our-history.

226. *News*, September 21, 1967; February 8, 1980; October 8, 1980; January 26, 1985; *Post*, January 3, 1968.
227. *News*, December 2, 1984; April 8, 1985; August 18, 1985; July 11, 1986; January 5, 1995; *Post*, May 2, 1980.
228. *News*, September 19, 1973; November 28, 1976; February 10, 1980; March 25, 1988; April 30, 1992.
229. Ibid., April 3, 1992; June 10, 1992; August 14, 1992; Abrams, "Hannah Levy," note 52.
230. *News*, May 21, 1994; January 5, 1995; May 2, 1995; January 31, 1997; author's memories of shopping at Palais Royal and Bealls when he lived in Houston, 1984–85.

Chapter 10

231. *News*, March 1, 1960.
232. *Republican*, November 24, 1912.
233. Zeckendorf, *Autobiography*, 108–9; *Post*, December 26. 1933.
234. *News*, June 5, 1945; December 27, 1946; February 20, 1949; *Post*, June 21, 1945; December 28, 1946; May 3, 1948; October 15, 1948; October 16, 1948.
235. *News*, July 7, 195; July 19, 1953; January 23, 1955; *Post*, July 7, 1953; January 23, 1954; June 20, 1954; January 23, 1955; November 4, 1955 (*Empire* magazine).
236. *News*, August 2, 1958.
237. Ibid., August 5, 1958; *Post*, August 3, 1958; August 4, 1958; author's conversation with Bob Rhodes, October 31, 2014.
238. *Post*, August 3, 1958; author's conversation with Bob Rhodes, October 31, 2014.
239. *Post*, July 22, 1962.
240. Ibid., July 22, 1952; author's conversations with Bob Rhodes, October 31, 2014, and November 21, 2014; "May-D&F Fortnights," notes in the files of Bob Rhodes.
241. *Post*, November 8, 1964; November 9, 1964; "May-D&F Fortnights" and "The Wonderful World of Winter," notes in the files of Bob Rhodes; "The Ski Chalet on 16th Street," flyer in the files of Bob Rhodes; *News* and *Post* clippings in files of Bob Rhodes (no dates given).

242. *News*, October 23, 1966; October 18, 1968; *Post*, October 21, 1968; "May-D&F Fortnights"; *News* and *Post* clippings in the files of Bob Rhodes (no dates given); Lego, "The Lego History," http://www.lego.com/en-us/aboutus/lego-group/the_lego_history/1960.
243. *News*, October 9, 1981; "May-D&F Fortnights"; script for Odyssey East slideshow in the files of Bob Rhodes.
244. *News*, April 29, 1972; March 2, 1976; February 25, 1977; February 12, 1978; February 18, 1983; *Post*, February 21, 1965; March 27, 1966; April 14, 1968; February 17, 1974; February 22, 1976; February 25, 1977; February 11, 1979; *Westword*, March 16, 1979.
245. *Denver Downtowner*, March 24, 1982; *News*, February 17, 1982; April 22, 1984 (advertisement); *Post*, November 25, 1977.
246. *News*, November 14, 1984; November 18, 1984; July 2, 1985; June 23, 1986; June 26, 1986; February 20, 1987; March 4, 1987; *Post*, June 23, 1986; June 24, 1986; July 17, 1986; January 31, 1987.
247. *News*, April 13, 1993; April 28, 1993; July 24, 1993.
248. Ibid., January 29, 1993; April 13, 1993; April 28, 1993; July 24, 1993; Federated Department Stores Inc. press release, "Federated and May Announce Merger."

Chapter 11

249. *News*, December 21, 1983; author's conversations with F. Joseph Hayes, February 20, 2016, and James O'Hagan, May 15, 2016.
250. Author's conversations with Bob Rhodes, October 31, 2014, and November 21, 2014

Epilogue

251. Thanks to Nan Walker.
252. *News*, March 13, 1955; August 8, 1958; June 6, 1959; *Post*, February 9, 1958; August 1, 1958; January 18, 1959; December 21, 1959.
253. *News*, November 19, 1968; *Post*, April 11, 1969; December 7, 1969; March 18, 1970.
254. *News*, December 19, 1979; February 17, 1981; *Post*, January 18, 1979; January 20, 1980.

255. *Denver Business Journal*, November 9, 1987; November 23, 1987; September 10, 1990; *News*, February 20, 1987; March 11, 1987; March 21, 1987; November 7, 1987; November 29, 1987; December 20, 1987; March 4, 1988; April 8, 1988; May 10, 1988; May 27, 1988; July 9, 1988; July 12, 1988; December 8, 1988; April 13, 1989; July 14, 1989; September 19, 1989; September 20, 1989; September 24, 1989; September 30, 1989; December 15, 1989; July 31, 1990; October 21, 1990; December 4, 1990; July 18, 1991; December 15, 1992; July 1, 1993; July 17, 1993; October 21, 1993; October 27, 1993; December 19, 1993; May 11, 1994; *Post*, July 14, 1989; January 26, 1997; Jonathan Rose Companies, "Denver Dry Goods Building," rosecompanies.com; Horizon International Solutions Site, "Downtown Redevelopment: The Denver Dry Building," solutions-site.org.
256. *News*, September 6, 1986; November 6, 1986; November 17, 1986; December 31, 1986; March 4, 1987; July 17, 1987; October 31, 1991; October 20, 1992; April 4, 1993; *Post*, January 21, 1987; November 18, 1987; July 14, 1989; October 22, 2003; author's employee training with Joyce Meskis, September 1994; author's conversation with an anonymous docent at the Vance Kirkland Museum of Fine and Decorative Arts, July 14, 2018.
257. *Denver Business Journal*, February 17, 1995; *Historic Denver News*, February–March 1997; *Post*, March 3, 1935; March 20, 1942.
258. *News*, August 5, 1995; April 25, 1996; *Post*, March 15, 1996; April 25, 1996; *Westword*, March 18, 2015; Wikipedia, "Casa Bonita." https://en.wikipedia.org/wiki/Casa_Bonita.
259. *News*, December 20, 1994; December 23, 1994; *Westword*, May 17, 1995; Gass, "Who Was Bill Zeckendorf?"; conversation between author and Gass, May 1, 2015.
260. *News*, October 25, 1959; *Post*, January 10, 1959; October 25, 1959; June 7, 1960; May 16, 1963; July 7, 1965; June 1, 1969; February 17, 1980.
261. Bretz, *Mansions of Denver*, 3–4; Stalnaker, *888 Logan Street*, 13; Zimmer, *Denver's Historic Homes*, 35.

BIBLIOGRAPHY

Books

Baker, James H., editor and Hafen, Le Roy R., associate editor. *History of Colorado*. Denver, CO: Linderman Co., Inc., 1927.

Barnhouse, Mark A. *Daniels and Fisher: Denver's Best Place to Shop*. Charleston, SC: The History Press, 2015.

———. *The Denver Dry Goods: Where Colorado Shopped with Confidence*. Charleston, SC: The History Press, 2017.

Barth, Gunther. *City People: The Rise of Modern City Culture in Nineteenth-Century America*. New York: Oxford University Press, 1980. Paperback edition, 1982.

Bretz, James. *Mansions of Denver: The Vintage Years, 1870–1938*. Boulder, CO: Pruett Publishing Company, 2005.

Byers, William Newton. *Encyclopedia of Biography of Colorado*. Vol. 1. Chicago: Century Publishing and Engraving Company, 1901.

Candelario, Elizabeth Moreland. *Northglenn*. Charleston, SC: Arcadia Publishing, 2013.

Clamme, Louise, and Sinuard Castelo. *Strangers Among Us: The Story of Blackford County Indiana Immigrants*. Bloomington, IN: AuthorHouse, 2011.

Gravenhorst, Edna Campos. *Famous-Barr: St. Louis Shopping at its Finest*. Charleston, SC: The History Press, 2014.

Haber, Francine, Kenneth R. Fuller and David N. Wetzel. *Robert S. Roeschlaub: Architect of the Emerging West, 1843–1923*. Denver: Colorado Historical Society, 1988.

Hall, Frank. *History of the State of Colorado*. Vol. 3. Chicago: Blakely Printing Company, 1889.

Hendrickson, Robert. *The Grand Emporiums: The Illustrated History of America's Great Department Stores.* Briarcliff Manor, NY: Stein and Day, 1979.

Howard, Vicki. *From Main Street to Mall: The Rise and Fall of the American Department Store.* Philadelphia: University of Pennsylvania Press, 2015.

Iversen, Kristen. *Molly Brown: Unraveling the Myth.* 3rd ed. Denver, CO: Johnson Books, 2018.

Johnson, Charles A. *Opera in the Rockies: A History of the Central City Opera House Association, 1932–1992*. Central City, CO: Central City Opera House Association, n.d.

Johnson, Charlie H. *The Daniels & Fisher Tower*. Denver, CO: Tower Press, 1977.

Leonard, Stephen J., and Thomas J. Noel. *Denver: Mining Camp to Metropolis.* Niwot: University Press of Colorado, 1990.

Lisicky, Michael. *Baltimore's Bygone Department Stores: Many Happy Returns*. Charleston, SC: The History Press, 2012.

Longstreth, Richard. *The American Department Store Transformed, 1920–1960.* New Haven, CT: Yale University Press, 2010.

———. *City Center to Regional Mall: Architecture, the Automobile, and Retailing in Los Angeles, 1920–1950*. Cambridge, MA: MIT Press, 1997.

Marcus, Stanley. *Minding the Store*. Facsimile ed. Denton: University of North Texas Press, 1997. Original publication, Boston, MA: Little, Brown, 1974.

Noel, Thomas J. *Denver Landmarks & Historic Districts: A Pictorial Guide*. Niwot, CO: University Press of Colorado, 1996.

———. *Denver's Larimer Street: Main Street, Skid Row and Urban Renaissance.* Denver, CO: Historic Denver Inc., 1981.

Noel, Thomas J., and Barbara S. Norgren. *Denver: The City Beautiful*. Denver, CO: Historic Denver Inc., 1987.

Parkhill, Forbes. *Donna Madixxa Goes West: The Biography of a Witch*. Boulder, CO: Pruett Press Inc., 1968.

Sheedy, Dennis. *The Autobiography of Dennis Sheedy*. Denver, CO: privately printed, 1922.

Smiley, Jerome. *History of Denver*. Denver, CO: Sun-Times Publication Company, 1901.

Soucek, Gayle. *Marshall Field's: The Store that Helped Build Chicago*. Charleston, SC: The History Press, 2010.

Vickers, W.B. *History of the City of Denver, Arapahoe County, and Colorado.* Chicago: O.L. Baskin & Company, Historical Publishers, 1880.

Zeckendorf, William, with Edward McCreary. *The Autobiography of William Zeckendorf.* New York: Holt, Rinehart and Winston, 1970.

Zimmer, Amy. *Denver's Historic Homes*. Charleston, SC: Arcadia Publishing, 2013.

Newspapers

Cervi's Journal.
Cincinnati Enquirer.
Colorado Statesman.
Colorado Sun.
Denver Business Journal.
Denver Catholic Register.
Denver Downtowner.
Denver Post.
Denver Republican.
Denver Times.
Historic Denver News.
New York Times.
Rocky Mountain Business Journal.
Rocky Mountain Herald.
Rocky Mountain News.
Westword.

Other Material

Abrams, Jeanne. "Hannah Levy (1905–1984)." Immigrant Entrepreneurship, May 2, 2016. https://www.immigrantentrepreneurship.org/entry.php?rec=268.

———. "Leopold Henry Guldman (1852–1936)." Immigrant Entrepreneurship, June 25, 2014. https://www.immigrantentrepreneurship.org/entry.php?rec=206.

Ballenger & Richards' Seventeenth Annual Denver City Directory. Denver, CO: Ballenger & Richards, 1889.

C.F. Murphy Associates. "Sixteenth Street Mall Plan." 1974.

Daniels and Fisher Stores Company. *From Prairie Days to 1907: Being a History of The Daniels & Fisher Stores Company*. Denver, CO: Press of the Smith-Brooks Company, 1907.

The Denver Directions. Employee newsletter, various issues between 1976 and 1985.

Denver Dry Goods Company. Clipping file, Denver Public Library, Western History Collection.

———. Downtown Store Directory, March 1957.

———. "Report of Operations for Month of December 1923."

Denver Dry Goods Telephone Directory, March 1, 1957.

Denver Planning Office and Downtown Denver Inc. "Downtown Denver Pedestrian Transit Mall Proposals." 1973.

"Dillard's, Inc., Announces Definitive Agreement for Acquisition of Mercantile Stores Company, Inc." Press release, May 18, 1998.

Doner, Phyllis J. "Denver's Merchant Princes: The Evolution of Denver Department Stores." M.A. thesis, University of Colorado–Denver, 1987.

Fashion Bar Clipping File. Denver Public Library, Western History Collection.

"Federated and May Announce Merger." Press release, Federated Department Stores Inc., February 28, 2005.

Gano-Downs Clipping File. Denver Public Library, Western History Collection.

Gass, Alan Golin, FAIA. "Who Was Bill Zeckendorf?" Typewritten manuscript, copy in author's files.

I.M. Pei & Partners, Architects and Planners. "The Transitway/Mall: A Transportation Project in the Central Business District of Metropolitan Denver." 1977.

Joslin's Clipping File. Denver Public Library, Western History Collection.

Lee, Michael. "The Patriarch of Denver Merchants: Leopold Henry Guldman and the Golden Eagle Dry Goods Company of Denver, 1879–1936." Unpublished thesis, Ira M. and Peryle Hayutin Beck Memorial Archives of the Rocky Mountain Jewish Historical Society at the University of Denver.

Levy, Hannah, and Jack Levy. Oral history interview by Jeanne Abrams. Beck Archives of Rocky Mountain Jewish History, Center for Judaic Studies and Special Collections, University Libraries, University of Denver. Recorded October 19, 1983.

Marguerite Riordan Papers. "Daniels and Fishers [*sic*]," unpublished manuscript. Denver Public Library, Western History Collection, WH1094, Box 6, FF19.

Mary Alice Fitzgerald Papers, 1948–58, 1997–2002 (MS). Denver Public Library, Western History and Genealogy Collection, MSS WH1800.

The May Company. "The May Story." *The Mayfare*, 1952. Special edition of employee newsletter.

Neusteter, Myron. Oral history interview by Eleanor Benson. OH no. 565, History Colorado. Recorded November 24, 1987.

Neusteter Company Clipping File. Denver Public Library, Western History Collection.

Stalnaker, Judith. *888 Logan Street: Home to the Prominent.* Booklet. N.p.: privately printed, 2015.

Willcox, Charles MacAllister, and the Willcox Family Papers. History Colorado, MSS #1606.

You and Your Store. "The Denver Dry Goods Company and How It Grew." May 11, 1957. Employee newsletter.

Zeckendorf, William. "Baked Buildings." *The Atlantic* (December 1951): 46–49.

———. "New Cities for Old." *The Atlantic* (November 1951): 31–35.

INDEX

I

J

K

L

M

ABOUT THE AUTHOR

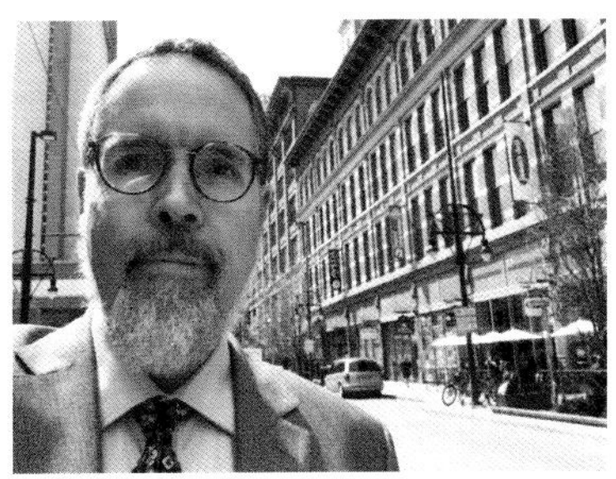

Denver native Mark A. Barnhouse has been fascinated by the city's downtown and its historic department stores from an early age, probably from the time he attended Breakfast with Santa at the Denver Dry Goods Tea Room at age seven. He chose Denver's Sixteenth Street as a research topic for a college paper at the University of Colorado Denver and has been researching and writing about it ever since, along with other Denver historical subjects. He is the author of *Daniels and Fisher: Denver's Best Place to Shop*, *The Denver Dry Goods: Where Colorado Shopped with Confidence*, *Denver's Sixteenth Street*, *Lost Denver* and *Northwest Denver*, all available from Arcadia Publishing/The History Press. He leads walking tours for the annual Doors Open Denver celebration of the city's built environment and is available for talks to groups. He lives in northwest Denver and is a member of the Denver Posse of Westerners. You'll find him on Facebook at "Denver History Books by Mark A. Barnhouse."